True Stories of the Korean Comfort Women

Edited by Keith Howard

Testimonies compiled by the Korean Council for
Women Drafted for Military Sexual Slavery by Japan
and the Research Association on the Women Drafted for
Military Sexual Slavery by Japan,
and translated by Young Joo Lee

CASSELL

Cassell
Wellington House
125 Strand
London WC2R 0BB

215 Park Avenue South
New York, NY 10003

Korean original © Korean Council for the Women Drafted for
Military Sexual Slavery by Japan and the Research Association on the
Women Drafted for Military Sexual Slavery by Japan 1993
English translation © Cassell 1995

English translation first published 1995

British Library Cataloguing-in-Publication Data
A catalogue record for this book is available from the British Library.

ISBN 0-304-33262-3 (hardback)
      0-304–33264-X (paperback)

Typesetting and Design Ben Cracknell
Printed and bound in Great Britain by Biddles Ltd, Guildford and King's Lynn

Contents

Introduction

Keith Howard

The bulk of this book comprises a collection of life stories originally published in 1993 in Korean as *Kangjero kkŭllyŏgan Chosŏnin kunwianbudŭl*
[The Korean Comfort Women Who Were Coercively Dragged Away
for the Military]. 'Comfort women' is a euphemism, translating the
Korean *wianbu* and the Japanese *ianfu*, that will regularly be repeated
in the pages which follow. An alternative Korean term, *chŏngshindae*
[literally, 'voluntarily offered body corps'], is also encountered both in
literature and when talking to Koreans. The meaning of both terms
becomes clear in the title of the body responsible for collecting these
interviews, *Han'guk chŏngshindae munje taech'aek hyŏbŭihoe* [The Korean
Council for Women Drafted for Military Sexual Slavery by Japan], and
one of its constituent bodies, the *Chŏngshindae yŏn'guhoe* [Research
Association on the Women Drafted for Military Sexual Slavery by
Japan].[1]

Rumours about the coercion of women as prostitutes for Japanese
forces have circulated for a long time, but it has only recently been
demonstrated that the policy began in the early 1930s – as the empire
began to spread its tentacles beyond Korea to mainland Asia – and lasted
until the end of the Pacific war. No reparation has been made by Japan to
any of the Asian women. Estimates of the numbers involved spiral
upwards to a high of 200,000. It is usually considered, following recent
revelations and a 1939 account by a military surgeon, Aso Tetsuo, that
between 80 per cent and 90 per cent of comfort women were Korean.
This, then, is a Korean tragedy, unique in terms of the numbers of
women used, although examples of the military appropriation of women
are known from elsewhere in the world. At the time of writing, accounts
of mass rape emerging from the conflict that has engulfed the former
Yugoslavia suggest that similar abuse continues.

Korean society, as it emerged after liberation in 1945, knew many
stories about the comfort women. Indeed, the term *wianbu* continues to
be used today to describe the prostitutes who work near the perimeters

of American army bases in South Korea, particularly Ŭijŏngbu and Kunsan, and to some extent for those in Seoul's red light districts. Yet the issue was, for almost 50 years, brushed under the carpet. Until recently, the South Korean government argued that no documentary evidence survived the defeat of Japan, hence the issue should not detract from the need to normalize Korean–Japanese relations. Those who studied the issue knew very little, and until the early 1990s many considered that coercive recruitment largely followed the setting up of a Women's Voluntary Labour Corps in 1944. The Corps was established ostensibly to provide labour for Japanese factories; according to Yun Chŏngok, writing in a Council publication, the recruits were 'forced to comfort the divine imperial troops at the battlefront while subsisting on day labour by laundering the soldiers' uniforms and cleaning the military mess'.[2] In January 1992, the Korean newspapers *Tonga ilbo* and *Chosŏn ilbo* reported the confession of a Japanese school teacher, Ikeda Masae, who recruited six pre-teen girls in 1944 in obedience to an imperial edict. The apparent discrepancies caused by supposing such a late date largely went unnoticed, even with suspicions roused by the knowledge that many Korean women were displaced to Japan in the 1920s and 1930s as labourers.[3] Further, female labourers, as with comfort women and the Corps, mostly had received little or no education.[4]

Public debate in Korea was further stymied by the lack of testimonies. By the end of 1991, only three Korean women had admitted their past as comfort women. The tragedy, then, was exacerbated by silence. The shame of a woman was the shame of her whole family. The poverty of colonial Korea meant that offers of work had held considerable attraction to both families and individual women, yet such paid labour countered the traditional view that a woman's place was within the home. The Confucian propriety of Korea stretched beyond economic power, since men held all legal and social mechanisms to represent their women. The resulting control and possession have proved powerful tools. Again, Korean society ascribed to a notion of defilement which expected and required chastity. Whatever the reason, sexual defilement tended to be associated with promiscuity.

The debate on comfort women has emerged in South Korea at a time of domestic realignment. The women's movement has gained considerable momentum just as economic development has led many to begin to take a stand against the might of Japan. In North Korea, the state has yet to normalize relations with Japan, and the issue of forced prostitution is seen as a potential and useful lever; media coverage, some of which has broadcast documentaries produced in Europe, has increased public awareness. On a broader canvas, memories of empire mean that the resurgence of Japan is feared throughout Asia. As Japan seeks a higher pro-file in the international community – and a possible seat on the United Nations Security Council – the comfort women issue allows smaller and poorer Asian states to reiterate that the Japanese have not yet atoned for war crimes. It can be argued that the lack of pressure by America and its allies on Japan began as an attempt to limit war reparations and aid the building of a Cold War balance in which Japan was to be a major capital-ist ally of America and Europe. The issue, therefore, was buried by the international community for reasons that lie beyond Korea's borders.

Here, our focus is on Korea. Koreans suffered. Nonetheless, this is a story in which nobody wins, and it is of note that both Koreans and Japanese took part in coercion. The 19 testimonies which we include tell a harrowing tale, insistently hammering home that to this day the women who suffered have received no appropriate recompense. The accounts follow a basic schema, covering childhood, recruitment, forced initiation as a comfort woman, routine and return. They are statements, given to the Council as a type of reporting, a coming out. They were collected as evidence, but just as importantly they have had a cathartic function, since they helped relieve the 50 years' oppression that keeping silent had imposed on survivors. The names of most victims are real, but contemporary social pressures still mean that six accounts – those of Kim Tŏkchin, Yi Sunok, Yi Tŭngnam, Kim T'aesŏn, Pak Sunae, Ch'oe Myŏngsun – are written under pseudonyms.

In this book an overview by Chin Sung Chung expands and replaces a brief chapter in the original Korean publication. This was prepared at the request of the Korean Council; Chung is a prominent member of the Council who holds a PhD in sociology and teaches at Duksung [Tŏksŏng] Women's University in Seoul. We have added an exploration by Etsuro Totsuka of the legal aspects surrounding the issue, and recent developments; Totsuka is a lawyer specializing in human rights who has lobbied at the United Nations in Geneva and elsewhere on behalf of the Council. The accounts, as they were first presented in Korean, were arranged for the Council by a number of scholars and others associated with the Research Association on the Women Drafted for Military Sexual Slavery by Japan. Those responsible, with chapter numbers in this book of the testimony they transcribed in brackets, are: An Yŏnsŏn (9 and 21), Cho Hyeran (12), Chin Sung Chung (4, 8), Kang Chŏngsuk (18, 20), Ko Hyejŏng (10, 16), Okuyama Yoko (17), Sŏ Ŭn'gyŏng (15), Yamasida Yŏngae (7, 13), Yi Sanghwa (3, 19), Yŏ Sunju (6, 11, 14) and Yun Chŏngnan (5).

The exigencies of translation, and a desire to keep the colloquial flow, has required the omission of several repetitive sections and many subtitles added by the compilers of the Korean volume. Many of the original footnotes, and a few clarifications, have been worked into the text. Footnotes are used sparingly to explain details about Korea, Korean lifestyles and the Japanese occupation of Korea which might otherwise elude all but a few. Romanizations, except for the given names of Korean authors, follow the McCune–Reischauer conventions, as recently adopted and revised by the (South) Korean Ministry of Education.[5] My aim has always been for clarity; the authentic text remains that of the Korean testimony. Thanks are due to many: Jane Greenwood at Cassell for patiently acting as go-between between Britain and Korea, to Young Joo Lee for the primary translations, to the members of the Korean Council who have contributed their time and energy and most of all to the living and dead who suffered as sex slaves.

Keith Howard

Notes

1 The division of Korea dates from 1945, hence the testimonies and the historical events to which they relate refer to a single state. The Council and the survivors who have been interviewed here operate and live in the Republic of Korea (South Korea). Much of the debate which we refer to has taken place south of the divide; less information about comfort women in the Democratic People's Republic of Korea (North Korea) is known.

2 *Chŏngshindae munje charyojip* 1 [Materials on the Problem of the Comfort Women], 6. Seoul: The Korean Council for Women Drafted for Military Sexual Slavery by Japan, 1991. The translation is cited in Chungmoo Choi, 'Korean women in a culture of inequality' in Donald Clark (ed.), *Korea Briefing 1992*, 99. Boulder: Westview, 1992.

3 One figure cited by Richard Mitchell, in *The Korean Minority in Japan*, 30 (Berkeley: University of California Press, 1967), from 1925 suggests that female labourers accounted for about 20 per cent of the 106,000 who had been moved to Japan. The proportion of female workers may have been rather less, for 1923 figures give 15,780 women from a total of 120,124. See Michael Weiner, *The Origins of the Korean Community in Japan, 1910–1923*, 79. Manchester: Manchester University Press, 1989.

4 See Chin Sung Chung, this book. Michael Weiner lists only six Korean women out of the 2969 resident in Osaka in 1923 who had reached an education level beyond lower elementary school (op. cit., p. 208).

5 Anon., 'The romanization of Korean according to the McCune–Reischauer system', *The Transactions of the Korea Branch of the Royal Asiatic Society* 38, 121–8; Anon., *P'yŏnsu charyo* II:4. Seoul: Kyoyukpu [Ministry of Education], 1988.

CHAPTER 1

A Korean Tragedy

Keith Howard

The story of the comfort women reflects an unhappy century of Korean development. Five hundred years into the Chosŏn dynasty, the late nineteenth century was a time of turmoil. Confucianism stifled intellectual debate and the land-owning *yangban* aristocracy had entrenched economic stagnation. The *yangban* controlled access to education and, because of a state examination system based on classical Chinese texts, held a monopoly of power. Commoners were throttled: by 1906 almost 70 per cent of government revenue came in the form of a land tax, when 75 per cent of farmers were tenants or part-tenants who worked smallholdings averaging out at less than 2.5 acres. From the eighteenth century, a law punishable by death prohibited Koreans from talking about their country with foreigners. But the 'Hermit Kingdom' found itself threatened by international realignments. The Chinese empire was in decline, and 600 years as a suzerain state left little scope for Korea to forge new political alliances. The 1860s Meiji restoration left Japan, towards which Korea held a long-standing enmity following several invasions, increasingly powerful. And new ideas in scholarship and learning, moulded from the Christian concepts of justice and the rights of man, had begun to filter into the Korean peninsula.

The Korean reaction was retrenchment. When Kojong (r. 1864–1907) ascended to the throne at the age of twelve, his father Yi Haŭng took effective power as the *Taewŏn'gun* [Prince of the Great Court]. Confucian propriety was reimposed. Much of the lineage power that ensured *yangban* control and had institutionalized corruption was curbed. The *Taewŏn'gun*, though, quickly lost local support, particularly when he imposed new taxes and viciously checked dissent from anyone such as Christians who stood for change. His myopic view of foreign relations could not be sustained as foreign powers began to jostle Korea to sign unequal treaties. New factions emerged. A mutiny in 1882 led to an attack on the Japanese legation in Seoul, which provided the excuse for Japanese troops to be sent in as guards. Then, in the 1884 *Kapshin chŏngbyŏn* attempted coup, the expected Japanese support failed to materialize, allowing the court to vacillate back towards Chinese protection. Later, the *Tonghak* peasant rebellion in 1894 threatened state control, and the king asked for Chinese assistance. This led directly to the Sino-Japanese war, as a result of which China was forced to rescind any claims on the peninsula. Japan manoeuvred into position as Korea's modernizing protector. For two years the *Kabo* reforms, financed partly with a Japanese loan, shifted social and political grouping away from the ascribed aristocracy/peasant duality. They initiated Western-style schools, monetary and judiciary systems, and a cabinet-centred constitutional monarchy. In 1896, an elitist Independence Club (the *Tongnip hyŏphoe)* began to argue for independence, but Korea was ill-equipped and unprepared to modernize at a pace dictated by foreign powers. The result was Japanese occupation, inevitable after Korea became a protectorate at the end of 1904, and official from 1910.

The Japanese approach to colonizing Korea was the summation of four modalities. First, Japan allowed few concessions to Koreans, the result of experience in Taiwan where they had had trouble controlling 'unsophisticated' tribes after their invasion of 1895. Second, Britain, other European states and America seemed relatively unconcerned, so Japan felt that in Korea they could emulate colonization practices employed elsewhere. Third, confidence was high, since Japan had triumphed in conflicts with China and Russia. Fourth, legend provided a divine mission, in which Korea could be exploited for Japanese good. Policy institutionalized discrimination: Koreans were to be made useful for the empire. The appropriation of resources moved beyond labour, industry and agriculture to encompass language and culture. Hence, in the 1930s, Koreans were eventually forced to adopt Japanese names and the Japanese language, and to discard shamanism in favour of Shinto. Koreans had no prior experience of democracy, and were used to living in a Confucian autocracy where hierarchical structures ensured that power must be obeyed, not questioned. Thus, and despite the nationwide demonstrations and widespread arrests that followed the 1919 Declaration of Independence, appeals for sovereignty came from competing groups of the educated or disenfranchised. There were two basic factions. Those on the right followed Yi Kwangsu's 1921 *Minjok kaejoron* [Treatise on National Reconstruction] and proposed that education and building wealth should be a higher priority than raising national consciousness. Those on the left soon splintered into Korean, Manchurian and Siberian camps.

To the Japanese, the appropriation of women was a further aspect of exploitation; they attacked at the point of least resistance as they took the young and uneducated. To the Koreans, the issue was never so clear-cut as it might seem from our contemporary viewpoint. There was little widespread understanding of human rights. Serving authority, even if disliked, was not widely questioned. And women had little value in the strictly patrilineal society, where the cost of bringing up a daughter and paying for her marriage put a heavy millstone around the necks of fathers who struggled to provide sufficient food for their families.

Emerging after liberation, the peninsula found itself divided for no reason except convenience. Two young Washington officers – one was Dean Rusk – had been instructed to find a way to divide responsibility for taking the Japanese surrender between the Soviets and the Americans. They suggested the 38th parallel, a line which corresponded to no single geographical feature or administrative boundary. The two halves of the peninsula were soon radically opposed. In the North it was inexpedient to be a former landlord, a collaborator with the Japanese or a Christian; in the South it was better not to be left of centre. The descent into a fratricidal war heaped physical destruction on the colonial inheritance of poverty. Until the late 1970s, rebuilding consumed the energies of both states and both Korean populaces. The Northern regime created a monochromatic socialist power pyramid that survived the death of its founder and single leader, Kim Il Sung, in 1994. After a military coup in 1961, the Southern government under Park Chung Hee accepted massive financial support from America and in 1965, in exchange for a normalization treaty, from Japan. Neither government was particularly concerned with human rights, hence war reparations of a more personal nature had to wait. Change is still to come in the North. In the South, increased individual wealth and greater access to higher education made change inevitable, even though it was held back by a second military coup that brought Chŏn Tuhwan to power in 1980. Chŏn's successor, Roh Tae Woo, initiated much of the needed democratization process while he served as president.

During Roh's administration (1988–94), four factors collided to push for the redress of wrongs committed against comfort women. First, the development of the fledging women's movement, particularly among female scholars, began to encourage primary research on former comfort women. Second, the Korean Legal Aid Center for Family Relations, founded by Tai-Young Lee, the first woman lawyer in Korea, succeeded in 1989 in persuading the government to revise the family law. Third, the 1980s had witnessed an outpouring of nationalism, directed primarily at what was perceived to be foreign cultural imperialism. Koreans had become secure in their economic development, and could now question the continuing influence of Japan, the neighbour on whom they still relied for a large proportion of technology transfers to their domestic industry. A fourth ingredient further focused attention: surviving sex slaves were prepared, at last, to tell their stories. The reason why they had kept silent for so long had much to do with the position of women in Korean society, and it is to this that I now turn.

Many would contend that a Korean woman's lot is not a happy one. The titles of three books in English on Korean women include, respectively, the phrases 'Shamans, housewives and other restless spirits', 'Virtues in conflict', 'View from the inner room'.[1] Women have lived with inequality.[2] During the Chosŏn dynasty, and still reflected in thought patterns today, women have been forced to live under the constraints imposed by Confucianism. Confucianism is a well-reasoned schema for ordering and shaping society, in which the *illyun* moral imperatives separate the functions of husband and wife. In practice, in Korea it enshrined patrilinealism, with male *yang* (Kor: *ŭm*) always above female *yin*. Marriage became a kin transaction to acquire a woman's domestic and procreative services. Male offspring ensured lineage survival, so girls were weak, and married women achieved status only as mothers. Still today, women's given names are often avoided; a girl, as the 'sister of x' (her brother), becomes a wife and the 'mother of y' (her son). Polygamy was until recently legally acceptable if a wife failed to produce a son; among the old, concubines and second wives can still be found, despite legal strictures in place since a 1921 revision of the Civil Code.

Girls were expected to be faithful and chaste (the terms *sujŏl* and *chŏngbu* applied) exemplary women (*yŏllyŏ*). Women were expected to be able to entertain guests and undertake household chores, roles which required little formal education. From the age of seven, strict segregation confined (and hid) women in the *an pang*, the inner rooms. Women, through exogamous marriage, became part of a husband's family. There, they enjoyed no rights to inherit. And virtue meant that even if a husband died his wife remained duty-bound to his family. The remarriage of widows was thus scorned. Further, women were not allowed to divorce until the 1890s *Kabo* reforms; then, divorce was allowed if the husband agreed, but a wife could still not set up her own home. A divorced woman became a *kich'ŏ*, an 'abandoned wife', not dissimilar to the *hwanghyang nyŏ* [returning woman], a category reserved since the seventeenth century for women who made an unwelcome return to their natal home. *Hwanghyang nyŏ* initially marked women sent away as tributes to China and Manchuria, and as in divorce, disdain came from the perception that in a marriage a woman should break all ties to her natal home.

The colonial administration inherited this social environment. The comfort women system could, nonetheless, only work because of Japanese importations. The Japanese licensed prostitution system was adopted – a system dating back to the Minamoto Yoritomo administration's 1193 guidelines and, more specifically, to Tokugawa regulations imposed ostensibly to avert potential Samurai revolts. Indeed, some Korean feminist writers downplay or deny the existence of prostitution in Korea prior to the twentieth century.[3] In Japan, the Meiji restoration had added new legislation in 1872, introducing the registration of brothel prostitutes, nullifying stultifying open-ended contracts and stipulating mandatory weekly check-ups. Money and the complicity related to its acquisition meant that prostitutes, even if no longer virtual prisoners, still tended to come from the countryside. Parents received money from brothel-keepers or middlemen and lost their daughters, in effect, as collateral for the loan. The patterns of recruitment continued as industrialization took hold, with contractors paying for a girl's labour over a fixed period. The image of Britain's dark satanic mills would not be out of place; girls shared squalid barrack huts and worked long hours for little food.

In Korea, given rural poverty, the same forces could be applied. At one end of the spectrum, the colonial administration upgraded *kwŏnbon* training schools for entertainment girls (*kisaeng*), and allowed the publication of catalogues of the most beautiful 'flowers', detailing artistic accomplishments as well as personal statistics.[4] Although the courtesan tradition once had little to do with prostitution – witness the *kisaeng* and poet Hwang Chini (?–1544) – it is clear that women who sang and danced in public fell foul of the Confucian view of appropriate virtuous behaviour. Partly because of this, many *kisaeng* were recruited from the low echelons of rural society, particularly from the *ch'ŏnmin*, a socially outcast group of artisans, traders and entertainers who, until the 1890s, were ranked below farmers in the official hierarchy. The testimonies included here make several references to *kisaeng* and *kwŏnbon*, and clearly demonstrate that women from the lower social orders were targeted by the military. Women were also actively recruited to work in factories, much along the lines already tried in Japan, as Kang Tŏkkyŏng (Chapter 20) relates. The testimonies make it clear that parents and elders remained reluctant to let daughters undertake paid work outside the home; this conflicted with the old sense of propriety. However, the crisis of poverty and the low value placed on daughters conspired to attract the young. Thus, a theme runs through this text: many of the former comfort women say they felt burdened to earn money for their families. This does not in any way diminish the Japanese crime; rather it demonstrates how the colonial authorities manipulated the desperation of Koreans.

After liberation in 1945, change slowly began to occur. Article 10 in the 1948 South Korean constitution guaranteed equality, but the state proved reluctant to allow this in respect of sexual equality. The reason probably lay in a perception that this might engender conflict between law and social custom. Certainly, the Civil Code, promulgated in 1958 to take effect from January 1960, remained discriminatory: women now had the right to inherit, but only half a son's entitlement; a mother/wife came third after sons and daughters; a woman had only limited parental rights, whereas a man could claim illegitimate children as his own; a woman could become household head only if there was no male heir.[5] From the 1960s onwards, women's organizations began to petition for revisions, particularly after members of 61 women's organizations inaugurated the *Pŏmnyŏsŏng kajokpŏp kaejŏng ch'okchinhoe* [Pan-Women's Committee for the Expedition of the Revision of the Family Law] in June 1973.[6] A revision of the family law was approved in December 1977. Now, in the absence of a will, sons and daughters could receive equal inheritance, except that the eldest son – whom tradition obliges to prepare and carry out appropriate ancestral observances – was to receive half as much again as his siblings. Married daughters received one quarter of their siblings' shares, and wives were now entitled to the same amount as the eldest son. Women also gained more parental rights, though the final arbiter remained the husband. And if a woman returned to her natal home after divorce or bereavement, she lost her rights as a parent, a regulation which in effect meant that the husband's family kept the children of a broken union.

The most recent revision, in December 1989, addresses issues of inequality, but continues to favour sons over daughters as family heads. There remain faint echoes of imbalance,[7] but it appears that the law has moved ahead of what remains a conservative society. Inequality is still widespread in everyday life. For example, one legacy of the Japanese colonial period in which the old and the new collide is working girls, *yŏgong*. Old Korea considered paid work unsuitable for women, but in new Korea girls labour to supplement family incomes until – and prior to 1987 this was specified in officially sanctioned contracts – they either marry or get pregnant. *Yŏgong* have provided much of the labour for Korea's economic development, but as cheap labour they institutional-ized a lack of training programmes and enjoyed few promotion opportu-nities. Thus, while women comprised over 40 per cent of the South Korean workforce in 1991, they earned 52.7 per cent of the average male wage.[8] In 1991, the 50 top Korean conglomerates recruited 1200 women but 19,000 men to white-collar and management-level jobs. And, at the same time, domestic work was accorded little monetary value, hence the average claim following the accidental death of a housewife was 276,250 wŏn (about £230).[9] Again, women remained peripheral in the National Assembly prior to 1993; no elected woman was able to take decisions or develop her own policies.[10]

Why, then, did comfort women not break their silence until recently? Apart from the four factors which collided during Roh Tae Woo's presidency, the reason lies primarily in social conservatism. Each revision of the family law has given women more power and control over their own lives, but social convention has taken some time to catch up. In 1945 and 1946, when the comfort women returned to Korea, they came back as *hwanghyang nyŏ*. To the Koreans around them, they were neither faithful nor chaste. They were not exemplary women. The families of comfort women feared the ostracism they would suffer if the shameful past was discovered; the women became an extra burden, and there was little chance to marry them off.

By the beginning of the 1990s social conventions had begun to change. But now, one further factor came into play: age. The former comfort women were now old. They had outlived their parents, and their families – where these existed –had grown up and married. The women had nothing left to lose. Their life stories complete a jigsaw begun in 1962 when Senda Kako, a journalist researching the war for the *Mainichi Shimbun*, uncovered a previously censored wartime photograph. It showed two women wading in the Yellow River. He was told they were 'P' women – Japanese slang that probably descends from a vulgar Chinese word *piya*, 'vagina house' – comfort women. Eleven years later his first book appeared.[11] Senda's efforts were verified and supported by Kim Ilmyŏn's 1976 account.[12] Kim mixed documentary evidence with testimony, notably referring to a 1965 account given under the pseudonym 'Kim Chŏnja', and Ito Keiichi's 1969 publication of Shanghai comfort station regulations promulgated in the late 1930s.

In 1982, Yun Chŏngmo's fictionalized account, *My Mother Was a Military Comfort Woman*, told of a comfort woman who had been sent to the Philippines. Yun was much more direct than the earlier allusions to a heroine's similar past in Hahn Musuk's (1918–94) 1948 novel, *Yŏksanŭn hŭrŭnda* [History Flows].[13] However, strict censorship under Chŏn Tuhwan's regime limited progress in Korea, and most of the debate took place in Japan.[14] A few military memoirs began to appear. Yoshida Seji's 1983 volume is perhaps best known. It describes how each Japanese regiment in Shanghai used one or more dedicated comfort station staffed mainly by Korean women, and recalled expeditions to Korea to recruit labourers in which some 1000 comfort women were taken.[15] By then, at least two documentary films existed. In *Karayuki-san* [Foreign-bound Women] in the late 1970s, the director Imamura Shohei travelled to Malaysia, and then accompanied a former comfort woman back to Japan.[16] In 1979, the director Yamatani Tetsuo in *Okinawa no harumoni* showed the life of a surviving Korean woman living in Okinawa, Pae

Ponggi (1915–91).[17] Pae is normally considered the first Korean comfort woman to have broken silence, and before her death she also appeared in a Korean documentary, Pak Sunam's 1991 *Chŏngshindae Arirang*.[18] Pieces of the jigsaw fell into place as former comfort women came forward – a memoir under the pseudonym Yi Namnim appeared in 1982; Yuyuta, a Korean living in Thailand, was interviewed by the *Asahi Shimbun* newspaper and brought to Seoul in 1985; Shirota Suzuko broadcast her story on Japanese radio in 1986.

International awareness grew. A Taiwanese novel by T'ang Te Kang based on comfort women testimonies appeared. Hung Kuei-chi edited a volume on Japanese atrocities in Taiwan which included information on forced prostitution.[19] Later, in December 1992, a Dutch woman, Jan Ruff, told a public meeting in Tokyo about her experiences;[20] a Javanese comfort woman described, in the May 1993 edition of the Indonesian magazine *Kartini*, how she and her sister were taken. But this is jumping ahead. A new Korean government under Roh Tae Woo was installed in 1988. At home, the climate was changing. On 7 January, more than 200 members of Korean women's groups drafted a protest letter against news that the government would send a representative to attend Emperor Hirohito's funeral. They staged a protest at the former Pagoda Park in Seoul, the site where in 1919 a declaration of independence was announced against Japanese rule. Yun Chung-ok and two members of the Korean Church Women United visited sites in Japan where comfort women had been stationed in February; in April, the church group sponsored a conference on women and tourism. The issue was increasing in importance, and then it exploded into public consciousness when Kim Haksun came forward to tell her story at the church group's offices on 14 August 1990. She was by then 67 years old. A year later, in December 1991, Kim and two other plaintiffs filed a lawsuit at the Tokyo District Court.[21] The full story could begin to be told.[22]

Notes

1 Laurel Kendall, *Shamans, Housewives and Other Restless Spirits: Women in Korean Ritual Life*. Honolulu: Hawaii University Press, 1985; Sandra Matielli (ed.), *Virtues in Conflict: Tradition and the Korean Woman Today*. Seoul: Korea Branch of the Royal Asiatic Society, 1977; Laurel Kendall and Mark Peterson (eds), *Korean Women: View From the Inner Room*. New Haven: East Rock Press, 1983.

2 The picture which emerges seems remarkably consistent. In addition to the books cited above see, in Korean, *Han'guk yŏsŏng undong yaksa*. Seoul: Han'guk puinhoe ch'ŏngbonbu [Korean Women's Association], 1986; and *Yŏsŏng paeksŏ*. Seoul: Han'guk yŏsŏng kaebalwŏn [Korean Women's Development Institute], 1991.

3 For example, Chin Sung Chung, 'Wartime state violence against women of weak nations: military sexual slavery enforced by Japan during World War II', *Korean and Korean American Studies Bulletin* 5.2/3 (Fall/Winter 1994), 21. To my knowledge, there is no adequate study of prostitution in Korea, and certainly no summary comparable to that in Nicholas Bornoff, *Pink Samurai: Law and Marriage in Contemporary Japan*. New York: Simon and Schuster, 1991.

4 An example is, in the Korean pronunciation and reproduced in a mimeographed copy, *Chosŏn miin pogam* [Handbook of Korean Beautiful Women]. Seoul: Minsogwŏn, 1984.

5 A number of discussions of the 1960 Civil Code have been published, among them Ko Chŏngmyŏng, *Han'guk kajokpŏp* [Korean Family Law], 32–7. Seoul: Komunsa, 1980; Yi Taehong, *'Han'guk yŏsŏng ui pŏpchŏk chiwi'* in *Han'guk yŏsŏngsa* [History of Korean Women] 2, 162–7. Seoul: Ehwa yŏja taehakkyo ch'ulp'anbu, 1972; and articles by Pak Pyŏngho and Kim Chusu in Pak Pyŏngho et al., *Modernization and Its Impact on Korean Law*. Berkeley: University of California Press, 1981.

6 One magazine, *Yŏsŏng* [Woman], has studiously followed the campaign. Judith Cherry has published an outline in English: 'Korean women's legal status: tradition and change' in Daniel Bouchez, Robert C. Provine and Roderick Whitfield (eds), *Twenty Papers on Korean Studies Offered to Professor W. E. Skillend. Cahiers d'etudes Coréennes* 5, 45–51. Paris: Collège de France, 1989.

7 '...Legal experts argue that [the 1989 revision] ameliorates only a certain de jure imbalance in practical matters and they expect that de facto discrimination against women may continue for some time': Chungmoo Choi, 'Korean women in a culture of inequality' in Donald Clark (ed.), *Korea Briefing 1992*, 106. Boulder: Westview, 1992.

8 *Chosŏn ilbo*, 15 August 1991.

9 *Chosŏn ilbo*, ibid.

10 Chunghee Sarah Suh, *Women in Korean Politics*. Boulder: Westview, 1993.

11 *Jūgunianfu, 'komaki onna': Hachimanjin no kouhatsu* [Military Comfort Women, 'Voiceless Women': The Indictment of 80,000 People], 1973. I have used a Korean translation by Yi Songhŭi, *Chonggun wianbu*. Seoul: Paeksŏbang, 1991. Senda has reflected further on his research in *Jūgunianfu to Tennō* [Military Comfort Women and the Emperor]. Kyoto: Kamogawa Shuppan, 1992.

12 *Tennō no Guntai Chōsenjin ianfu* [The Emperor's Forces and Korean Comfort Women]. Tokyo: Sanchi Shobo, 1976.

13 Kashima Setsuko translated Yun's book into Japanese as *Haha Jūgunianfu*. Kobe: Gakusei Seinen Senta, 1992. I am grateful to Hyun-ki Kim Hogarth, the author's daughter, for alerting me to Hahn's novel.

14 This does not preclude the considerable discussions between Japanese and Korean scholars. Yun Chung-ok [Yun Chŏngok], a professor at Ehwa Woman's University in Seoul who in the closing days of World War II had narrowly escaped being drafted to the Women's Voluntary Labour Corps, has been particularly active. Her reports dot the available literature in Korean, particularly publications from the Korean Council and its constituent bodies such as the series *Chŏngshindae charyojip* [Materials on the Comfort Women]. A good example of her work is an analysis of 39 former comfort women, '*Chonggun wianbu, 39 myŏn-e taehan shilt'ae chosa pogowa chŏngŭiwa in'gwŏn-e taehan hoso* [Military comfort women, documentation on 39 people, definitions, and appeals about human rights]' in *Kukche in'gwŏn hyŏpyakkwa kanje chong-gun wianbu munje* [International Human Rights Agreements and Questions on the Coerced Military Comfort Women], 2–12. Seoul: The Korean Council for Women Drafted for Military Sexual Slavery by Japan, 1993. Yun is also the primary author of a collection of articles issued in Japanese in 1992, *Chōsenjin josei ga mita ianfu mondai* [The Comfort Women Issue As Seen by Korean Women]. Tokyo: Sanchi Shobo.

15 *Watakushi no sensō hanzai: Chōsenjin kyōsei renkō* [My War Crimes: Forced Drafting of Koreans]. Tokyo: Sanchi Shobo, 1983. Translated into Korean by the Hyŏndaesa yŏn'gushil and issued as *Nanŭn Chosŏn saramŭl irŏkke chabagatta* [This Is How I Abducted Koreans]. Seoul: Ch'ŏngge yŏn'guso, 1989. See also the 1977 volume, *Chōsenjin ianfu to Nihonjin: Gen Shimonoseki rōdō hōkoku dōin buchō no shiku* [Korean Comfort Women and the Japanese: Memoir of a Former Shimonoseki National Service Corps' Recruiting Chief].

16 Later, in 1986, Imamura produced a feature film, *Zegen*, about a comfort station.

17 A brief version of Pae's life story was published posthumously together with documents from North Korea in the English language booklet *Fact-Finding Work and Compensation of 'Comfort Girls' and Forced Labourers*. Tokyo: The Fact-Finding Team on the Truth About Forced Korean Labourers, 1992.

18 This film was reviewed by Kim Kyŏngyong in '*Chŏngshindae arirang: muryo ch'ulhyŏn* [Comfort Women's *Arirang*: benefit performance]', *Tonga ilbo*, 15 October 1992. Several other films exist. The Korean Broadcasting System issued a documentary *Ch'immuk ŭi han* [Suffering of Silence] in August 1990. A film by Sekiguchi Noriko and titled *Senso Daughters* is noted by Alice Yun Chai in her article 'Asia–Pacific feminist coalition politics: the *chŏngshindae/jūgunianfu* ('comfort woman') issue', *Korean Studies* 17 (1993), 67–91. This was distributed by First Run/ICARUS Films. More recently, *Najŭn moksori* [The Murmuring: A History of Korean Women], produced by Byun Young-Joo [Pyŏn Yŏngju] and issued by the Docu-Factory VISTA, was being shown in Seoul cinemas in spring 1995. I am grateful to Brother Anthony for this last information.

19 *Jihpen Tsai-Hua Paosing lu 1928–45* [Japanese Atrocities in China, 1928–45]. Taipei: Kuoshih Kuan, 1985.

20 Evidence given to the war crimes tribunal held by the Dutch in Batavia (Jakarta) in 1948 was meant to be sealed until 2025, but some documents kept in The Hague were made public shortly before Ruff came forward.

21 This is the starting-off point for Seong-Phil Hong, 'A quest for accountability: redressing the wrongs of the comfort women', *Korean and Korean American Studies Bulletin* 5.2/3 (Fall/Winter 1994), 28–37. The background, and early stages in the court proceedings, are detailed in George Hicks, *The Comfort Women*, 148–52, 158–68, 179ff. St Leonards, NSW: Allen and Unwin, 1995.

22 English language materials still remain sparse. Apart from sources already mentioned, I have been introduced to the following by Helen Oh: Jin Sook Lee,'The case of Korean comfort women: women forced into sexual service for Japanese soldiers during World War II seek justice', *Korea Report* (Spring 1992), 18–20; 'Questions of responsibility', *Japan Times*, 5–7 August 1992; Lisa Go, '*Jugunianfu, Karayuki, Japayuki*: a continuity in commodification', *Japanese Militarism Monitor* 53 (January/February 1992), 9–16; Kano Mikiyo,'The problem with the comfort woman problem', *Japan-American Quarterly Review* 24/2 (1993), 40–3; short articles in the *Far Eastern Economic Review*, 18 February 1993, by George Hicks ('Ghosts gathering: comfort women issue haunts Tokyo as pressure mounts') and Louise do Rosario ('A quest for truth: sex slavery issue affects ties with Asian nations'); Watanabe Kazuko, 'Militarism, colonialism, and the trafficking of women', *Bulletin of Concerned Asian Scholars* 26.4 (October–December 1994), 3–17.

CHAPTER 2

Korean Women Drafted for Military Sexual Slavery by Japan

Chin Sung Chung

The extent of the damage which the Japanese inflicted on Korea during their occupation, especially during the Asia–Pacific war, need not be repeated here. Still there are numerous unsolved problems such as the Korean expatriates who remain in Sakhalin, Korean victims of atom bombs, Korean forced labourers, soldiers and civilian employees, and war crimes committed against Korea which fall into the recognized classes B and C. The most tragic issue, however, is the case of comfort women. Only recently have facts begun to emerge about women forcibly drafted between 1930 and 1945 for military prostitution from Japanese colonies and occupied territories, including Korea.

The monstrosity remained buried on the dump of history primarily because the Japanese government and military authorities kept all relevant documents hidden. Documents recently uncovered reveal that the Japanese military not only secretly operated the comfort woman system,[1] but also instructed soldiers who were in charge to destroy records at the end of the war.[2] Japan, unlike Germany, has never tried to resolve post-war issues. It has not concerned itself with fact-finding, restitution and punishment. I consider this to reflect Japan's contempt for other *Asian* nations and the American desire to see their capitalism spread in Asia. In respect of the former, those responsible for drafting Dutch women to serve as comfort women in Indonesia were punished, but the same crime against Asian women has not been dealt with punitively in any way. In respect of the latter, America's priority was to keep Japan on their side in the Cold War. America was lax in its condemnation of Japan's ferocity, and thereby helped Japan dominate Asia once more.[3] Another factor is a culture based on Confucianism which discriminates against women and fosters the shame and silence of sex victims. Therefore, although Japan perpetrated the crimes, responsibility for failing to deal with the issue properly, for concealing it and for not publicizing it as a historical lesson, belongs not only to them but to the sex-discriminating culture of Asia and to the consciousness of the whole world, particularly America.

In late 1991 and early 1992 a number of military documents were discovered in America and Japan[4] and research, which had so far only been attempted in an extremely fragmented fashion through short autobiographical accounts, rapidly progressed. In this new-found atmosphere, victims and assailants began to give testimonies, and both Korean and Japanese governments extended help in unearthing material.[5] Starting with Kim Haksun in August 1991, a number of former Korean comfort women began to report. The Korean Council for Women Drafted for Military Sexual Slavery by Japan [Han'guk chŏngshindae munje taech'aek hyŏbŭihoe] was inaugurated in November 1991 and opened a telephone line to encourage other women to report. In Japan, 'Call 110' was set up as a hot-line for the reports of victims and assailants. The facts about military comfort women, although still vague at times, have slowly begun to take shape. In Korea, the Research Association on the Women Drafted for Military Sexual Slavery by Japan [Chŏngshindae yŏn'guhoe] was established in July 1990 and started research on the former comfort women. It soon took over documenting those who had reported to the Korean Council for Women Drafted for Military Sexual Slavery by Japan.

This book was begun in March 1992, when members of the society began speaking to about 40 former comfort women who had given their addresses and had indicated a willingness to be contacted. In the process of recording testimonies, the number of women we decided to include here was narrowed down to 19. We eliminated those who were reluctant to talk about the details of their experiences, those whose stories contained inconsistencies and those who contradicted themselves. The surviving comfort women are now quite old, and have lived through so much adversity that many can only faintly remember the sufferings they endured. To help them remember their experiences more clearly, all the researchers compared the details of the accounts with what we know about the military history of Japan through documents. In an attempt to obtain accurate testimony, researchers had to interview each survivor more than ten times. They were forced to restrain their emotion and to maintain an objective attitude while talking about heart-breaking experiences.

This chapter studies how the detailed testimonies of these 19 witnesses supports the evidence of documents and previous interviews, along with recently discovered facts. I attempt to reconstruct a more complete picture of the lives of military comfort women than has been possible to date.

The Comfort Stations

Japanese military comfort stations were set up from the time of the invasion of Manchuria to the Second World War. Military regulations allowed only soldiers and civilian employees to visit them.[6] Local civil servants and the general public were specifically forbidden, while soldiers and civilian employees of the military were prohibited from visiting non-military comfort stations, private prostitutes or civilian women.[7] All of the 19 women interviewed said that only soldiers came to their comfort stations, but that there were some rare visits from civilian employees. The military authorities usually directly established and managed the comfort stations. In some cases, the authorities delegated civilians to carry out the whole process. All comfort stations were under strict military protection, assistance and control. The military provided condoms and regular medical check-ups for the women. Women had to obey sanitary and hygiene rules and other regulations set out by the military authorities. Activities in the comfort stations were reported to the military on a regular basis, and even the transfer of women was subject to army orders.[8]

Military comfort stations began to be set up as Japanese forces advanced on the Asian mainland in the early 1930s. In 1932, the increase of Japanese soldiers sent to Shanghai to cope with the Shanghai Uprising was accompanied by the establishment of comfort stations for sailors.[9] A record shows that a request was put to the authorities at about this time for comfort women who could prevent the sailors from raping local women.[10] Fresh documentary evidence unearthed in late 1992 shows that the army set up comfort stations in April 1933. These were managed systematically, with regular medical check-ups and so forth.[11] This supports testimony from a former Japanese soldier who visited Manchurian comfort stations around the same time.[12] Other records show that there were 14 navy comfort stations in Shanghai by 1934, with the military imposing control and assistance, and check-ups carried out once or twice a week.[13] Later, with the increase of stationary troops, the number of comfort stations increased until, by the late 1930s, the number reached its peak and in some areas had begun to decline once more.[14] Therefore 1937 cannot be the year when military comfort stations began to be formed, as has widely been stated, but the year when the stations were systematically expanded.[15]

The 1933 medical record of comfort women in Manchuria shows that 35 women out of 38 who received examinations were Koreans, confirming that Koreans made up the majority of women from the start.[16] From the testimonies of the 19 included here, it is clear that recruitment was actively pursued in later years. Table 1 shows the year in

which the 19 were recruited. From this, we can surmise that the recruitment of comfort women from colonies intensified after 1937, the year
when systematization was firmly imposed.

Table 1

1936	1937	1938	1939	1940	1941	1942	1943	1944	1945
1	4	1	2	1	3	1	2	3	1

A recent study confirms that the comfort women policy was planned,
established and managed, and the women recruited, by the chiefs of the
army and navy General Staff. It further reveals that the commanding officers of the Chosŏn (Korea) Unit, Taiwan Unit, Guangdong Unit, and
Chinese and South Pacific Unit were responsible for their own areas.[17]

Why did the Japanese military need comfort stations? The direct purpose, as presented in military documents was, first, to encourage the spirit of the soldiers. As the war continued, soldiers began to lose their fighting spirit, which had grave consequences for their psychological state and
caused many difficulties in managing occupied territories. The authorities saw the sexual comfort facilities as a means of reducing these
problems.[18] Second, the main purpose in strictly forbidding soldiers from
using other brothels was to protect them from venereal infection. This
meant they must use military stations established exclusively for them. It
is a known fact that venereal infection was widespread among soldiers
when the Japanese advanced into Siberia during the period 1918–22.
The claim that this past experience was one main reason for setting up
comfort stations is persuasive.[19] The fact that the military saw it as important to give comfort women regular medical check-ups, and oversaw
management, surely reinforces this claim.[20]

Third, the most direct reason for expanding military comfort stations
during the war was the frequent rape of women carried out by Japanese
soldiers. Soldiers plundered towns, raped women, started fires and
brutally killed any captives. Rape, in particular, tended to provoke strong
anti-Japanese local feeling.[21] This made it difficult to rule the occupied
territories, hence the military ordered: '…each soldier's behaviour must
be tightly controlled and sexual comfort facilities should soon be set up'.[22]
Besides this, the military authorities imposed a business and luxury tax on
comfort stations that were not directly established and managed by the
military but, rather, were operated by civilians.[23] Some claim this is an
indication that the military was actively involved in setting up comfort
stations in order to expand their sources of revenue.[24]

It is, however, important to consider Japan's unique historical and social background under these superficial, even if direct, reasons. Under the Meiji system, freedom of movement had been repressed and the position of the monarchy strengthened. This institutionalized a discriminative imperialism that soon produced a social structure which lowered the position of women. The imperial government imposed a family system which completely ignored women's rights in society. It established a licensed prostitution system to meet the desires of men, especially the military, and to protect the family system it had already imposed.[25] Military comfort stations, established to satisfy and raise the spirits of soldiers, can be seen as a variation on the licensed prostitution system. The characteristics of the military system clearly distinguish it from the licensed prostitution system since it forcibly recruited vast numbers of women from the colonies. From this it is clear that the military system was established in direct relation to the Japanese policy of obliterating colonial races, Koreans in particular.[26] The system did not recruit Japanese prostitutes, but forcibly took Koreans, most of whom were to die on the battlefield, while those who survived would be unable to rear children.

It would not be an exaggeration to say that comfort stations were established wherever Japanese military units were stationed. An American report states that 'comfort girls' were found wherever it was necessary for the Japanese army to fight.[27] Testimonies of former Japanese soldiers show that comfort stations were located in many areas, not only in the occupied territories of China and Manchuria, but also in colonies such as Taiwan and Korea, and even at home in Japan.[28] A record showing about 50 Koreans who worked on Sumbawa island, at the southern tip of Indonesia, indicates how far afield the Korean comfort women were dispersed.[29] The areas to which former comfort women whom we have interviewed here were sent are various. Many did not stay in one place but moved with troops or for personal reasons. They continued to be forced to serve soldiers wherever they were. In Table 2, the areas where women stayed for the longest periods are given:

Table 2

Manchuria	4
China (except Manchuria)	7
Pacific islands	2
South Asia	5
Taiwan	2
Japan	2
Korea	1

Stations varied in kind according to the time and place of their establishment. They can be divided into three types: those established by the military authorities;[30] those established by civilians but licensed by the authorities;[31] existing private brothels which the authorities subsequently requisitioned for military use.[32] It is clear that comfort stations established by civilians had to obtain permission and licences from the military authorities, and civilian managers paid a fixed business tax each month.[33] Stations established by the military were either managed directly by a unit or by civilians appointed by the army.[34] Those established by civilians were mostly managed by civilians and were located outside units. In contrast, stations controlled directly by the military were located within army compounds or were sited adjacent to units housed in converted residences or schools. Of the stations to which the 19 interviewees were sent, seven were established and managed by the army, seven established by the army but managed by civilians and five were set up and run by civilians. Although some of our informants could give us no direct information as to who established their stations, it is possible to deduce the responsible agents from meal provisions and the condition of buildings. One informant told us of a civilian manager in a station established by the military who received a monthly salary directly from the army. The military's serious and systematic involvement in establishing and managing comfort stations is evident throughout the testimonies in this volume.

The Comfort Women
Who were the women mobilized for comfort stations during the 15-year war period?

Nationality
The nationality of women is of major interest, but remains the most difficult aspect on which to obtain accurate information. It has been generally accepted that between 80 per cent and 90 per cent of the women were Korean. This reflects one of the earliest documents on military comfort stations, the testimony of Aso Tetsuo, a former military surgeon, which documented a comfort station in Shanghai in 1939.[35] It is also accepted by Senda Kako, one of the earliest researchers on military comfort women.[36] The fact that Korean women constituted up to 90 per cent of comfort women is also supported by a military document disclosed by the Japanese government in July 1993 and by documents on the Manchurian army revealed by the Seoul-based Fact Finding Committee for Coercively Drafted Koreans [*Chosŏnin kangje yŏnhaeng chinsang chosadan*].[37] Furthermore, Japanese soldiers who responded to the hot-line 'Call 100' installed by a Japanese non-governmental office testified that most of the

women in stations located in South Asia, the Pacific islands and remote areas of the Philippines were Koreans.

Recently, new records have been found in Nanjing and elsewhere in China which state that there were more Japanese and Chinese than Korean women, but these records cannot be considered sufficient to counter the Korean majority theory.[38] Other records show that women from China and other occupied territories were also forced to become comfort women, but the exact number remains unknown.[39] Some of the testimonies recorded here accept that there were a small number of Japanese and Chinese women, but report that women of other national-ities were rarely, if ever, seen.

Some Japanese soldiers have testified that Japanese women were reserved for officers and Koreans for the ratings. Some add that Taiwanese women were meant for civilian employees.[40] The regulations in most documents allow the officers and the ratings to visit the same women during different parts of the day.[41] Clearly, the separation of women and their duties by nationality does not seem to have generally been practised. Only one woman interviewed here stated that Japanese women served officers, and Koreans the rank and file: this was at the Akyab (Sittwe) comfort station. Eighteen testify that they, sometimes along with a small number of Japanese women, together served both officers and rank and file at different times. One states specifically that officers preferred Korean women, since the Japanese were older and had worked in brothels as prostitutes before they came to the comfort station.

Age

The legal age for licensed prostitution was 18 in Japan and 17 in Korea.[42] In contrast, there appear to have been no age restrictions for comfort women. One 1940 document left by an army unit in China states that a prostitute must be aged 16 or over, but the regulations of other stations discovered so far do not mention anything about age.[43] One woman interviewed by us said she was taken to Taiwan when aged 11 and had had to run errands in the comfort station because she could only obtain a licence when she reached 15. The accounts of two others we have not included here reveal a similar age restriction. One of these latter unfortunates was forcibly taken to somewhere near Shimonoseki when 13, where she was grouped by age along with many others brought from other parts of Korea. She was taken with other young girls to a fabric factory in Tokyo, where she worked for two years before moving to a comfort station in Osaka once she turned 15. The second woman was taken to Japan but was allowed to return to Korea because she was too young. Of the 19 we have interviewed here, one was 11 when taken, one 14, two 15, five 16, four 17, two 18, two 19, one 21 and one 22. This would suggest that an age restriction was imposed in only a few places. It also appears that young girls were preferred.

Financial background

Most of the comfort women came from poor farming families, and had received little formal education. Of the 19, four had had no education, four had only attended night school, ten had gone to elementary school and one was still attending secondary school when sent to Japan. This last woman was first mobilized in the Voluntary Labour Corps and sent to a factory. She ran away but was captured by the military police and taken to a comfort station. It is plain that the Japanese government took women from the working class to minimize public criticism and any potential condemnation of their forceful and deceptive ways.

Marital status.

Only one of the 19 was married, but she was living alone in Seoul when taken away. All the rest were unmarried, although one woman had been registered by her parents as married as a disguise to avoid suffering this sort of fate at the hands of the Japanese. None came from brothels.

Place of birth and recruitment.

Of the 19 women, one was born in Japan while 17 came from the southern provinces, of Korea. Those born in Kyŏngsang provinces, the southeastern part of the peninsula adjacent to Japan, constitute the majority. Although most came from farming backgrounds, their place of birth and the place where they were living when taken away varies. Many were taken in Seoul, and some in other cities. Comfort women were clearly recruited from a wide area, not only from the rural countryside but also from cities. Table 3 shows their place of recruitment.

Methods of recruitment

The ways in which Korean women were drafted has become a matter of controversy between Korea and the Japanese authorities. No military documents so far uncovered have explained the methods of recruitment in any detail. Only Yoshida Seiji, one of the men responsible for drafting Korean comfort women, has testified that army headquarters supplied him with trucks and soldiers to take women away by force.[44]

As defined by an international regulation contemporary to the time, taking anybody through deceit, violence, threat, misuse of power or any other coercive means constituted an act of forced drafting.[45] The methods used against the women we have interviewed here consequently constitute coercive recruitment. Our research shows that the method of

Table 3

	Birth place	Place of recruitment
Seoul	1	3
Kyŏnggi province	1	
South Ch'ungch'ŏng province	1	
North Ch'ungch'ŏng province		
South Chŏlla province	1	2
North Chŏlla province	2	1
South Kyŏngsang province	6	5
North Kyŏngsang province	5	3
South Hamhŭng province	1	1
Japan	1	2
Manchuria		1
Beijing		1

recruitment divides into four types: recruitment by violence, including threats of violence and the misuse of power; false promises of employment; abduction; human traffic. In the cases of violent recruitment, soldiers and the military police were largely responsible, though there are a few documented cases where civilian employees took part. The most commonly used method was to tempt women with false promises of employment in Japan. Civilians were mostly responsible here, but we have also recorded instances which involved the complicity of people in authority such as village heads, community officers, soldiers and civilian employees. Abduction and human traffic were usually carried out by civilians, but occasionally soldiers were involved. Even when coercive recruitment was organized by civilians, it is evident that the military controlled and intervened by providing transport such as boats or trucks, or by raping the women during transit. A military document dated 4 March 1938 actually records that 'personnel in charge of drafting women must be selected with great care to minimize commotion during the process', thus implying that civilians could be appointed or licensed by the military to recruit women.[46] The fact that both mobilizer and women needed a travel pass also confirms that the military systematically intervened in the whole recruitment operation.[47]

Table 4 shows how the women we have interviewed here were drafted. Two were actually drafted twice, one recruited initially for the women's Voluntary Corps.

Table 4

Recruitment method	Recruited by			
	Civilians	Local authority	Military/ military police	Civilian employees
Violence			3	1
False employment	6	2	1	4
Abduction	1		1	
Human traffic	1			
Other			1	

The women drafted through these various underhand methods were forced to become comfort women. So, they were taken by deception, and once they reached their destination they were forced to serve men as sex slaves, often through the use of further threats and/or violence. Therefore, mobilization was entirely violent and coercive.

The Running of Comfort Stations

Military comfort stations were managed according to rules set by the army. These rules typically allocated different hours for different ranks of soldiers, set out fees and regulated regular medical check-ups and the allowable standards of sanitation. The details varied slightly from station to station, but each place seems to have been subject to written regulations dealing with these same points. The regulations were meant to be strictly obeyed, although we have no way of finding out how well they were adhered to in reality.[48]

Hours

The hours for visitation were fixed and were meant to be strictly kept.[49] If a station was used by several units, each unit was allowed to visit women on a certain day of the week.[50] The ratings, non-commissioned officers and officers were given different visiting hours, which varied according to each comfort station and seem to have been adapted according to local circumstances.[51] I have noted that in a few places Japanese women served only officers and Koreans the lower rank and file. In most places, women had to serve all ranks.

The time allowed for each man was either 30 minutes or an hour. Those who came after regular hours and stayed overnight were charged extra.[52] In spite of regulations concerning the hours, and according to the testimony of former soldiers, most men only took a few minutes each because there were so many others waiting. These same soldiers say that between 20 and 30 soldiers would queue up outside the women's rooms, with their trousers down, waiting their turn.[53] Of the women we have interviewed here, ten said there were time regulations while nine could remember no limits on time. Most of the former ten said that the regulations were not enforced properly or adequately. Especially at weekends, soldiers would crowd in regardless of the set time limits, and in extreme cases a woman had to serve 100 men in a single day. As a result of being forced to endure such an excessively unnatural life, most comfort women contracted diseases such as venereal infection and many were injured on occasions by violent soldiers. The women still suffer from the resulting physical ailments.

Fees

Fees specified in station regulations varied according to rank and the hours of visiting. For example, one station in 1942 charged the lower rank and file 1 yen for 30 minutes or 2 yen for an hour, non-commissioned officers 1.5 yen and 2.5 yen respectively, and officers 3 yen and 4 yen. Officers were charged 8 yen to stay overnight.[54] Charges also varied in different areas and at different periods of the war. Mostly, the fees were paid through the purchase of tickets that helped to prevent confusion.[55] Regardless of the fees, comfort women were not paid in accordance with what was actually stipulated in the regulations. Only three of the women we have interviewed say that they were paid for their services, either with money or with tickets. One testifies that she was able to save a substantial amount and send money home. Seven say they received cash or tickets from soldiers which they were then forced to give to proprietors. These same seven say they were never repaid for the tickets or the cash. Four say that the proprietors managed money and/or the tickets. The remaining survivors remember nothing about fees. Several report that they received occasional pocket-money from soldiers, but insist that this did not take the form of direct payment for services rendered. One reports how she prayed every day for Japan to win the war, because her proprietor had promised she would be paid in one lump sum after the conclusion of hostilities.

The regulations of one comfort station specified fees according to the nationality of women. Here, to serve a non-commissioned officer a Japanese woman was to receive 2 yen, a Korean 1.5 yen, and a Chinese 1 yen.[56] Some soldiers who responded to the Japanese hot-line said that fees reflected a descending order from Japanese, through Korean, to Chinese women. However, this system was never mentioned by any of the women we are concerned with here.

Medical check-ups and sanitary conditions

As I mentioned earlier, regular medicals to check for venereal infection were considered a matter of great importance. Regulations that specify check-ups every week, every fortnight or every month appear in many military documents. A considerable number of records that show the results of such check-ups have also been discovered.[57] Only three of the women say they never received check-ups, but the rest report that they were regularly examined, either at a clinic or by military surgeons who visited the comfort stations. The frequency of examinations varied.

The military authorities ordered soldiers to use condoms to prevent the spread of venereal disease. Sheaths were given to soldiers, but were also distributed to comfort stations to make sure that all men would use them.[58] Most women say that the soldiers had to use condoms, and one reports that if any man refused, she was instructed to report him to the military police. However, in spite of the strictness of these regulations, many survivors state there were soldiers who refused to use protection. And, although soldiers were meant to bring their own condoms, many used those provided at the comfort stations. It is because of this that several women say they washed used condoms, finally throwing them away after anything up to five separate uses. These same women confess that they felt wretched when they had to wash sheaths.

Military documents which stress thorough sanitation, including the regular disinfection of women, have been discovered.[59] Three interviewees say they washed themselves every time they served a man. Yet, in spite of such strict controls, venereal disease was common. The medical records of comfort women discovered to date show that many were infected with disease and were hospitalized to receive treatment.[60] Given such circumstances, the authors of some documents argued that medical check-ups were useless.[61] Those who were diagnosed as being infected were generally not allowed to serve men until they recovered.[62]

Of the women interviewed here, seven say they caught venereal infections. They were usually given an injection, always called 'No. 606', and did not serve soldiers for a few days. One woman remembers how one of her colleagues was treated in isolation because she was so severely infected. This woman never returned to the station. Military surgeons treated most of those who were suffering, but there were cases where the proprietor himself gave the required injections. Only two women report that they had to continue to serve men while infected. Besides venereal infections, the women suffered from all sorts of other diseases such as malaria, jaundice, mental disorders and vaginal swelling. The ailments caught and suffered 50 years ago still trouble them today. Two became pregnant: the baby of one died in her womb and the other child was given to an orphanage.

Regulations banned soldiers from drinking in comfort stations, and soldiers who were drunk were generally not allowed to visit women. Violence directed at women was also specifically forbidden. In spite of such rules, however, it is clear that soldiers were abusive. Most women say that they feel they were not treated as human beings. Not only the soldiers, but proprietors also were cruel. As a consequence, women were forced to serve men even during menstruation, and if they refused or resisted they faced harsh treatment from the soldiers and proprietors alike. Most women still bear the marks of such abuse. All the women interviewed in this book used Japanese names, most given them in the stations while they were comfort women. This shows that attempts were made to destroy their identities. Most testify that in addition to serving soldiers they had to wash their own clothes, clean, serve food, cut hay, receive training while wearing the armband of the National Defence Women and regularly recite the Oath of Imperial Subjects. One notable case is the woman who first worked as a nurse's assistant before she was forced to transfer to work as a comfort woman. Four others were given work assisting nurses after they had served a period of time as comfort women. This once again demonstrates that women in all types of comfort stations, along with military nurses and orderlies, were under the supervision and control of the military authorities.

After the War

Although the Japanese military exploited comfort women to such an extent, hardly any were taken back to Japan after the war. The treatment received by the women after Japan capitulated was in a way much more cruel than what they had been subjected to when they were initially drafted or when they later worked in the comfort stations. Many soldiers have stated that women were abandoned in their stations, were forced to take their own lives along with soldiers or were taken to caves or submarines and murdered.[63]

Among those interviewed here, eight were able to leave their comfort stations before the war ended. Two ran away, one was sent home because she had a serious venereal disease, four received travel passes with the help of officers they had grown close to and one returned home with her proprietor. One went back to her first comfort station, and a total of 12 were able to return to Korea once the war ended. Only one of the 12 who returned to Korea initially left her comfort station with Japanese soldiers, while the other 11 say that soldiers simply suddenly stopped coming to the station. After the soldiers fled, abandoned women found their own way home or stayed in American refugee camps before they were shipped to Korea.

Those who had been comfort women suffered greatly back in Korea. They still suffered from diseases they had contracted while working in the comfort stations. They bore guilty consciences, simply because of the knowledge that they had been prostitutes. They suffered from the prejudice and discrimination of their relatives and friends. Many still had venereal disease or from time to time suffered its recurrence. The son of one became mentally disordered because his mother had venereal infection at the time of conception. Many women subsequently found they were barren, and many still suffer from ailments, from womb infections, high blood pressure, stomach trouble, heart trouble, nervous breakdowns, mental illness and so on. The psychological aftermath is far more serious than the physical suffering endured in the comfort stations. Apart from nervous breakdowns or mental disorders, the effects of which can be noticed externally, the minds of former comfort women are haunted by delusions of persecution, shame and inferiority. They tend to retain a distrust and hatred of men. They want to avoid contact with other human beings. Taken together, all of these make it difficult for the women to carry on any normal social life. The prejudice and discrimination heaped on them by society makes them feel particularly wretched. People around the women tend to despise them, guessing even if never told that they were sexually victimized while abroad. One woman we interviewed was thrown out of her house when her husband discovered the secrets of her past.

According to our research, women were most resentful of the fact that they were unable to lead ordinary married lives after their return.[64] Six of the women we interviewed married, and five became second wives. But all marriages failed. Eight experienced some form of family life by moving in with men without marrying, but most of these relationships also ended in breakdown. Five women never married. Only two live with their own children; one stays with an adopted son, and one with a grandchild. The remaining 15 women now live on their own. All once tried to make a living on their own. They have, however, suffered from poor physical and mental health, hence work is difficult and all have consequently endured great financial difficulties. The women managed to survive an extremely harsh life on the battlefields of a foreign war, but the reality they have been forced to face since their return to Korea in peacetime has been nothing short of a continuation of their hardship, even though in a different form.

Conclusions

Many of the details concerning the operation of the comfort women system, including its overall scale, have yet to be uncovered. Yet, we have been able to discover a number of facts about Japanese military comfort women from military documents, the testimonies of former soldiers and through close scrutiny of the accounts of former sex slaves themselves. From what we have discussed so far, we can conclude that the Japanese comfort station system had its own characteristics; it was unique in world history. The stations were strictly and exclusively for the use of soldiers. They were systematically planned, established and controlled by the Japanese imperial government and they were set up almost wherever military units were stationed. Most of the comfort women were supplied by Japanese colonies. The women were drafted by force; they were not treated as human beings but merely as military necessities. As I discussed at the outset, these characteristics have much to do with Japan's unique cultural history.

From the perspective created by this consideration we can begin to uncover a more fundamental infrastructure of human behaviour. This can be defined as violence inflicted by one nation on the women of another nation. The women will mostly be from the lower classes and are used by a nation taking advantage of the chaotic situation which we call war. It is possible that this same behaviour can be repeated in any country when nations, people, women, class and confusion combine, either in totality or selectively. Similar crimes can arise when only some of these elements combine. The similar issues in Bosnia which recently astonished an unsuspecting world were cases of violence on the women of another nation carried out during war. Although we cannot know whether the government actually planned what occurred, Bosnia was a case of large-scale, mass rape carried out by the army. It bore all the traits of public, rather than private, violence. Indeed there are a large number of cases in world history where women have been violated on an organized basis by military forces in war. The Japanese military took their own prostitutes along during campaigning in the Sino-Japanese and Russo-Japanese wars prior to their colonization of Korea, and when they invaded Siberia. Florence Nightingale states that the British military took comfort women with them during the Crimean War. It is true that prostitution prospers wherever military units are sent.[65]

In conclusion then, we can see that the system of military comfort women had its roots in Japan's unique social background, but also holds a form of universality: it can arise and occur anywhere in the world. Nonetheless, the issue has never been evaluated, let alone condemned, by the international community. As a specific case, the issue of women drafted for military prostitution has never been resolved between Japan and Korea. Right now, while some of the comfort women are still alive, the world must re-examine the social conditions of this case, examine how ignoring such tragedies has allowed Japan to achieve its position today, and take positive steps to protect the world from similar things ever happening again. Finally, I would like to emphasize that, in the light of the present worldwide situation, where nationalism is resurgent and state intervention in civilian society is more pervasive than ever, the characteristics and universality of the issue of Japanese military sex slavery must be noted and properly understood.

Notes

1 All documents concerning military comfort stations were classified as top secret. Documents cited in the following pages are used to support the statements given in the interviews which follow.

2 One document discovered states: 'Accurate data are missing because many of the records of the 48th Division were destroyed at the end of the war, following orders from superiors, and the remainder was submitted to the Australian army. Therefore we have had to focus on the memories of the soldiers...': *Dai-48 shidan senshi shiryō narabi shūsen jōkyō* [Military History Material of the 48th Division and End of War Condition], 1946.

3 Takaki Kenichi, 'P'yŏnghwarŭl mandŭnŭn yŏsŏng [Women making peace]' in *Ilbonŭi chŏnhu posange daehaesŏ* [On Japan's Post-war Compensation], Kidokkyo yŏsŏng p'yŏnghwa yŏn'guwŏn [Christian Women's Peace Research Centre], 56–7. Seoul: 1992.

4 In November 1991 a record entitled 'Headquarters, US Naval Military Government' dated Okinawa, November 1945, was discovered. In December, the report of the United States Offices of War, Information Psychological Warfare Team dated August, September and October 1944 was released. In January 1992, Professor Yoshimi Yoshiaki of the University of Chuo unearthed several documents concerning military comfort women in Japan's Defence Library. These played an important role in increasing public interest in the issue.

5 On 31 July 1992, the South Korean government's *Chŏngshindae munje shilmu taech'aekp'an* [Board for Military Comfort Women] published an interim report entitled *Ilcheha kundae wianbu shilt'ae chosa* [Survey on the Reality of Military Comfort Women]. On 6 July 1992, the Japanese government had issued a research report, *Chōsen hantō shusshin no iwayuru jūgun ianfu mondai ni tsuite* [Concerning the So-called Comfort Women of the Korean Peninsula Serving the Army] based on documents preserved in the Police Agency, the Defence Ministry, the Foreign Ministry, the Ministry of Culture, the Ministry of Welfare and the Ministry of Labour. On 4 August 1993, a second report was issued which re-examined the data preserved in these six government departments, and investigated other documents kept by the Ministry of Justice, the National Library of Official Documents, the National Congress Library and the American Library of Official Documents. This second report also added the testimonies of former soldiers and comfort women.

6 'Use of the comfort stations is restricted to soldiers and civilian employees in uniform' states '*Iansho kitei sōfu no ken* [Concerning comfort station regulations]' in *Gunsei hanbu Bisaya shibu Iroiro shutchōjo* [Military Authority, Bisaya Department, Iroiro Branch Office], November 1942.

7 '...they are never to serve local men' states '*Gaimushō keisatsushi, Shina no bu: Shōwa 13 nen ni okeru zaihōnin no tokushu fujo no jōkyō oyobi sono torishimari narabi ni sokai tōkyoku no shishō torishimari jōkyō*

[Foreign Office Police History, China Section: Condition of Japanese authority in dealing with special women and private prostitutes]' in *Zai Shanghai sōryō jikan* [Shanghai Consular Division]. Also: '...local officials and civilians are prohibited at all times' and '...soldiers and civilian employees are strictly forbidden to use other comfort stations': '*Gunjin kurabu ni kan suru kitei* [Regulations on the Military Clubs]' in records of the *San dai 3475 butai* [The 3475th Division], December 1944. And: '...any contact with prostitutes besides these recognized by the military authorities or with any local residents is strictly forbidden': '*Senji fukumu yōbō* [Outline of War-time Duties]', *Kyōiku sōkanbu* [Education General Office], 1938.

8 '...the managers of comfort stations ... should report circumstances in their stations to the military authorities ...': '*Iansho kitei sōfu no ken* [Concerning comfort station regulations]' in *Gunsei hanbu Bisaya shibu Iroiro shutchōjo* [Military Authority, Bisaya Department, Iroiro Branch Office], November 1942. And: '...the women in the special category are being transferred by military orders': '*Gaimushō keisatsushi, Shina no bu* [Foreign Office Police History, China Section]' 1 in *Zai Kyūshū ryōjikan* [Kyūshū Consular Division], December 1938.

9 '*Gaimushō keisatsushi, Shina no bu* [Foreign Office Police History, China Section]' in *Zai Shanghai sōryō jikan* [Shanghai Consular Division], 1938.

10 Inaba Masao (ed.), '*Ajia Taiheiyō sensō Kankokujin giseisha hoshō seikyū jiken* [Demands of compensation by Korean victims of the Asia–Pacific War]' in *Okamura Neiji taishō shiryō* [Data on General Okamura] as cited in *Sojō* [Petition] (2nd edition), 1992.

11 '*Eisei gyōmu junpō 34 hen* [Hygiene Duty 10-day Report, 34th edition]' of the *Konsei dai 14 ryodan shireibu* [Mixed 14th Brigade Command Office], September 1932–December 1933. And: '*Gei shōgi shakufu kenkō shindan jisshi yōryō* [Outline of medical check-up plans for geisha, prostitutes and barmaids]', *Konsei dai 14 ryodan shireibu* [Mixed 14th Brigade Command Office], cited from an article in the *Asahi Shimbun*, 6 December 1992.

12 '*Jūgun ianfu 110 ban* [Military Comfort Women, No. 110]', edited by *Jūgun ianfu 110 ban henshū iinkai hen* [Editorial Committee for the Military Comfort Women hot-line], 1992.

13 '*Shōwa 13 nen Zai Shanghai sōryō jikan Keisatsu jimu jōkyō* [Shōwa, 13th year, Police Duty Condition of Shanghai Consular Division]', *Zai Shanghai sōryō jikan* [Shanghai Consular Division], 1935: '*Gaimushō keisatsushi, Shina no bu* [Foreign Office Police History, China Section]', *Zai Shanghai sōryō jikan* [Shanghai Consular Division], 1936; '*Gaimushō keisatsushi, Shina no bu* [Foreign Office Police History, China Section]', *Zai Tianjin sōryō jikan Tanggu shutchōjo* [Tianjin Consular Division, Tanggu District Office], 1937.

14 'Recently, with the increase of other comfort facilities (restaurant, cafés, and so on) the number of military comfort stations has begun to decline': '*Sinji junpō* [Wartime 10-day Report]' of the *Nami shūdan* [Nami Command Office], 10–20 April 1939.

15 For example, the date 1937 is given by Suzuki Yūko, Kim Ilmyŏn and others.

16 '*Eisei gyōmu junpō 34 hen* [Hygiene Duty 10-day Report, 34th edition]', *Konsei dai 14 ryodan shireibu* [Mixed 14th Brigade Command Office], September 1932–December 1933. And: '*Gei shōgi shakufu kenkō shindan jisshi yōryō* [Outline of medical check-up plans for geisha, prostitutes and barmaids]', *Konsei dai 14 ryodan shireibu* [Mixed 14th Brigade Command Office], cited from an article in the *Asahi Shimbun*, 6 December 1992.

17 Yoshimi Yoshiaki, '*Chŏnggun wianbu munje ŭi yŏksahakchŏk kyumyŏng* [A Historical Study of the Issue of Military Comfort Women]', a paper read at the Joint Symposium of the Japan War Data Centre and *Han'guk chŏngshindae munje taech'aek hyŏbŭihoe* [The Korean Council for Women Drafted for Military Sexual Slavery by Japan], in December 1993.

18 '*Shina jihen no keiken yori kan taru gunki shinsaku taisaku* [Policy to raise the military spirit based on the China Incident experience]', *Hōjūtai honbu* [Artillery Unit Headquarters], September 1940.

27

19 Kŭm Pyŏngdong, '*Jŭgun ianfu gokuhi shiryō* [Top secret material on military comfort women]' in Kŭm Pyŏngdong (ed.), *Kaisetsu* [Commentary]. Tokyo: Ryokuin Shōbō, 1992.

20 This argument can be traced back to the Meiji restoration, when the government created a law which made it compulsory for prostitutes to be examined regularly for syphilis. For details (in Korean) see Yamasida Yŏngae, *Han'guk kŭndae kongch'ang chedo shilshi-e kwanhan yŏn'gu* [A Study on the System of State Regulated Prostitution in Modern Korea], MA dissertation, Seoul: Ewha Women's University, 1991.

21 For example, see '*Shina jihen no keiken yori kan taru gunki shinsaku taisaku* [Policy to raise the military spirit, based on the China Incident experience]', *Hōjūtai honbu* [Artillery Unit Headquarters], September 1940, and '*Jinchū nisshi* [Battlefield Diary]', *Hohei dai-9 ryodan* [9th Infantry Brigade].

22 '*Jinchū nisshi* [Battlefield Diary]', *Hohei dai 41 rentai* [41st Infantry Regiment], 1–31 July 1938.

23 '*Ryo shūdan tokumbu geppō* [Ryo Group Special Duty Section Monthly Report]', April 1940.

24 For example, see *Sangiin yosan iinkai giroku* [House of Representatives' Budget Minutes] for 8 April 1992.

25 See Fukae Seiko, '*Baishun seido to tennōsei* [Prostitute system and emperor system]' in Suzuki Yūko and Kondō Kazuko (eds), *Onna tennōsei, sensō* [Women, the Emperor System, and War]. Tokyo: Orijin-senta, 1989.

26 Japan tried to make Koreans Japanese. They forced them to take Japanese names, to worship the Japanese emperor and forbade them to speak Korean. Japan tried to eliminate Korea as a nation by moving Japanese migrants to the Korean peninsula and expelling Koreans to other countries such as Manchuria. The case in relation to comfort women is made by Yun Chŏngok, '*Chŏngshindae, muŏshi munje in'ga*? [Sexual slavery, what is the problem?]' in *Chŏngshindae munje charyojip* [Research Data on Sexual Slavery] 1, 12. Seoul: Hanguk chŏngshindae munje

taech'aek hyŏbŭihoe [Korean Council for Women Drafted for Military Sexual Slavery by Japan], 1991.

27 United States Offices of War Information, Psychological Warfare Team, 1944.

28 '*Jŭgun ianfu 110 ban* [Military Comfort Women, No. 110]', edited by *Jŭgun ianfu 110 ban henshū iinkai hen* [Editorial Committee for the Military Comfort Women hot-line], 1992.

29 *Dai-48 shidan senshi shiryō narabi shūsen jōkyō* [Military History Material of the 48th Division and the End of the War Condition], 1946.

30 'Each unit must immediately report details on opening a comfort station': *Dae 62 shidankai hōtei*, 17 September 1944. Also: 'Order: A company must install the temporary facility of a comfort station in a [specified] house on the 5th of the month': *Jinchū nisshi, Yōsai kenchiku kinmu dae 6-chūtai* [Fortress Construction Duty, 6th Troop], 1–30 June 1944. And: 'Five people from and below *Yamaguchi gunsō* of *Kanriban* rank should start installing the facilities for comfort stations': *Jinchū nisshi, Dai-62 Shidan fuku kanbu* [62nd Division, Adjutant Section], January–February 1945.

31 'Those who wish to open comfort stations must apply to the Medical Section of this department': *Ryo shūdan tokumubu geppō* [Monthly Report, Ryo Group Special Duty]', *Ryo shūdan tokumubu* [Ryo Group, Special Duty Section], 4 May 1940.

32 '…about an existing comfort station … one part must be set apart and managed for special purposes for the convenience of local residents', stated in '*Gaimushō keisatsushi: Shina no bu* [Foreign Office Police History: China Section]', *Zai Nanjing sōryō jikan* [Nanjing Consular Office], 16 April 1938.

33 'Managers must renew their licences every three months; 50 sen [0.5 yen] for a licence, 7 yen for the monthly business tax': '*Ryo shūdan tokumubu geppō* [Monthly Report, Ryo Group Special Duty]', *Ryo shūdan tokumubu* [Ryo Group, Special Duty Section], 4 May 1940.

34 'Officers must control, supervise and guide the management of the clubs so that business can run smoothly and properly.... Medical officers must be responsible for sanitation facilities ... and administrative officers for book keeping...': *Gunjin kurabu riyō kitei* [Regulations on the use of Military Clubs], *Nakayama keibitai* [Nakayama Patrol Unit J], May 1944. See also '*Gunjin kurabu gyōmu buntamhyō* [Military Club Duty Rota Chart]' in *Gunjin kurabu ni kan suru kitei* [Regulations on Military Clubs], *San dai 3475 butai* [The 3475th Division], December 1944.

35 Aso Tetsuo, *Karyūbyō sekkyokuteki yobōhō* [Positive Methods to Prevent Venereal Disease], 26 June 1939.

36 Translated into Korean by Yi Songhŭi, *Chonggun wianbu* [Military Comfort Women]. Seoul: Paeksŏbang, 1991.

37 *Zairyūhōjin tōkei*, 1939, and a medical report which states '35 out of 38 women were Koreans' in '*Gei shōgi shakufu kenkō shindan jisshi yōryō* [Outline of medical check-up plans for geisha, prostitutes and barmaids]', *Konsei dai 14 ryodan shirebu* [Mixed 14th Brigade Command Office], cited in the *Asahi Shimbun*, 6 December 1992.

38 For example, '*Fukukan gōdō jisshi no ken* [On the Joint Practices of Adjutants]', *Shina haken gunsō shireibu* [General Command Office, Dispatched to China], October 1942; '*Gokuhi Shōwa 18 nen nigatsu eisei gyōmu yōbō* [Top Secret Hygiene Duty Report, Shōwa 18th year]', *Nanjing Dai 15 Shidan Gunibu* [Nanjing, 15th Division Military Medical Section].

39 For example, '*Dai 14 gun kenpeitai gunji keisatsu geppō* [14th Military Police Unit, Military Affairs and Police Monthly Report]', *Takurobaso kenpei buntai, Begio Buntai* [Takurobaso Military Police Unit, Begio Squad], 1943.

40 For example, '*Jūgun ianfu 110 ban* [Military Comfort Women, No. 110]', *Jūgun ianfu 110 ban henshū iinkai hen* [Editorial Committee for the Military Comfort Women hot-line], 1992.

41 For example, '*Jinchū nisshi* [Battlefield Diary]', *Dokuritsu sanpō hei dai 3 rentai* [3rd Regiment, Independent Mountain Artillery], 1–30 April 1941; '*Jinchū nisshi* [Battlefield Diary]', *Dokuritsu shubi hohei dai 35 daitai* [35th Company, Independent Defence Infantry], 1 April–30 June 1942.

42 Yamasida Yŏngae, op. cit. (note 20 above).

43 *Ryo shūdan tokumubu geppō* [Ryo Group Special Duty Section Monthly Report], April 1940.

44 Yoshida Seiji, '*Nanŭn Chosŏn saramŭl irŏkke chabagatta* [This Is How I Abducted Koreans]', translated into Korean by *Hyŏndaesa Yŏn'gushil* [The Modern History Research Institute]. Seoul: Ch'ŏnggye Yŏn'guso, 1989.

45 Yoshimi Yoshiaki, *Jūgun ianfu to nippon kokka* [Military comfort women and Japan]' in Yoshimi Yoshiaki (ed.), *Jūgun ianfu shiryōshū* [A Collection of Materials on Military Comfort Women], 34–5. Tokyo: Ōtsuki shoten, 1992.

46 '...*zhi shou da ri ji mi* [Expense Account, Great Diary Secret]', 4 March 1938.

47 See, for example, *Shina jihen ni sai shi hōjin no toshi seigen narabi torishimari kankei zantei shori yōbō* [The China Incident and Japan's Limits on People Crossing to China, and an Outline of the Temporary Treatment of People Related to Management], May 1940.

48 'The rules on the use of military comfort stations should be strictly followed', stated in '*Jinchū nisshi* [Battlefield Diary]', *Dokuritsu konsei hei dai 15 rentai honbu* [15th Regiment Headquarters, Independent Mixed Army], 1–31 October 1945.

49 '*Jinchū nisshi* [Battlefield Diary]', *Dokuritsu konsei hei dai 15 rentai honbu* [15th Regiment Headquarters, Independent Mixed Army], 1–31 January 1945.

50 A May 1938 entry in '*Iansho shiyō kitei* [Rules on the Use of Comfort Stations]', *Dokuritsu kōjōjū pōhei dai 2 daitai* [2nd Company, Independent Assault Artillery] states: 'Sunday for the *hoshi* unit, Monday for the *kuriiwa* unit, Wednesday for the *matsumura* unit ... separate instructions will be given to other units stationed here on a temporary basis.'

51 *'Jinchū nisshi* [Battlefield Diary]', *Dokuritsu san pōhei dai 3 rentai* [3rd Regiment, Independent Mountain Artillery], 1–30 April 1941.

52 *'Jinchū nisshi* [Battlefield Diary]', *Dokuritsu shubi hohei dai 35 daitai* [35th Company, Independent Defence Infantry], 1 April–30 June 1942.

53 *'Jūgun ianfu 110 ban* [Military Comfort Women, No. 110]', *Jūgun ianfu 110 ban henshū iikai hen* [Editorial Committee for the Military Comfort Women hot-line], 1992.

54 *'Jinchū nisshi* [Battlefield Diary]', *Dokuritsu shubi hohei dai 35 daitai* [35th Company, Independent Defence Infantry], 1 April–30 June 1942.

55 'A ticket system must be applied to prevent confusion': *Dai 2 gun jōkyō gaiyō* [Outline of the 2nd Army Situation], *2A shireibu* [2A Command Office], 10 December 1938.

56 *'Jinchū nisshi* [Battlefield Diary]', *Dokuritsu kōjōjū pōhei dai 2 daitai dai 2 chūtai* [2nd Company, Independent Assault Artillery], 1 January–30 April 1938.

57 '*Iansho shiyō kitei* [Rules on the Use of Comfort Stations]', *Dokuritsu kōjōjū pōhei dai 2 daitai* [2nd Company, Independent Assault Artillery], March 1938; *'Jōhō junpō* [10-day Information Report]', *Dokuritsu shubi hohei dai 35 daitai* [35th Company, Independent Defence Infantry], December 1942; '*Shina jihen dai 8 kai kōseki gaiken hyōsō* [The China Incident, 8th Merits Table], *Kaigun bukō chōsa* [Navy Military Merits Investigation]' in *Tokusetsu butai, Tokusetsu kansen* [Special Unit, Special Fleet], April–November 1940.

58 'Condoms will be distributed by the unit responsible for welfare facilities…': *Dai 62 Shidanka Hōtei*, 2 October 1944. Also: 'Until now, the army has distributed condoms to soldiers every two months. Now the managers will be responsible for this for the following reasons: for soldiers who do not bring their own condoms, for those using them in places other than comfort stations, and for those who might cause trouble in places other than military comfort stations': *Shōwa 17 nen riku shi mitsu dai nikki* [Shōwa, 17th year, Army Secret Diary], Volume 39, *Rikugunshō* [Army Office].

59 For example, '*Iansho kitei sōfu no ken* [Concerning Comfort Station Regulations]', *Gunsei hanbu Bisaya shibu Iroiro shutchōjo* [Military Authority, Bisaya Department, Iroiro Branch Office], November 1942; '*Gunjin kurabu ni kan suru kitei* [Regulations on Military Clubs]', *San dai 3475 butai* [The 3475th Division], December 1944.

60 For example, '*Sinji junpō* [Wartime 10-day Report]', *Nami shūdan* [Nami Command Office], 10–20 April 1939; '*Gokuhi Shōwa 18 nen nigatsu eisei gyōmu yōbō* [Top Secret, February Shōwa 17th-year Hygiene Duty Report]', *Nanjing dai 15 shidan Kunibu* [Nanjing 15th Division, Military Medical Section]; '*Shina jihen dai 8 kai kōseki gaiken hyōsō* [The China Incident, 8th Merits Table], *Kaigun bukō chōsa* [Navy Military Merits Investigation], *Tokusetsu butai, Tokusetsu kansen* [Special Unit, Special Fleet], April–November 1940.

61 For example, see Aso Tetsuo, op. cit. (note 35 above).

62 '*Gunjin kurabu ni kan suru kitei* [Regulations on Military Clubs]', *San dai 3475 butai* [The 3475th Division], December 1944.

63 Yun Chŏngok, op. cit. (note 26 above).

64 Yi Sanghwa, *Kunwianbu kyŏnghŏm-e kwanhan yŏn'gu: Kyŏrhon kwajŏngesŏ nat'ananŭn inshik pyŏnhwarŭl chungshimŭro* [A Study on the Life of Military Comfort Women: Changes of Understanding and Their Marriage], MA dissertation, Seoul: Seoul Ehwa University, 1993.

65 This is argued by Kŭm Pyŏngdong, op. cit. (note 19 above).

Survivors Tell
Their Stories

CHAPTER 3

Bitter Memories
I Am Loath To Recall

Kim Haksun

Kim Haksun was born in 1924, in Jilin, China. When she was three months old her father died, and she returned with her mother to P'yŏngyang, in present-day North Korea. After her mother's second marriage, she was put into foster care, and entered a kisaeng (entertainment girl) training course when she was 15. After graduating two years later, she was considered too young to be a kisaeng, and crossed back to China. Immediately after her arrival in Beijing she was forcibly taken to a military unit, and began the life of a comfort woman.

Childhood

I was born in Jilin, Manchuria. My mother told me she had married my father when she was 15, and they lived in P'yŏngyang before moving to China, fed up with continual harassment from the Japanese occupation forces. My mother gave birth to me in 1924, and she told me that my father died before I was three months old: what caused his death I cannot say for sure. My mother, a woman alone and friendless in a foreign land, found it difficult to survive. She returned to P'yŏngyang with her two-year-old daughter.

Back in P'yŏngyang with a small child, she was forced to resort to begging from her brothers and sisters to live. Maybe because she had nobody to rely on, she attended church faithfully and regularly. I can still remember going to church with her when I was little. I liked it, because I enjoyed the singing and our pastor was very friendly. I was constantly told off by my mother for being stubborn and disobedient. Whenever I paid no attention to what she said, she would bewail her misfortune, telling me: 'You finished off your father' or 'Your father was nothing but trouble and heartache when he was alive – has he passed his character on to you?'

In P'yŏngyang I attended a missionary school which charged no fees. I went for about four years, until I was eleven. I enjoyed lessons, sports and playing with friends. I was good at running and often won relay races. Throughout my life, the memories of those years have remained dear. I recall them fondly. I was able to learn when I wanted to learn; I was able to play when I wanted to play. In my early years, my mother did all sorts of work. She was a domestic help, a farmhand and a washerwoman, often leaving home early with a packed lunch. But by the time I started school she had hired a machine that could make woollen socks and she stayed at home knitting. I used to help her when I came home from school.

During the year in which I turned 14, my mother remarried. My step-father came with a son and a daughter – both of whom were older than myself. The son was about 20 and the daughter 16, but before long the daughter married and left home. I didn't like living with a stepfather, but I got on well with his son. I had been so used to living alone with my mother that I found it difficult to have a man around. I couldn't call him 'father' and I avoided him as much as possible. I became detached from my mother and eventually rebelled. I drifted away. She sent me as a fos-ter-child to a family who trained *kisaeng*, entertainment girls who sing, dance and generally serve men. I was 15. She sent me to the family, and I was accepted after I sang in a sort of audition. I remember how my mother made a contract with the foster father, taking 40 yen[1] and agree-ing that I should live with them for a certain number of years. Staying at home had become so uncomfortable, and I hated it so much, I felt relieved to be able to leave.

My foster home was 133 Kyŏngje village, P'yŏngyang. There was another girl there who had been taken in a little earlier. I was given a new name, Kŭmhwa, and I began to attend the *kisaeng* academy (*kwŏnbŏn*) with the other girl. The academy was a two-storey building with a large sign outside. It had about 300 pupils. We attended for two years and learned to dance, and to sing, *pansori* ('epic storytelling' through song) and *shijo* (short sung poems). When a girl received her graduation certificate she could go into business as a qualified *kisaeng*. But she had to be 19 before the local authority would issue a licence. I was only 17, so I was not allowed to go into business. My foster father took me from place to place, trying his utmost to obtain a licence for me. I looked older and more mature than my real age, so he lied about me, but the authorities knew the truth and refused to grant me a licence.

---

1 In the interviews, many women refer to the Korean currency, wŏn. Yen was the cur-rency during the occupation; hence currency mentioned in the text is referred to as yen, divided into 100 chŏn.

Unable to earn money from me and the other girl in Korea, he thought we would find business if we went northwards to China. So we left. The year was 1941, and I was 17. Before we left, my foster father contacted my mother and asked her for permission to take me abroad. My mother came to P'yŏngyang station, gave me a yellow cardigan as a leaving present and saw me off. We boarded a train and went to Shinŭiju. We were to continue to Shanhaiguan by crossing the Andong river, but the Japanese military police stopped our foster father. They inspected his documents and took him into the police check-point for a few hours. We waited. When he returned, we continued our journey for several days. Sometimes we would spend the night on the train, and sometimes we would stay in guest-houses. We went as far as Beijing, because our foster father had heard that business there was very good.

When we finally arrived, we had lunch in a restaurant. We were about to leave when a Japanese soldier beckoned our foster father over. He was a military officer with two stars on his lapel and he asked if we were Koreans. Our foster father explained that we were indeed from Korea and that we had come to China to find work. The officer retorted that we could have stayed in Korea if we had just wanted money, and led him away, saying 'You must be a spy, come with me'. My friend and I were bustled away by other soldiers. We were led along a back street and came to a place where an open truck was parked. There were about 40 or 50 soldiers on board. They told us to jump on and, when we resisted, they lifted us into the mass of soldiers. After a few minutes the officer who had taken our foster father off returned, and the truck immediately sped off. The officer sat next to the driver. Crouched in a corner at the back of the truck we wept, shocked at what had just happened. We were terrified. Some minutes later we noticed another truck, just like ours, following us.

We had been seized in the afternoon, and our journey continued through the night. As we travelled, when shooting was heard everyone got off and crouched underneath the truck. We were given balls of cooked rice for food. Some soldiers tried to give us biscuits, but we were so frightened we didn't even look at what was being offered. At dusk the next day we all got down, and some of the soldiers took us to a house. Later we found out that it was empty, that it had been abandoned by fleeing Chinese.

It was dark. We weren't aware of what was going on and couldn't even guess where we were. My friend and I were sent into a room, where we sat and looked at each other. We had no idea what was going to happen. A little later, the officer who had taken our foster father away came in. He began to take me to an adjacent room, divided only by a curtain. I was scared to be alone, and resisted. He dragged me off and held me close to him, trying to take my clothes off at the same time. I struggled, but in the end my clothes were all torn away. He took my virginity. During the night he raped me twice.

The following morning he left while it was still dark. I managed to cover myself with my torn clothes, but as he left he told me that I would be no longer be able to wear such clothes. I wept. I lifted the curtain to see if my friend was still there. A soldier in a brown uniform was lying fast asleep. My friend was weeping; she like me had covered her body with her torn clothing. I was shocked and dropped the curtain. When day dawned, and after the soldier had left her, my friend came over. We wept aloud, cuddling each other. She said she had been beaten when she tried to resist. I had been so occupied fighting off the officer that I hadn't been aware what had been going on beyond the flimsy curtain.

My Hateful Life as a Comfort Woman

We heard women's voices outside. They were speaking Korean. One opened the door and came in. She asked us how we had got there. My friend told her about our journey. She said: 'Now that you're here there isn't much you can do. There is no way you can run away. You'll have to stay and accept your fate.' Later, soldiers brought wooden beds into our curtained room. We were allocated one portion each, and our lives as comfort women began.

The house was built of red brick and had two entrances. Right next to it was a military unit, and sometime later we were told by the soldiers that the place was called Tiebizhen. The village had originally been Chinese but, perhaps because a Japanese military unit had long been stationed there, we never saw a single Chinese person. There were five women in the house. They all had Japanese names. Sizue, at 22, was the oldest. Miyako and Sadako said they were 19 years old. Sizue gave us Japanese names: I was called Aiko, my friend Emiko. The soldiers brought us rice and other groceries, and we took turns to cook. Since I was the youngest I had to do much more cooking and washing-up than the others. If I asked the soldiers for some cooked rice from time to time, they would bring me the rice and soup that they had prepared to eat themselves.[2] They also smuggled us occasional dry biscuits. We wore a sort of cotton underwear that had been discarded by the soldiers. Sometimes they would

---

2 The staple Korean diet is rice and soup complemented by vegetables, or occasionally fish or meat side dishes. Glutinous Annam rice and a soup made with yellow bean/soya bean paste are typical foods. Japanese rice balls and *misō* soup are mentioned regularly in the interviews. The most famous side dish in Korea is fermented Chinese cabbage, *kimch'i*, but pickled radish, in either Korean or Japanese varieties, seems to have been a more common accompaniment.

bring us clothes raided from Chinese houses. Sizue spoke very good Japanese, and mainly entertained officers. Miyako and Sadako, on the grounds that they had been there long before us, sent us the rough soldiers they didn't want to deal with. I didn't like their haughty attitude, because I thought we all shared the same fate, so I kept my distance. Sizue said she had come from Seoul, but not being very close to Miyako and Sadako I had no idea where they came from nor how they had got there.

There were five rooms in the house. Each had a bed, blankets and a basin by the door. Sizue gave us bottles of an antiseptic solution, which went pink when diluted and we were told to wash ourselves with it after serving a soldier. There was no one to manage us directly, but as the unit was right next door we were checked if we tried to go out. We couldn't venture out and we had nowhere to go. When the soldiers came to the house they went to whatever room they wanted. When I had been there about a month, I began to realize that the same men kept coming back, and that there were no new soldiers. We thought that we had been allocated for just these soldiers.

The soldiers often went out on punitive expeditions. They would go out at night, stay away three or four days, and return in the early hours of the morning, singing as they marched. When they came back, we had to be up early to meet them. Usually they would come to us in the afternoon, but when they had been out they came in the early morning. On such days we had to serve seven or eight men a day. When they came in the afternoon, each would stay about half an hour. When, more infrequently, they happened to come in the evening, they were often drunk and bothered us by asking us to sing or dance. On such occasions, I would try to get out to the backyard to avoid them. But if they found me there they would treat me even more roughly.

Because the soldiers chose which rooms they fancied, each of us had regular customers. They varied in the way they treated us: while one soldier was so rough as to drive me to utter despair, another would be quite gentle. There was one who ordered me to suck him off, while he held my head between his legs. There was another who insisted that I wash him after intercourse. I was often disgusted by their requests, but if I resisted they would beat me until I gave in. They brought their own condoms: we weren't allowed to keep any. Once a week, a military surgeon visited us with an assistant and gave us routine check-ups. If he was busy he would sometimes miss a visit. Whenever he was due, we gave ourselves a thorough scrubbing with the antiseptic solution. If he checked us and found anything even slightly wrong, he would inject us with 'No. 606'. If we burped after an injection, a strong smell would trace itself upwards to our nostrils, making us feel sick.

When our menstruation was due we used cotton wool obtained from the surgeon. We had to serve soldiers during our periods. We tried to avoid them at this time, but they just forced their way in and there was nothing we could do to stop them. We had to make small cotton wool balls and insert them deep inside our wombs so that no blood leaked out. When we didn't have enough cotton we had to cut cloth into small strips and roll this up to use instead.

It seemed to us that the soldiers received special permission to visit. At first I didn't know whether they paid for our services or not, but later I heard from Sizue that the rank and file paid 1.5 yen a visit and the officers 8 yen to stay the whole night. I asked who received the money. All she replied was that we were the ones who should be paid. I never received any money all the time I was a comfort woman. I don't know what Sizue knew to make her say such things.

During the mornings when the soldiers didn't come, we used to spend our time washing clothes or talking to each other. But by nature I am not docile, and my head was full of ideas about ways to escape. Because of this, I didn't get on too well with the others except for my friend, Emiko.

One morning as we were having breakfast, a soldier rushed in and told us to pack quickly. He kept calling us to hurry out and get on a truck, rushing us. We left in a great hurry, not knowing what was happening. I had only been there about two months. There were two trucks waiting, already filled with soldiers, and the officer was on horseback, with a long sword at his side. Before evening we got to a new place. It wasn't too far away, but seemed to be more remote, further out in the countryside. From here, we could hear much more shooting than previously. The house was smaller, and the rooms were divided by walls, not curtains.

Our lives continued without much change, except that there seemed to be fewer soldiers who came. The surgeon hardly bothered with us. The soldiers went on more frequent expeditions and some brought us bottles of alcohol on their return when they visited us. Life seemed more bleak than before. I continued to look for ways to escape. Emiko and I discussed many different possibilities, but because we didn't know anything about the area where we were held we would have been lost if we had ever got away. We promised each other to escape together when an appropriate opportunity came.

Escape

I had been in the new house just over a month when a Korean man in his forties came into my room. No one except a soldier was allowed to come to the house. But he said that he had heard there were Korean women there and had managed to furtively find his way in, avoiding the watchful eye of the guard. The soldiers were away on an expedition at the time. He claimed he was a silver coin pedlar. With a mind half-glad and half-apprehensive, I asked him to take me with him when he left. Japanese or Korean, men all seem to be the same. He, too, satisfied his desires with me and then tried to leave. But I clung to him and begged him to take me with him. I threatened that if he left without me I would scream. All this wrangling went on in hushed voices so that Emiko in the next room couldn't hear. I was afraid that if she did hear us and wanted to come along, we would be seen trying to flee. He asked me how old I was, and how I had been brought there. He said he travelled all over China, never settling in any one place, and that it would be very hard and possibly dangerous to accompany him. I pleaded. Even if I died or he abandoned me I wouldn't mind, I said, as long as he got me out of that place.

I cannot remember the exact time, but it must have been around two or three in the morning when we escaped from the comfort station together. I left what little I possessed and came out with empty hands. I was so scared that I cannot remember how we passed the guard and the military unit. Even though the soldiers were supposed to be out on expedition, there must have been a few guards stationed at the unit. Heaven must have helped us avoid their eyes.

Four months had passed since I had been captured in Beijing by the time I escaped. Summer had ended, and it was early autumn. We walked for a while until my accomplice discovered a house that had been deserted by its Chinese owners. He went in and found some clothes for me to put on. He knew his way around and could easily find empty houses. He spoke very good Chinese and at times he successfully pretended to be Chinese. Not only did I speak no Chinese but I was in constant fear of being arrested. So I followed him wherever he went. He introduced me as his wife. He said he had studied at Kwangsŏng High School in P'yŏngyang, and gave his home address as Namhyŏngjesan district, Taedong county, P'yŏngyang. He said he had a son at home. He also spoke and wrote Japanese. I suggested we should return to P'yŏngyang, but he replied that he could not go back. He gave no reason. He seemed to know every nook and cranny of China. We travelled to Suzhou, Beijing, Nanjing and elsewhere. I could never make out exactly what his business was, but could only assume that he was a sort of middleman, delivering opium for the Chinese.

In the winter of 1942, when I was 18, I became pregnant. He decided we should settle down in one place to have the baby, and he chose Shanghai. We crossed the river Huangpu, and settled in the French judicial district. There were consular offices there from 53 different countries. We went to that district because it was said that the Japanese and British districts were easy military targets for attacks. A year later, on 20 September by the lunar calendar, I gave birth to our first child. It was a girl. Later, in 1945, when I was 21, I gave birth to a boy. Both children were born in Shanghai. We managed a pawn shop called Songjŏng. Our financial capital was provided by a Chinese man, and in effect we just ran the business for him. Sometimes we lent money out, and the profits were divided 50/50 with the investor. The business went reasonably well.

Home and Misery

After Korea was liberated in 1945, Yu Ilp'yŏng, the head of the Korean residents in Shanghai, told us to board a ship to take us home. In June 1946, we boarded and returned to Korea. The ship was large, with two decks, and carried the Liberation Army on board. The fare was 1000 wŏn for adults and 500 wŏn for children, so the four of us paid 3000 wŏn altogether. We arrived at Inch'ŏn but, due to an outbreak of cholera, we couldn't disembark. We had to remain on the ship for a further 26 days. After that we stayed in a refugee camp in Changch'ung-dong, Seoul for three months. It was there that our daughter died of cholera. As winter drew on, my husband went around his acquaintances trying to find us a room to rent. He managed to find space at the house of a friend, and in October we left the camp.

I sold vegetables while my husband worked on a construction site to make a living. From 1953, after the Korean War ended, he ran a scrivener's office and served as a local community head. He also delivered groceries to a military unit. One day after he had gone out to have the groceries inspected before delivery, I was called and told that the building had collapsed where he was working. I rushed over and found the roof of the building had fallen in as a result of the heavy rain of the previous days. Quite a number of people had been hit, and some had died. Some were covered in blood and could only breathe with great difficulty. My husband was moved to the Red Cross Hospital, but he died within a couple of months.

I had suffered so much, living with this man who had supposedly been my husband. When he was drunk and aggressive, because he knew that I had been a comfort woman, he would insult me with words that had cut me to the heart. After we had returned to Korea I hadn't wanted him to come near me. My life seemed to be wretched. I had refused to do as I was told and I had received more and more abuse from him. When he called me a dirty bitch or a prostitute in front of my son, I cursed him. Now, though, once my husband was cremated, my son and I lived alone. He had tortured me mentally so much that I did not miss him a lot. I began to buy underwear from factories and sell it to shops around the country, travelling as far afield as Kangwŏn province. Whenever I travelled to the provinces, I had to stay away from home several days, so I took in a girl from a poor family in Sŏkch'o to help. When my son was in the fourth grade of primary school I wanted to show him the sea, so I took him back with me to Sŏkch'o during the summer vacation. He suffered a heart attack and died while swimming in the sea. I hadn't been blessed with good parents, I had been unfortunate with my husband and children. Now I lost all my will to live.

I determined to end my life. I tried to take drugs several times, but I didn't die. In 1961, I moved down to Chŏlla province. I had no definite plans, and didn't know what I would do. For roughly 20 years I did all kinds of hard work, drinking and smoking away anything that I earned. Then I began to reflect upon my miserable, wandering life. Yes, I would die when my time came, but in the meantime I realized that there was no need for me to squander my life so pitifully . So I returned to Seoul. A friend from Chŏlla found me work as a a domestic help, and I stayed with one family for seven years. But my heart was weak and the work tired me out, so I left them in 1987. With the money I had saved over the years I rented the room where I live today.

I became involved in a job creation project through the local government office. While on this project I met an elderly woman who had been a victim of the atomic bombs dropped on Japan. I harboured a considerable grudge against the Japanese, and my whole life had been loathsome and abhorrent, largely because of them. I had been wanting to talk to someone about my past for a long time, and I told this woman that I had once been a comfort woman. Since then I have been called to speak in many different places, because I was the first of the comfort women witnesses to come forward. I find it very painful to recall my memories. Why haven't I been able to lead a normal life, free from shame, like other people? When I look at old women, I compare myself to them, thinking that I cannot be like them. I feel I could tear apart, limb by limb, those who took away my innocence and made me as I am. Yet how can I appease my bitterness? Now I don't want to disturb my memories any further. Once I am dead and gone, I wonder whether the Korean or Japanese governments will pay any attention to the miserable life of a woman like me.

CHAPTER 4

I Have Much to Say to the Korean Government

Kim Tŏkchin

Kim Tŏkchin was born in 1921 in South Kyŏngsang province, where her whole family lived at an uncle's house, farming the land but scarcely making a living. After her father had been arrested and beaten to death by the Japanese police it became harder than ever to survive. In 1937, when she was 17 and working as a domestic help, she heard that a factory in Japan was recruiting workers. She left the country, only to become a comfort woman. She returned to Korea in 1940 with the help of a Japanese officer.

Escape from Poverty

I was born in Taeŭi district, Ŭiryŏng, South Kyŏngsang province,[1] in 1921. My family owned no land that they could till, and they found it extremely difficult to live. So we went to my uncle's home – he was the older brother of my father. He made a living making bamboo baskets in P'yŏngch'on village, Samjang district, Sanch'ŏng county at the foot of Chiri mountain. There, my father began to cultivate tobacco. We gathered mushrooms and wild vegetables on the mountainside, some of which we ate ourselves and some of which we exchanged for rice or cash at the local market. Tobacco was a government monopoly. The leaves which my father grew were sold to the state, and my father received only a small amount of money. After the main crop was harvested, new shoots sprang up from the tobacco stalks and he would dry these small leaves and smoke them himself. He continued to put the dried leaves aside until he was caught by the Japanese police. He was taken to the police station and subjected to a heavy beating. As a result of this, he took to his bed and eventually died.

---

1 Throughout the text, the following translation conventions have been used to cite addresses: 'village' for *ri* and *maŭl*, 'ward' for *tong/-dong* in a city or township, 'township' for *ŭp*, 'district' for *myŏn*, 'county' for *kun* and 'province' for *to/-do*.

Mother had to carry on life with the five of us – two elder brothers, one elder sister, one younger sister and myself. Making a living was not easy by any means. We were desperate for food. We dug up the roots of trees to eat, and my mother would work on a treadmill all day to bring back a few husks of grains as payment which we would boil with dried vegetables for our supper. Those who flattered the Japanese were able to get help from them; they might get rubber shoes. But those who kept firmly apart were forced into extreme poverty.

My sister-in-law and I would dry and store the leaves from bean and pea plants and boil them for winter food. My big brother had gone to China to earn some money, but his wife was staying with us. As I ate watery rice and barley gruel, I began to realize that we would all die of starvation. If I left home and found work, though, I thought that not only would there be one less mouth to feed but I could earn some money. So I decided to leave to find work as a domestic help. At that time, a neighbourhood friend came home for a short holiday. We had often gone to the mountains to collect wild vegetables together when we were younger, but she had left to get a job with a wealthy family in Chinju. She introduced me to the family of a bank clerk. I was twelve. The family consisted of a large household with five children and six adults, but the lady of the house was a spiteful woman who gave me a hard time. There were times when, having washed up all the supper dishes, I had to keep going back and forth to the well some two kilometres away to fetch water. I would continue doing this until one or two in the morning. Words cannot express the pain I endured. Several years passed. I was 15 before they began to pay me the small sum that they had until then said I was too young to receive. I saved up the money, and a year later bought some fabric to make a dress for my mother and beans to make soy sauce. I made my way home. During the years I had been away my family had moved to an old house in Samga district, Hapch'ŏn county, where my aunt lived and cultivated a small rice field. I began to help my mother with the housework and the collection of wild vegetables as before, but then I heard a rumour that one could earn money in Japan.

It was the middle of January or perhaps a little later, say the beginning of February 1937. I was 17 years old. I heard girls were being recruited with promises of work in Japan. It was said that a few had been recruited not long before from P'yŏngch'on where we had lived with my uncle. I wished that at that time I had been able to go with them, but then I suddenly heard a Korean man was in the area again recruiting more girls to work in the Japanese factories. I went to P'yŏngch'on to meet him and promised him I would go to Japan to work. He gave me the time and place of my departure and I returned home to ready myself to leave. In those days people were rather simple, and I, having had no education, didn't know anything of the world. All I knew – all I thought I knew – was that I was going to work in a factory to earn money. I never dreamed that this could involve danger.

On the day set for my departure, I went to the bus stop in Ŭiryŏng as I had been instructed to do. The man who had come to recruit us was there, and he took 30 of us to Pusan. Some were older, some were younger than me, and some were married with children. The married women told me that their husbands were already in Japan. We were all to stay together until our return to Korea. An empty coach came to Ŭiryŏng, and our party, but nobody else, boarded it. We were on our way. As we crossed Chŏngam Bridge, we held on to each other and wept: 'Goodbye, Chŏngam Bridge, goodbye until we return with money lining our pockets.' Soon we became very close, calling each other sisters. I belonged to the younger group, where there was a girl three years older than me. She was an orphan, and had been working as a housemaid. She, like me, wanted to go to Japan to make money. Later on, after we had returned to Korea, I bumped into her on the street one day and we stayed in touch until the Korean War.

We arrived at Kunbuk station and transferred to a train. It was a public slow train, and travelled slowly down to Pusan, where we boarded a boat. The man who had brought us this far left us, and a Korean couple who said their home was in Shanghai took charge of us. The boat was huge. It had many decks, and we had to climb down many flights of stairs, right to the bottom of the boat to find our bunks. It was a ferry and took many other passengers. The crew brought us bread and water, and we sailed to Nagasaki. At Nagasaki, a vehicle resembling a bus came and took us to a guest-house. From that moment on we were watched by soldiers. I asked one of them: 'Why are you keeping us here? What kind of work are we going to do?' He simply replied that he only followed orders. On the first night there I was dragged before a high-ranking soldier and raped. He had a pistol. I was frightened at seeing myself bleed and I tried to run away. He patted my back and said that I would have to go through this experience whether I liked it or not, but that after a few times I would not feel so much pain. We were taken here and there to the rooms of different high-ranking officers on a nightly basis. Every night we were raped. On the fifth day, I asked one of the soldiers: 'Why are you taking us from room to room to different men? What is our work? Is it just going to bed with different men?' He replied: 'You will go wherever orders take you. And you will know what your job is when you get there.' We left Nagasaki after a week of this gruelling ordeal.

Led by our Korean guides, we boarded another boat for Shanghai.

This was even larger than the ferry we had taken from Pusan. It was as big as a mountain, and we had to take a small boat to reach this huge monster floating out at sea. We climbed on to the boat holding its iron rails. There were soldiers as well as civilians on board. We walked down some stairs to a huge room that looked like a deserted field. If you looked from where you lay you could see endless rows of people lying on the floor. We travelled for a few days then disembarked at what we were told was Shanghai.

Moving With the Troops

There was a truck waiting for us at the pier, which whisked us away. There were no rail tracks, and nò buses or taxis to be seen. We passed through disordered streets and arrived in a suburban area. There was a large house right beside an army unit, and we were to be accommodated there. The house was pretty much derelict and inside was divided into many small rooms. There were two Japanese women and about 20 Koreans there, so with the 30 of us who had arrived from Ŭiryŏng there were about 50 women in total. The two Japanese were said to have come from brothels. They were 27 or 28, about ten years older than all the Koreans. The soldiers preferred us Korean girls, saying we were cleaner. Those who had arrived before us came from the south-western provinces of Chŏlla and the central provinces of Ch'ungch'ŏng and were of similar age to us. Those of us who had travelled together kept ourselves very much to ourselves. I was called 'Lanchang' there. From the 50 of us, excluding those who were ill or had other reasons, 35 girls on average worked each day.

The big house was divided by wooden panels into a lot of small rooms, each just big enough for one person to lie down in. There was a bed in each cubicle, and we spent most of our time incarcerated. There was a separate dining room. It was a single-storey building, and on the gate was a sign saying 'Comfort Station'. The Korean man who brought us there seemed to be the owner, but Japanese soldiers came and inspected what we ate and checked whether the house was clean. Several times, we were moved to different front lines with the troops, finally spending time in Nanjing before we returned home to Korea. The comfort station we were in didn't belong directly to the army. So, when the troops moved to a new place the comfort station along with us women would follow shortly afterwards. Sometimes we went by boat, and sometimes we went by truck but we never moved with the troops. The comfort station was always positioned in a remote place, usually avoiding built-up areas such as cities, and our living conditions were practically the same wherever we went. As a result of the war that was going on conditions around us were tragic. We heard guns firing every day. There were bodies lying all over the place, and dogs would drag corpses around. We wore skirts and blouses of the sort that are quite common today, but we were also given heavier clothes for winter.

We rose at seven in the morning, washed and took breakfast in turns. Then from about 9 o'clock the soldiers began to arrive and form orderly lines. From 6 o'clock in the evening high-ranking officers came, some of whom stayed overnight. Each of us had to serve an average of 30 to 40 men each day, and we often had no time to sleep. When there was a battle, the number of soldiers who came declined. In each room there was a box of condoms which the soldiers used. There were some who refused to use them, but more than half put them on without complaining. I told those who would not use them that I had a terrible disease, and it would be wise for them to use a condom if they didn't want to catch it. Quite a few would rush straight to penetration without condoms, saying they couldn't care less if they caught any diseases since they were likely to die on the battlefield at any moment. On such occasions I was terrified that I might actually catch venereal disease. After one use, we threw the condoms away; plenty were provided.

About once every two months, an army surgeon gave us check-ups. If any of us had a problem, she was ordered to rest for a few days. We had to go to the army hospital for check-ups, and while we were in Shanghai we saw many women like us who were kept at other comfort stations. We even saw Chinese women standing in the queues. You could tell them, since they had unusual and large earrings and they dressed differently from the Koreans and Japanese. One person who ran errands at the comfort station said that many Chinese ran away or committed suicide when they were captured as comfort women. At the hospital, there was an examination table on which we were made to lie with our legs spread wide apart. The surgeon would insert an instrument that looked like a trumpet or a duck's beak and with this he examined us. If we had any disease we would be given the 'No. 606' injection, but I was never diagnosed as needing such an injection. Yet, even though I had no venereal disease, I had to have treatment, because I kept bleeding and couldn't pass water. Perhaps it was a bladder infection. There were some women whose vaginas were so swollen and were bleeding so profusely that there was no space for a needle to be inserted inside. How could one expect anything to be otherwise when an innocent girl was subjected to such torture day and night? None of us had children, but I heard that some became pregnant and were forced to abort with an injection or drugs. Even though I had no disease, I was told at a recent check-up that my womb is malformed from the abuse it received in my youth.

When I was in pain and distressed I tried to die, but I couldn't. I thought of jumping into the river, jumping down from a high place or running into a car, but I never managed to do anything remotely like this. Whenever I was in such a sombre mood, I missed my mother greatly. And, even though I wanted to run away, it wasn't possible since I didn't know the area where I was being held. So I gave up any hope and I didn't rebel. I was so scared that I did whatever I was told to, and I would even have pretended to die if I had been told to do so. Maybe because of this, the soldiers didn't treat me as cruelly as they could have done.

Among us, there were some who fought against the men. Some were accused of stealing, some tried to escape only to be dragged back. Some were beaten and kicked by the soldiers. But I don't remember being hit, slapped or cursed. Soldiers who returned from the battlefield were wild. They would try not to use condoms. Their faces, their clothes and shoes, were all covered with dust. The soldiers who were about to leave for combat were somewhat more gentle and a few of them would give us their loose change, saying it wouldn't be of any use to them if they died. There were even some who wept, they were so scared to go to fight. I would comfort them and tell them to come back safely from the battle. When any returned alive, I would be genuinely glad to see them again. I acquired quite a few regular customers, and one or two confessed their love to me and even proposed.

Whenever they came, the soldiers gave us a small ticket which looked just like the pensioner's card today. We collected these tickets and gave them to the manager, who recorded them in his notebook each day. He promised to improve our conditions once Japan won the war, but we received no wages. I even prayed for Japan to win the war, thinking we would be paid when there was peace. The manager provided us with clothes, cosmetics and food, all free of charge. But he said he would deduct the sums we owed him from the promised final lump payments. If we needed anything we asked him to buy it when he went to the market, and he was very obliging. But he reminded us that the more we bought the less we would be paid later. For our meals we had rice, soup and two or three vegetable side dishes.

Pretty and intelligent girls were selected for very high-ranking officers and taken into the army unit by car. I was chosen in this way and developed a special relationship with an officer called Izūmi. When I asked how old he was, he spread five fingers before me, and so I guess he must have been about 50 years old. He seemed to be of quite a high standing. Whenever I entered the unit to meet him or whenever he and I went out for a walk, neat rows of soldiers on either side of the road shouted a greeting out loud, holding their guns aloft. Izūmi's room was large, and in it was a large bed, a shining gun and his neat uniform. On his lapels he wore sparkling rank badges. When there was no combat taking place and things were calm, he used to send for me and keep me in his room for two or three days. When there was combat going on, I didn't hear from him for several months at a time, until the situation quietened down. Then he would call for me frequently once more. When his troops were moved away and his base was at a distance from the comfort station, he took me with him by boat. One day as I was crossing a river to meet him, I saw the river dyed red with blood and bristling, crowded with bodies from bank to bank that parted on either side of us as our boat crept forward.

I continued to meet Izūmi often and came to regard him almost as my father, husband and family rolled into one. Guiding my hand in his, he taught me numbers and how to write Japanese script, and through it all I could feel great affection. Every day, he said he loved me. He said that when the war was over he would take me to Japan where I could live an easy life. He said that I would go to school and live with him. Even after I returned to Korea, we wrote to each other for quite some time.

Back Home

About three years after I had become a comfort woman, in February or March 1940, Izūmi said that I should go back home since my health was getting worse just as the war was becoming more serious. He promised that he would come for me when the war was over. He asked if I had any friends with whom I would like to go home to Korea. I named four. Izūmi ordered the manager to let me and these four return home. It was an order from an officer, so the manager had to obey, although he was clearly not happy to let us go. He asked why we wanted to leave, when Japan was about to win the war and we would all be paid for our services. Izūmi sent someone to escort us, and the five of us left the comfort station. Izūmi told me that we might be invited to Japan and he offered to settle payment for our services later. He instructed us never to return. We didn't receive any money from the comfort station, but Izūmi gave me 100 yen as we left.

Izūmi issued many travel permits and handed them to me in an envelope. The permits had official seals and they looked very much like our contemporary family registration certificates. When we showed these at the station, the guards allowed us to board trains, and when we got off the trains we were able to get lifts in trucks and boats. We were provided with food and sleeping places without any difficulty. At one station, we were even given lunch boxes. On the way – it may have been at

P'yŏngyang – a Korean asked me how I knew Izūmi. He said that the travel permits had this script on them: 'These women have become ill while working in an army unit and are returning home to receive treatment. Please provide them with transport, food and accommodation until arrival at a certain place in South Kyŏngsang province.' After about 20 days of travelling, I got home to Samga district in Hapch'ŏn county. I was 20 by this time. The linen skirt and blouse that my mother had given me left me feeling cold: it must have been around early April.

In my home, people seemed to be talking about me behind my back, and we were still very poor, so I left and came up to Seoul. Izūmi wrote to me constantly. I would reply to him, and I even sent him packages of chilli powder or toasted grain powder every now and again. He would thank me for the parcels, saying he enjoyed them very much, and once he joked that the chilli powder had been so hot that it had almost killed him, asking if I had intended to murder him with it! He would also correct my Japanese spelling. He wrote such amusing letters. Although I couldn't reply to all of the letters after I had come up to Seoul, he continued to write for some time from Nanjing, but his letters abruptly stopped one or two years before the Liberation in 1945. All the letters I had kept were destroyed by a bomb during the Korean War.

I lived by working in a guest-house in Chongno and as a housemaid. For a time I worked in a factory making bags, then I ran a small shop. Just before the Korean War, I met a man whose wife had been left behind in Sariwŏn, in part of what had become North Korea. He was living alone with his children, and soon I moved in with him. His parents lived nearby, and I helped them with their housekeeping. Then during the war, his wife managed to escape southwards and started to live with her parents-in-law. Her husband continued to live away from her with his children and me. We sent his children through school. His son went to university and still writes to me, although he now lives in Los Angeles in America. The wife lives with her daughter now. She and I got on well right from the start and we are still on good terms. I had two sons and a daughter with this man, but my daughter died during the Korean War, and I am now living with my eldest son. My children were initially registered under the wife's name, but I recently managed to have them transferred to my name. Her husband, the father of my children, died of a heart attack about 20 years ago. He was an assistant in the Railway Bureau. The husband of Mun P'ilgi at the Korean Council for the Women Drafted for Military Sexual Slavery by Japan was head of the section where my husband worked at the Bureau. P'ilgi and I bumped into each other when we went to the Council to register. We were glad to see fellow spirits and marvelled at the strong human ties that could bind us together. My eldest son drives a truck now.

He moved out when he married but has since lost his wife.

So, I went to live with him and his two children, and I now keep house for them.

The gifts of my days as a comfort woman still trouble me. I have bladder infections, womb diseases, a restlessness of mind and many other ailments. I suffer from a gallstone and also have severe anaemia. Since I registered with the Council I have been feeling oppressed whenever I am indoors. The four of us, my son and his children, live in one crowded rented room in a terraced house in Puch'ŏn.

I have watched various television programmes about the Council, including the testimony of Kim Haksun. Until now I have lived with all my resentment and anger buried deep in my heart. But the programmes left me unable to sleep at night. I went to one of my nephews, my brother's son, a high school teacher, whom I had helped to educate. I told him about my past and asked if I should register at the Council. He said 'You know how the case of the Survivors Association of the Pacific War led to nothing. You will only bring trouble on your family and your children will be traumatized.' He pleaded with me not to register. I discussed the matter with another nephew living in Taejŏn. He wept as he listened to my story and advised me not to register. He said 'It will break your son's heart. What will your stepson in the United States say when he hears all this?' But I felt uneasy and couldn't sleep at all. So one day I went to a broadcasting station and told my story. They gave me the telephone number of the Council. Next day, I went to the local police station, and with the help of an officer I made a report. I came home and slept soundly, making up for the troubled nights of the previous weeks. After having poured out what I had to say for so long, I felt that half my problem was solved. I told my son about the whole thing, and he wept uncontrollably, saying 'Mother, you have lived so courageously even with such a rough past. I am proud of you.' But the wife of my youngest son became despondent, and even my son is now disheartened. I feel very sad and guilty when I see them. But my heart moves more and more towards the meetings of the Council. I haven't missed any rallies arranged outside the Japanese Embassy.[2] As I go out often, my sister from Pusan comes up and helps with the housework.

Of course Japan is to blame, but I resent the Koreans who were their instruments even more than the Japanese they worked for. I have so much to say to my own government. The Korean government should grant us compensation. Life is very hard without a place of my own to live. I think accommodation should be provided, at the very least.

---

2 Since January 1992, weekly lunchtime rallies have been mounted outside the Japanese Embassy in Seoul by comfort women survivors and other members of the Korean Council.

CHAPTER 5

I Will No Longer Harbour Resentment

Yi Yŏngsuk

An orphan, Yi Yŏngsuk lived with a family in Osaka until the age of ten. Her parents were Korean, and she left for Korea in 1937, when she was 15. Because she was an orphan, she found it hard to find work even as a housemaid. Through a friend, she heard of someone who was promising work in Japan. The friend asked her to go with her, and the two travelled through Sinŭiju, Shimonoseki and Taiwan, before being taken to an army unit in Guangdong to start life as comfort women.

Until I was about ten years old, I lived with a family in Osaka. I helped with the housework. I don't know why my parents had gone to Japan, nor whether I was born there or in Korea. Neighbours said to me, 'Both your parents have died, and you are a Korean. Don't you think you should go back to your own country?' I thought that if I was indeed Korean, I must go to Korea. I cannot remember whether I had any brothers or sisters. At that time my name was Yi Ch'anam and my Japanese name was Yasunaka Kasūnai. My nickname was Ttonam. I was badly treated in that family.

In 1937, the year I turned 15, I met someone who was going to Korea and asked him to take me along with him. I arrived at Pusan on board a ship but, having nowhere to go, I began working in a café selling noodles. The owner was a single Korean woman who had returned from Japan just like me. As we were able to communicate in Japanese she was quite pleased to have me around, but I often quarrelled with her children. Finally, I had to leave the café to find other work as a housemaid for a family. This family paid me only meagre wages, but I was able to stretch them to meet my needs. People looked down on me because I had no parents. I was beaten by my employers for the smallest mistakes. I moved about from one family to another, as I continued to be beaten a lot. When my employer's children beat me, I had no choice but to let them continue. My life was worthless, so I tried to end it all, but that didn't work out

50

as I wished; I couldn't kill myself. In this way, then, I moved around Pusan and nearby Yangsan, going from one family to another.

While working in Yangsan, I made friends with a girl two years older who lived alone with her father. It was December 1939, and I was 17. My new friend told me that there was someone locally promising work in Japan; she said she was going to go and asked if I wanted to go along with her. Whether I lived in Korea or in Japan made no difference, so believing that life in Japan would be easier than in Korea, I left the family I was working for. We met a couple who were said to have come from Sinŭiju, and who had recruited four girls in addition to us. They provided us with room and board and bought us some simple clothes. They got us all to have our hair bobbed and encouraged us to put make-up on.

We waited with them in a guest-house in Pusan for a ship to arrive. But the ship never came, so finally they suggested that we should change our plans. We went northwards, travelling to Sinŭiju by train. The husband of the couple became quite nasty, and if he was displeased with any of us he would torture us, twisting our fingers around a steel spit. In Sinŭiju we stayed with a Korean family for about a week, then were suddenly awoken and taken off early one morning aboard a train. We returned to Pusan. It was pitch dark when we arrived. We were handed over to a Japanese man, a civilian employee for the military, who was dressed in a uniform without badges. We called him *Otosang*, a word roughly equivalent to 'father'.

We boarded a ship at about 11.30 p.m. I had travel sickness and had thrown up what little I had eaten. I was completely exhausted. We were on the bottom deck of the ship, along with some Chinese. Once aboard we hadn't been allowed to speak in Korean. Whenever we did, our guards shouted at us and told us to shut up. As I spoke Japanese, I didn't have too much of a problem, but there were those who didn't speak any Japanese and so had to use Korean. There were other women who looked very much as if they were in a similar desperate situation to us in that bottom cabin, but they were supervised by another person. The guards kept their eyes glued on us all the time. I suppose they had been instructed to watch us in case any one of us went up on deck and tried to leap overboard.

We had to ask the crew for meals, and each of us was given a bowl of rice and two vegetable side dishes morning and evening. Beside these two meals, I ate small strips of dried octopus I had bought when I first met the Korean couple in Pusan. Other girls snacked on dried squid they had brought along. The ship passed Shimonoseki and continued to sail on towards the wide, limitless sea to the south-east. We became more and more uneasy, not knowing where we were being taken. I looked down into the sea and wanted to throw myself in, but the blue-black depths terrified me and robbed me of all courage. We sailed for about a fortnight before finally arriving at a place which I later learned was Taiwan. As we landed, we saw people walking around barefoot. As soon as we had disembarked, the Japanese man who had brought us so far went through all the wrongs he claimed we had committed on board, and beat us with a steel rod in punishment. We felt like slaves who could do nothing but follow orders.

We stayed in the port overnight, and the following morning sailed on to Guangdong. When we arrived there were many soldiers walking about the dockside with long swords hanging at their sides. We were taken by truck to a three-storey red brick house. As soon as we got off, we were led into a large room on the ground floor. The room had a double steel door, and each window was barred with iron rods. It had once been occupied by a Chinese family. We soon discovered that there were many other comfort stations near this one, and the number of Korean comfort women appeared to be several hundred. The road that led to the houses was always guarded by a Chinese man who also acted as both interpreter and military policeman. He and his colleagues would rush in if soldiers became violent or whenever the proprietor of the comfort station telephoned for assistance. Sometimes they came to check the place.

When we arrived, there were already 15 Korean women there, who all spoke good Japanese. They told us how to carry on our lives, and we started to call them our big sisters. There were 21 of us altogether, and there weren't enough rooms to accommodate us all. Each of the 15 rooms contained a large mirror and a chest one could use to store things and put bedding in. The bathroom and dining room were on the ground floor, and I was allocated a room on the first floor. All the comfort stations on the road had signs, some hung horizontally, some vertically. Every sign was written in Chinese characters, and because of that, I didn't know what they said. Once we had arrived and had been herded into the large room, I felt really miserable and began to sing a Korean folksong. A soldier rushed in from outside and threatened me with his sword. This incident made the proprietor very angry. He scolded me and beat me with an iron rod. Those who had been there already told me never to sing in Korean — if we did so, the soldiers would think we were making fun of them.

Cooking and cleaning was done by a Chinese couple. Their situation was no better than ours. The proprietor and his wife were Japanese, the husband about 40 and the wife a little younger, say 35. We were told to call him 'big brother' and her 'big sister'. They gave me a Japanese name, Aiko. Two days after our arrival, soldiers came who wanted sex with us, and we began to serve them from that day on. My vagina was torn and bled for a week. I began to menstruate only when I was 19, and each month from then onwards I suffered severe back pain.

We would rise around seven each morning. We cleaned our rooms, had breakfast in the dining room and then began to serve soldiers. We had two meals a day, one in the morning and one in the evening, and the main dish was cooked rice. In the hall on the ground floor there were chairs arranged along three sides of a square, and we had to sit there every morning after we had tidied ourselves up. There was a placard on the wall behind each of the chairs which bore our name and number. We remained seated as the soldiers came in to choose whoever took their fancy to take to bed. We generally served five or six soldiers a day. There were days when men didn't come at all, and at times one or two would stay overnight. On Saturdays and Sundays, that is at weekends, we had to serve 15 men a day, and sometimes we didn't get time to eat. Both officers and the lower rank and file came. When a soldier chose me the proprietor, or one of the women who had been there before us, followed us into my room and took money from him. When he had paid, I was given a ticket with the amount written on it and a condom. There were times when I took the money directly from soldiers and passed it on to the proprietor. Normally, though, we collected the tickets and handed them to the proprietor each evening. Once a month he counted them. He would compliment the girls who had collected many tickets and verbally or physically abuse those who had few. I collected an average number of tickets, but I often got venereal disease, which had the effect of reducing the men I could serve and, consequently, the number of tickets I could get. Because of this I earned myself regular beatings.

My relationship with the proprietor was neither good nor bad. My spirit had been broken through frequent beatings, so I was quiet and obedient. Once I heard him remarking how silent I was. During the first year I did whatever he told me to do and didn't say a word about how harshly he treated me. We went to hospital to have a check-up once a week. If the slightest symptom of venereal disease appeared, we had to have the 'No. 606' injection in gradations numbered from 1 to 6. The injection was so strong that once you had it you couldn't touch water for a whole week. We were told that if the soldiers were infected it would dampen their fighting spirit. Therefore, we weren't allowed to serve any men if we caught V.D. Of course this upset the proprietor as it reduced his income, but he was forced to stop us serving men.

Having to serve so many men made my sexual organs swell up, and I had to go to see a doctor. When I went the first time, my stomach hurt to the extent that I thought it was going to burst. If I showed the slightest abnormality, I was not allowed to serve men. My abdomen often became swollen, and I had to stay in hospital three or four times a year. After one exhausting year at the station, I realized I should look after my own body a little better. So I began to play tricks now and then. Whenever we went for check-ups we had to wash ourselves thoroughly with salt water, but sometimes I would pretend to be ill by stepping on to the examining table without having washed myself. Then I had to go through a period of treatment, during which I didn't have to serve the soldiers. It was good to be hospitalized, as I didn't have to work, but I hated the daily inspections. The proprietor gave me mugwort heat treatments on my abdomen, and this treatment was repeated again and again even before the burns from his previous administrations had disappeared. Due to this, I am still scarred. In those days, as soon as I was better I had to serve men again. We used to say to each other, whenever we had sufficient spare time to relax, that we would never be able to use our wombs as nature intended when we grew older. Apart from sleeping with the soldiers, we had to do various chores. The proprietor nagged us to wash our bedding every two days, and we had to change the sheets every day.

It was like a living death. If someone died, no one would have known. One of the girls from my home town became very ill. She actually died. They burnt her corpse, and the smell of burning flesh was like rotten fish as it drifted on the air into our rooms.

When we needed money, we had to ask the proprietor. Sometimes he gave the amount we asked for, and sometimes he did not. With money from him we bought underwear and cosmetics whenever we had a chance to go out. We were allowed out once or twice a month, always on the days when few soldiers were expected. Sometimes we went to the cinema to watch films. Sometimes the proprietor accompanied us, but sometimes we were allowed to go by ourselves, riding in rickshaws drawn by Chinese men who, since they thought we were Japanese, were very obliging. Clothes and other essential articles were provided by the proprietor, and we had to wear Japanese kimonos. There was a hairdresser run by a Chinese man on the road, and we sometimes had perms there.

After about two years, I got to know how things were run. One of my friends tipped me off that my contract time had expired and that I could do whatever I wanted to do. A few days had passed since the end of my official term, although the proprietor hadn't said a word about this to me. So, one day, I got drunk and complained to him. Surprised at my unusual behaviour, he said he would report me to the military police. I threatened him, 'If you want to report me, by all means go ahead. I am going to report you as well. I know my contract is over. I am going to tell them how badly you treat me.' I refused to serve any soldiers from then onwards. On our street there lived an old Japanese man whose job was to introduce comfort women to proprietors, and one day he came to me and asked me, in confidence, if I would like to go somewhere else. He said he could find another place. I told him to go ahead, and after a few days he came back to introduce me to a new station. I moved that very same day. As I left I took with me the money I had earned since my contract had expired. I had found out that once our contract was over we were meant to share our earnings with our proprietor, on a 50/50 basis.

The women in the new station were all Japanese. I was the only Korean. It was more spacious, since each woman had a room to herself. The proprietors were a Japanese couple who lived with their seven-year-old son and the husband's parents. The wife's name was Eiko. It was much more comfortable. Most of the soldiers who came were officers, although a few NCOs visited as well. I was able to serve them when I wanted to. My fee was divided with the proprietor on an equal basis. If I earned enough money, I knew I would soon be able to return to Korea. But I had given up the idea of going home. At the time, I still didn't have enough money and just carried on living and working there. One day, there was a party for us women and our customers. We were meant to order our own food, but the wife ordered noodle dishes for us all. I didn't like anything made with flour, so I alone ordered rice. It was at that point that I overheard the proprietress saying 'A Korean bitch can't be helped'. It was meant to be whispered, but I heard her. After the party was over I kept drinking, since the wine tasted nice. In the end I got quite drunk. In this intoxicated state I shouted at all the women, asking who had called me a Korean bitch. I told them to own up. The women said none of them had said such a dreadful thing. I pointed to the proprietress and asked if it was her. I used her name, Eiko. I grabbed her by the throat and beat her up. Now, I knew she was having an affair with a military policeman behind her husband's back. So, as I beat her, I screamed my head off about this. I told her that she had no right to treat me differently from the other girls since I had been brought to this land specifically for her people. I said I would report her to the police for discrimination; the police had clearly stated she should treat us all equally. In the end she reported me to the military police and they took me to the station and kept me there overnight.

A soldier named Takano Kyōichi was one of my regulars. He was very fond of me. One day he brought me a white gold watch, then he never turned up again. I made enquiries and was told that he had been taken to prison because he had stolen money. I saw him once more, just a few days before the war ended, but I have never seen him since. Some soldiers brought us dried biscuits and gave us tips now and again.

Sometimes bombs dropped all around us, and we used to shelter under the staircase. Wherever a bomb had hit, bodies would be scattered around. People were killed while eating or sleeping. One day as we were sitting around in the yard, a Chinese woman came by and stuck a red card on the gate. When we asked what she was doing, she replied that she was reclaiming her house. We guessed that the war must be coming to an end. Suddenly the Chinese returned, and we were all driven out of the house. We got on a truck and were taken to a makeshift tent set up by soldiers. We stayed there for two months. One day, some Koreans came by and asked for any Koreans to step forward. They transferred me to a refugee camp for my own race. I stayed there until a ship came to port. In the camp, we sang the Korean national anthem each morning while Korean guards watched over us. Men and women were put into separate rooms, each shared by about 80 people. Even here, anyone who broke the rules was beaten by the Korean guards.

We spent New Year in the camp, and in 1946, the year I turned 24, a ship came to take us back home. I didn't want to return, but I had to get on board as all Koreans had been ordered by the government to return home. The ship was filled with comfort women. I had no family, no relatives and no home to go to. It would be impossible for me to find a husband. I thought it would be better to drown than to return to my country, but I didn't have the courage to throw myself overboard.

After 15 days sailing we arrived in Pusan. We had to stay on the ship for another 15 days because cholera had broken out. During this second fortnight many people died and were carried to the shore. We were paid 100 wŏn each as we disembarked. Of the six girls who had left Pusan together, only three returned: Yachio, Kiyoko and myself.

I couldn't speak good Korean anymore. I managed to live for a while on the 100 wŏn. By the time that money ran out, someone had asked if I had returned from Japan. When I replied in the affirmative, she said she knew a place where I could work and took me to a drinking house. I helped in the kitchen, but before long I left because I couldn't stand the way men and women flirted with each other. Then I worked in a restaurant as a cook's assistant. This was followed by a swift succession of many different jobs. I sold ready-made side dishes, worked as a domestic help, wandered about in Pusan, Yŏngch'ŏn and Taegu, and then sold fish on Inch'ŏn pier.

It was so terribly lonely living on my own, so I tried to form the ties of blood sisterhood and to care for an elderly couple as if they were my parents. While I was trying this and that, I was introduced to a man. I started a relationship. I was lonely, and had found it hard to live on my own, so I started to live with him without getting married. I was 28. We had no children. When I was over 40, he began to distance himself. I left him, in order that he could take another woman and have children.

There was a time when I wished to be a nun and live in a temple, buried somewhere deep in the mountains. It was only in 1975 that I registered myself in the local office. Until then I had no official identification card, even though the law said I should, and I had no family registration. When I registered I changed my name from Yi Ch'anam to Yi Yŏngsuk.

After I started once more to live alone, I wasn't able to get much work. I soon spent all the money I had saved. I rented a small room, but this was destroyed by a fire from which I barely escaped in 1991. I had to leave all my belongings to burn. The government offered me 5,000,000 wŏn ($6500) as a loan, but since I could never repay it, I didn't apply formally. Then the local government office asked me to apply for a loan of 3,000,000 wŏn ($3750) they were offering to the homeless at an interest of 15,000 wŏn ($19) a month. With this I was able to rent my present room, paying the 3,000,000 won as key-money. Since I turned 65, the local government office has started to give me 10 kg of rice, 2 kg of barley and between 28,000 and 30,000 wŏn a month, with which I have been able to support myself. Sometimes, when there are job-creation projects, I take part and earn some extra pocket-money.

Let me finally say something I consider to be important. The Japanese were bad. But the Koreans were just as bad because they put their own women through such terrible ordeals for personal profit. It was bad enough that I had to suffer what I did. But it is worse that I was made barren because of this ordeal. I am bitter when I think of this, but I am not going to blame others any longer. What happened was destiny. We are finished, and our bodies are useless after so much abuse. It doesn't matter whether we receive compensation or not. After all, what could we do with money, with so few years left before we die? All I can wish for is that my country and my people will prosper so that history can never be repeated.

CHAPTER 6

I Would Rather Die

Ha Sunnyŏ

Ha Sunnyŏ was born in 1920 in Chinju. Because her family was poor, she began school later than was usual. Her school friends teased her for this, and she hated going to class. Her father was insistent that she should graduate, so she eventually left home. For a long time she worked as a domestic help in Kwangju, and when she was about 21 or 22 she set out with others to earn money. Instead, she was taken to Shanghai, and had to serve as a comfort woman.

I was born in Chinju in 1920. My family moved to Mokp'o as soon as I was born, then, following my father's illness, we had to move to Yŏngam where we had relatives. I remember more about life in Yŏngam than anywhere else. My mother gave birth to eight daughters, all of whom died apart from me. I was the second to be born, but my eldest sister died when she was nine, so I became the eldest child. My father cultivated someone else's land, and as a consequence we were very poor.

My parents weren't able to afford my school fees, so I was twelve before they sent me to start elementary school.[1] I was older, so other children used to tease me about my age. I hated this and sometimes I ran home during lessons, or I tried to get out of going to school first thing in the morning. Most children started school at the age of eight and were already in the fifth grade when they reached my age. Because of this, they teased me as soon as I started: 'We will soon be finishing school. You, fat one, when will you ever finish? Aren't you a bit too big to be in the first grade?' Whenever I tried to miss going to school, my father cajoled me into going, saying he was sending me there not because we could afford it, but because he wanted to bring me up like the son he never had. However, I didn't like studying. I would have rather played and run around with other children of my age.

1 The Japanese colonial regime instituted a six-year school curriculum at what Koreans refer to as *pot'ong hakkyo* (ordinary school). It is this school I have glossed as 'elementary school'. High schools were optional, and few Korean girls attended them.

58

My father was determined to educate me, but since I couldn't stand school any longer, I finally left home. There was no money in the house that I could take, so I just got on a train with nothing, and with no particular destination in mind. I got off at Kwangju and, having eaten food that some passers-by gave me, I spent the night at the station. The next day a lady who was about 50 years old told me to go with her. I went to her house, and stayed there the night. The very next morning she took me to a relative's house, and I started to work there as a live-in maid. The couple I worked for ran a business.

Every day, after the couple left for work, I looked after their baby, did the dishes and did the housework. I lived there for about three years. They fed and clothed me, but paid me no wages. After this time a neighbour coaxed me to move and work for them, saying that they would give me a monthly allowance. So I moved to this new household. After only a fortnight my former employer came to fetch me, and the two women had a huge row. At the end I was taken back to the first place, where I stayed a couple more years. My employer said she would find me a good husband when I reached 20 or 21. I found my job as a housemaid quite comfortable and I never had to go hungry, so I didn't contact my parents at all. Later, I learned that they had been trying everything they could to find me. They even resorted to consulting fortune tellers.

One day, I think I must have been about 20 or so, my employer's baby was fast asleep and I was outside talking with some girls. They were also housemaids in the same neighbourhood. A Korean man approached us together with a Japanese man as we chatted. They wore suits and looked quite young and dashing. They asked us how much we were paid for our work. We answered that we didn't receive any monthly wages, but were given food and clothes for free. To this they responded, saying that the Koreans were thieves. They said that if we went to Osaka with them we would be able to earn lots of money. We were fascinated by the prospect of earning our own income so, without even asking what kind of work we would do, we went with them. We didn't even stop to tell our employers.

Eight of us went altogether. There were girls from Kwangju and girls from Changsŏng. I remember I was wearing a long-sleeved dress, so it must have been spring. At about 2 p.m. we got on a train and went to Yŏsu with the men. We stayed overnight, then took a ship bound for Japan. There were many Korean men on board, all of whom were going to Japan to work. We disembarked at Osaka the following morning, at about 10 a.m., and were led to the home of the Japanese man. In his house there was an elderly lady and two young children. He said we would be moving again to go to Shanghai. We asked him why, when he had earlier said we were going to Osaka. He replied that he ran a big business in Shanghai and needed people to work for him there. We believed him. After spending the night at his house, the very next morning we boarded a ship for Shanghai.

The ship was crowded with civilians, and we sailed for many days. We were given maize for food. When we landed at Shanghai, the Korean and the Japanese, who had accompanied us all the way so far, parted. A military truck was waiting and this took us to a house. The house was next to a military unit. When we entered we found that the same Japanese man was the owner. His wife, a woman from P'yŏngyang, and a Chinese couple who did cooking for them, lived there. The wife was also Japanese even though she came from a Korean city, and she looked older than her husband. She scolded him for his delay in arriving, and they started by having a row. The other girls were taken to different places, leaving me alone. It was a single-storey house with many small rooms. I was told it had formerly been a guest-house or a boarding house, but that it had been confiscated from a Chinese owner.

The Japanese man was in effect the proprietor. He brought more women to join us until we numbered about 30 altogether. Except for two Chinese and two Japanese who arrived about three or four months after me, the other girls were all Korean. Some came from P'ohang and some from Pusan, cities in Kyŏngsang province. The Chinese women were residents of the local district. An introduction agency in Shanghai informed the proprietor when there were new arrivals at the port, and he went to fetch girls. The Korean man who had accompanied us turned out to be a dealer in women. There was a sign on the front door, which I wasn't able to read because I was virtually illiterate. The house was right in the centre of Shanghai, and I was later told it was situated in what had earlier been the French judicial area. There were a few Japanese military units there and, alongside them, brothels.

We were each given a room and told to serve soldiers. The room allocated to me was just big enough for two people to lie down in, and the floor was covered with paper and two blankets. There was a small wastepaper basket.

For the first two weeks, I had to serve one or two soldiers a day, but after that many more came. I said to the proprietor that I'd rather die than keep doing this job. We would sell wine to the soldiers, too, but when they got drunk they became unbearably rough. I begged the proprietor to let me do the cooking and washing-up instead of serving soldiers. He just slapped my face. He kicked me and told me to continue my work. I was given a Japanese name, Odomaru. I can remember there was another girl also named Odomaru and another named Takeko. The soldiers who came to the house were in the army. Some had no commissions and some were officers. Civilians weren't allowed to come in at all. If a sailor came by, he was chased out with people shouting to him to go to the place where the navy was allowed. This sort of segregation often led to fights among the men.

We had to get up at 4 o'clock every morning to clean our rooms. On Sundays, the soldiers came from 9 o'clock in the morning until 4 o'clock in the afternoon, without respite. Sometimes we had to serve 20, 30, 40 or even more men without pausing for a break. We gave up counting. While some finished what they had come to do with us in a short time, there were some who held on and delayed, wearing us out. How can I recount everything that I was subjected to in words?

Most of the soldiers used condoms.

If, for any reason, the visits of regulars became less frequent, the proprietor would beat us, saying that because we had treated them badly the last time they were not coming anymore. For about three or four months, I didn't serve soldiers. I was allowed to help the Chinese cooks with cooking and shopping. The other girls said that I cooked so nicely and begged me to continue to cook for them. But the proprietor nagged at me and beat me, telling me to serve soldiers rather than cook. If I boiled water to wash the dishes, he would throw the pan out, saying that I was deliberately taking time out to heat the water so that I could avoid the soldiers.

Whenever we had time to spare, we Koreans sat around talking about our homes and families. One of the Chinese women was 31 years old and one was 29. The Japanese women were 25 and 27 respectively. Of the Koreans, a few were about 30 years old, and some were younger than me. There were girls who were still teenagers. The younger girls were frightened and refused to serve the men, so they were sent to different houses. Yes, the proprietors in Shanghai sometimes exchanged girls. Our proprietor favoured the women who earned him the most by serving as many soldiers as possible. The two Chinese were pretty and amiable, and served more men than anyone else. So, on special occasions they were given new clothes and good food. When I first arrived, the proprietor gave me two pretty dresses. The soldiers paid their money direct to him, and he managed this himself since he didn't trust anyone. We never knew how much the men paid, nor were we paid directly.

We had to go to a military hospital once a month for check-ups. Those who developed any venereal disease then had to attend regularly for treatment. The check-ups were carried out either by a Japanese doctor or by a Japanese nurse. The hospital was in a large, two-storey building, and it housed many wounded soldiers. As far as I could see, three doctors and two nurses worked there.

Not long after my arrival, I asked the woman from P'yŏngyang to write a letter to my parents for me. A reply came saying that my father was very ill, asking me to go home immediately. Since I hadn't written the letter myself, I don't remember the exact address where I was being kept. I wasn't allowed to go home. Later I heard that my father had died, so greatly was he disturbed by my letter. That letter of mine was lost during the Korean War.

After about a year in Shanghai, I ran away from the comfort station on a snowy winter's day. I ran as far as the rickshaw terminal. It was late at night. But there was nowhere for me to go. I couldn't communicate with anyone, because I didn't know Chinese. I crouched in the corner of the terminal and tried to sleep, waking frequently. I was frightened. In the morning, I still didn't have anywhere to go, so I returned to the comfort station. I crept back to the kitchen. I cooked breakfast, as usual, and sat down to have my own meal. But the proprietor knew. He came in and beat me all over, saying that he would teach me a lesson once and for all. When my wounds had almost healed, soldiers began to come looking to have sex with me. I resisted them, so then the proprietor hit me on the head with a club. I can remember blood gushing out from the wound but then nothing else. I blacked out. Later, I heard that he had put some soya bean paste on my head to stop it bleeding, but I was saved because a Western woman living in the neighbourhood saw me from over the wall and brought ointment to put on my wound. I am told that the proprietor told her to leave me alone to die. The woman was about 40 years old and she sold clothes in the neighbourhood. I had once bought a dress from her with a tip given to me by an officer I had served. She had remembered my face, and came to my aid when she saw me bleeding.

Lieutenant Yamamoto, who was one of my regulars, found me in bed with my head all bandaged, and took me to the hospital to have the wound treated properly. Not all the Japanese soldiers were bad. He and another soldier from Akasima were kind. Yamamoto was about 30. He was tall and healthy. After about eight weeks' treatment, the wound healed and the swelling went down. I still have the scar, some 15 cm long, on my head. After that time I was allowed to just do the cooking. The officer who had taken me to the hospital ordered that I should not serve any more soldiers. Until Korea was liberated in 1945, I cooked and washed for the others. Yamamoto gave me pocket-money now and again to buy things with.

On our free days, we took turns to go out in groups of ten with the proprietor's wife. There were restaurants and cinemas in the area, but our outings were limited to an hour and a half, so we were unable to look around much. If we were late back, we were beaten by the proprietor. Not far from our house was a place that only accepted sailors. The proprietor there was a much nicer man, even though he was Japanese. Whenever I went over to his place, he invited me in to eat and told me how pretty I was. He said he was from Tokyo. When I went there I told our Chinese cook where I was going, but never my proprietor. There were more rooms there than at my place, and he had about 40 women from Korea, Japan and China. One of the Japanese women was called Sanai, and she and I became good friends. If I didn't visit her for a while she would telephone to ask me over. She was from Nagoya and quite a bit older than me. She would often come to see me if I was ill.

Two women in the station caught cholera nostras and died in hospital while undergoing treatment. After two or three years, the woman who had written the infamous letter for me died of opium addiction. She used to sniff white powder at the dinner table and, when I asked her what it was, she used to say it was just a kind of medicine. After she had snorted, she would get high and dance about. We took our meals in the kitchen while the proprietor and his wife ate in their own rooms. This meant that they remained ignorant of what was going on. Some other women also took opium behind their backs. If the proprietor had found out he would have beaten them up, just as he had hit me. The woman who died had graduated from school and started taking opium while she was still living in P'yŏngyang. Her habit had begun as a boost to give her strength because so often she felt weak. But gradually she became more and more addicted. Anyone could buy cheap powder from a Chinese shop right opposite our place. Anyway, that woman used to serve many soldiers and she saved up her tips to feed her habit. Quite a few Japanese women took it, but very few Koreans were interested.

On my visits to the house which served only sailors, I met a Japanese woman and a Korean woman who were both pregnant. I also met two Korean soldiers in my own place, one from Chinju and one from Pusan. Those Koreans were allowed in, but they pitied us and spent their time talking instead of making us serve them.

Towards the end of the war we were bombed several times. If air raids were announced we would be evacuated to the piers. When Japan was defeated, the proprietor promptly disappeared, leaving us penniless. For a while we stayed with the Chinese cook at his home. There were five of us left, including one girl from P'ohang and another from Kwangju. One day our host told us that there was a ship in port leaving for Korea, and we rushed out to get on it. We were afraid that we might not be allowed to board, since we did not have any money to pay the fare with. But our host explained everything about our circumstances, and we were allowed to get on the last ship to be found in the port.

It was 1946, the year after our country had been liberated. I disembarked at Pusan and went home to Yŏngam. My father, remember, had died of grief at my letter. My 14-year-old sister welcomed me. As my mother was too poor to keep me, I quickly left home again and went back to Kwangju to find work as a domestic help. I moved around many different places trying to eke out something of a living. Between moving from one household to another, I briefly lived with a man. But I soon left him because he was a heavy drinker and a gambler. At present I live with my sister, surviving on government aid. All the beatings I received in Shanghai have so affected my health that on wet days my body aches all over and I am unable to move about. Even now, I can't bear to watch violent scenes on television.

CHAPTER 7

I Thought I Was Going to a Textile Factory

Oh Omok

Oh Omok was born in 1921, in Chŏngŭp, North Chŏlla province, the first child in a poor family of five children, two boys and three girls. In 1937, at 16 years of age, she was promised work in a textile factory in Japan by a Mr Kim from her home town. She left home with a friend. When they arrived in Manchuria, where Mr Kim handed them over to a Japanese man, they were taken to a Japanese unit and forced to become comfort women.

I was born into a poor family on 15 January 1921, in Chŏngŭp, North Chŏlla province. I was the eldest child, and I soon gained two brothers and two sisters. My father had been in poor health since I was very little and was now no longer able to work. My mother ran a small shop next to the police station where she sold vegetables. I couldn't go to school, because we were too poor to pay the fees.

It was 1937, and I was 16. My parents had begun to try to find me a husband. One day a Mr Kim, from Chŏngŭp, visited us and said that he could get me a job in a textile factory in Japan. He also offered to find work for a friend of mine. He said that our job would be as weavers and added that we would be paid such and such a month. I forget the actual amount. After the visit he didn't come back. We had almost forgotten about him when he suddenly reappeared and urged me to take the job which was on offer. I needed to earn money, so I went along with him, taking an old friend of mine called Okhŭi. She was two years younger than me. She used to visit me often and I had shown her how to embroider.

When I left home for the factory, my mother was expecting another child. It must have been winter, since I remember wearing padded clothes. Okhŭi and I arrived at Chŏngŭp station with Mr Kim, where there were three other girls waiting. We all got on board a train and travelled to Taejŏn, where Mr Kim bought us lunch. Then we boarded the train again and travelled for three or four days, all the way to Manchuria.

Somewhere around Fengcheng we asked Mr Kim why he had brought us to China instead of Japan. He had, after all, promised to take us to Japan. He bluntly told us we must follow him. He handed us over to a Japanese man and promptly disappeared. From then on, with this new man, we continued our journey further north until we finally arrived right at the top-most tip of Manchuria, although I still don't know what the place was called. It was very cold, and it was crowded with soldiers. There were mountains and rivers, and there were thousands of Chinese and Koreans milling around.

The five of us from Chŏngŭp were led to a village of tents on the outskirts of the place where the Japanese military units were based. There was a sea of tents surrounding the troops. Whenever new soldiers arrived, they would set up even more tents, because there was not enough room for them in the barracks that had already been built. There were already some 30 Korean women. We entered one tent. A soldier there cut my hair short and gave me a Japanese name, Masako.

There were women in every tent. They washed the soldiers' clothes and they cooked for them in the kitchens. There was no fresh water supply in the whole village. The soldiers delivered meals to us. We had cooked rice mixed with barley, spinach or pickled radish, soup and occasional fish balls. We could often hear guns firing in the distance, and whenever there were air raids we were not allowed to light anything.

At first I delivered food for the soldiers and had to serve the rank and file, to have sex with them. There were Japanese as well as Koreans among the managers who instructed us where to go each day. On receiving orders we were called to the appropriate unit and served five or six men a day. At times we would serve up to ten. We served the soldiers in very small rooms with floors covered with Japanese-style mats, *tatami*. There were many rooms. We lived in the tents and were summoned to the barracks whenever required. We were given blankets by the army, and when it was very cold we used hot water tins. The only toilets were outside the tents, as were the bathrooms, and such facilities were separated for men and women. When the soldiers were away on an expedition it was nice and quiet, but once they returned we had to serve many of them. Then they would come to our rooms in a continuous stream. I wept a lot in the early days. Some soldiers tried to comfort me saying '*kawaisōni*' or '*naitara ikanyo*' which meant something like 'you poor thing' and 'don't cry'. Some of the soldiers would hit me because I didn't understand their language. If we displeased them in the slightest way they shouted at us and beat us: '*bakayarō*' or '*kisamayaro*', 'you idiot' and 'you bastard'. I realized that I must do whatever they wanted of me if I wished to survive. There was no payment given to any of us for cooking or washing clothes, but we were paid whenever we slept with soldiers. The bills they handed over were blue and red. There were some women who set up home with soldiers in tents, and a few of them even had children.

The soldiers used condoms. We had to have a medical examination for venereal infections once a week. Those infected took medicine and were injected with 'No. 606'. Sometime later, I became quite close to a Lieutenant Morimoto, who arranged for Okhŭi and me to receive only high-ranking officers. Once we began to exclusively serve lieutenants and second lieutenants, our lives became much easier. When I was 21, in 1941, I had to have my appendix out, but the operation didn't go well and I was readmitted to hospital for a second, follow-up operation. I remember Morimoto coming to see me. The hospital chief was Japanese, and the patients were mostly soldiers and Chinese women. The fee for the operations must have been paid by the army. Afterwards I was able to take a break from serving soldiers. During my convalescence I did various chores: I cooked, filled bathtubs, heated the bath water and so forth.

We moved along with the army. I cannot remember what it was called. We moved south in China. When we were stationed in Nanjing we were sometimes able to see films with the soldiers. We mainly watched war films. The comfort station there was housed in a Chinese building. It was not so cold there. We wore Western style dresses and occasionally were able to buy Chinese clothes. Fukiko, Masako and Fumiko were among the five of us who went there together, but all the others died except Fukiko. One of them died of serious syphilis. There was a sign in front of the house, but I don't remember what it said. In Nanjing we had to serve many soldiers, just as usual. Whenever they came into the building, we had to say '*irassyai*'. This meant 'welcome'. There was a bed and a mirror in each room.

I cannot remember where it was, but we had to do training under the supervision of the soldiers. Each of us wore a sash on our shoulder with *Women's National Defence Society* written on it. We wore caps and baggy black trousers. There were Japanese women and civilians who trained with us, and after each training session we returned to our station.

It was while we were there that we were liberated. There was a Korean man from Kwangju who lived in Nanjing with his wife and family, trying to run a business. I used to call him my big brother, and we got on very well. After Korea was liberated Okhŭi and I returned with this man and his family. On our way back, many people with us died in a train accident, but we were delivered safely. I wept and wept as we travelled back to our homeland, and 'big brother' tried to console me. He, with his wife and family, went their own way half-way through the journey, and Okhŭi and I were left alone. We noticed lots and lots of Russian troops on the way, and there was a rumour going around that they would take away young women, just as the Japanese had done before them. So we smudged our faces with soot, and continued our journey looking like tramps. In Shinŭiji we stayed overnight in a Korean guest-house. Russian soldiers rushed in during the night, apparently looking for young women, so we hid in a wardrobe. They must have gone, but we stayed confined in there all night.

We got on a ship from Shinŭiju to Inch'ŏn, and then took a train to Chŏngŭp. I was wearing flat yellow shoes I had bought in China, and a short-sleeved blouse. We bid goodbye to each other at the station, and I took a rickshaw home. My brother, Kŭmsu, who was in primary school at the time, still remembers me arriving on the rickshaw! My other brother was cutting firewood, and when he heard I was home he dropped everything and ran back to the house. My parents said that they had given me up for dead. My mother was so shocked to see me after such a long time that she fainted. After nine years in China, I found it hard at first to understand my own language. I had a small bamboo bag from Japan with me in which I carried some photographs and Chinese shoes. But in order to forget that part of my life, I burnt these souvenirs later on.

For a few years I stayed with my parents. I lied to them about my life in China, saying I had worked as a domestic help. I was still young, and felt that I could do anything with my life. My parents tried to find me a husband, but I said I wanted to live alone. They finally found me a room, and my mother bought me a pair of beautiful shoes, even though she was still very poor. She also got me many herbal cordials to build up my strength. After 1945, my parents were running a small restaurant in a boarding house for policemen. My father died of illness in 1951, and at the age of 33 I married a farmer whose wife had also died. I had been told that he had two children from his first wife, but after the marriage I found out that he had five! Marrying him meant I had to move to Seoul, and I lived with him for a number of years, looking after those five children. I found it hard to bring up someone else's kids, and I soon discovered that I wasn't able to have any of my own. When I was 48 I left him, taking with me the baby of my housemaid. I adopted that baby girl and lived back in Chŏngŭp for three years, without letting anyone know my exact whereabouts, not even my own brothers. It was hard to bring up a child on my own. I lived on cooked barley, working at silkworm farms on a daily wage of 2500 wŏn. I could not afford to send my adopted daughter to school until she was nine but, seeing me struggling to survive, she left school during her sixth grade and began to work in a

factory that made bamboo umbrellas. I didn't tell her that she had been adopted, just that her father had died. She is 21 now, married to a stonemason. They live in Asan county, South Ch'ungch'ŏng province. They have a three-year-old son and are expecting a second child soon. So that they were able to register the birth of their child, I had to register the birth of my adopted daughter as my own daughter. I had been scared to do this earlier.

Okhŭi used to say that, since we couldn't have children or be married, we should live on our own. She used to visit me often and we would cry together, talking about our miserable past. She, too, lived on government aid until she died of cancer last year. I have been on the list to receive state benefit for the past three years. In the autumn I work, picking red peppers from their stalks. If I work from dawn until dusk, I get paid something between 3000 and 5000 wŏn ($4 to $6) a day. I have very little income, so I don't pay any tax, but I have to pay 300,000 wŏn ($375) every ten months for my room. Last year I wasn't able to pay it. My only wish is to be able to live without worrying about rent. And I still feel resentful that I haven't been able to have children because of what happened almost 50 years ago.

CHAPTER 8

I Want to Live without Being Treated with Contempt

Hwang Kŭmju

Hwang Kŭmju was born in 1922 in Puyŏ, the first daughter in a scholarly family. When her father became critically ill, the family fortunes sank and in 1934, at the age of 13, she left home and began work as a housemaid. The Japanese head of the community was saying that one could earn a great deal of money working in Japanese factories manufacturing military necessities and said, almost as a threat, that at least one girl from each household should work in such a factory. Taking the place of the daughter of her employer, Hwang left Korea in 1941, when she was 20 (in Korean reckoning). She was taken by force to an army unit and became a comfort woman.

Youth

I came from a well-born, scholarly, gentry family. My paternal grandfather was from Puyŏ in Ch'ungch'ŏng province and my maternal grandfather from Suwŏn in Kyŏnggi. They had been close friends for many years, and it is said that they promised to marry their children to each other's children before they were even born. My paternal grandfather died earlier than was normal. The year when my mother turned 17 and my father 12 they married.[1]

I was their first child, born in Puyŏ on 15 August 1922 according to the lunar calendar. A second girl and a boy were born after me. We were not financially well off, but my father was very bright and went to Japan to study after graduation from a high school in Seoul. My maternal

---

1 Until the early twentieth century it was not uncommon, particularly amongst aristocratic or wealthy families, to arrange marriages before children reached puberty. The custom of marrying a son at 12 or 13 meant that a child could be conceived at the earliest opportunity. The mention of Puyŏ, once the capital of a Korean pre-modern kingdom, and Suwŏn, a city to the south of Seoul, emphasizes the claimed aristocratic roots of Hwang's family.

uncle, who was 20 years older than my father, ran a judicial scrivener's office in Suwŏn and helped my father pay for his education. This support was insufficient, and he had to do various odd jobs like shining shoes or delivering newspapers in order to complete his studies. Just as he was about to finish, his health began to fail. He returned to Korea and helped my uncle at the office, but his illness gradually grew more serious. He eventually came home to Puyŏ for treatment, but nothing seemed to make him better, and the cost of the treatment used up what little money we had. Father took to his bed, reading newspapers which were not freely available to the general public. I often had to go and fetch these papers from the town office in the centre of Puyŏ.

One day, we heard of a special drug which cost 100 yen. We didn't have so much money sitting around, and could only continue to worry, until a friend of my mother introduced us to a man from Hamhŭng who ran a big business in Seoul. We told him of our predicament. He took pity on my father and gave us the 100 yen. It wasn't a free gift. In exchange for the money, I was fostered to him and started to help with housework at the house of his mistress in Seoul. Later, I learned that although my father had used the money to buy the medicine, he didn't benefit from it. He died within a year. When I left home, I made up my mind not to contact any of my family until I became successful. I thought I was doing my duty as a filial daughter. I was 13.

The man I went to work for was a Mr Ch'oe. His mistress was a cruel woman who often beat me. I tolerated her harshness for two years before I told Mr Ch'oe how I was being treated. He said he had guessed as much and sent me to his own wife, who was then living in Hamhŭng. The man who accompanied me on the journey to Hamhŭng was paid 100 yen by my foster mother. So the debt I had to pay back was now increased to 200 yen, and knowing this always lay heavy on my mind. Mr Ch'oe had two sons and two daughters. His wife was a kinder woman and she sent me to evening school when I turned 17. It was called the Hamhŭng Ladies Institute, and was run by a large church. It had four classes, grades one through four. I attended the first two grades, studying mainly Japanese and mathematics. We had only two hours a week for Korean lessons. By now, I was particularly good at knitting and sewing.

I took a year off after two years at the Institute. The community head of the village where we lived was Japanese, and he stayed in a rented house right behind ours. We often saw his wife and children, but we saw very little of him. His wife went around the village, saying 'If you go to work for three years in a military goods factory in Japan, you will earn a lot of money. At least one person from each household *must* go to work there.' I had heard of a government official who had sent his daughter to a factory to work, and there was a woman in our neighbourhood who had returned after having earned a great deal of money in such a Japanese factory. So I had no doubt that these factories actually existed. There were three girls, including me, with my foster parents. I felt that at least one of us would have to agree to go to a factory to work. The eldest son of my foster parents was at university in Seoul, and the second was attending a university in Japan. The youngest daughter was in high school and the eldest had finished Hamhŭng Girls High School and was preparing to go to Japan to further her education. My foster mother was worried, because the head's wife kept nagging her to send one of the girls. So I volunteered to go. I thought it wouldn't do for the daughters, who should be studying, to go. And I reckoned that if I went I would be able to pay my 200 yen debt. I thought I would easily be able to pay the money back if I worked for three years. My foster mother was touched with my idea and promised to find me a good husband once I returned after the required period away. It was February 1941 according to the lunar calendar, and I was 20.

Two girls were drafted from the neighbourhood. The community head's wife told us when and where to meet, and I accordingly went to Hamhŭng station at the appointed hour. There, I found about 20 girls gathered from different counties. Most of them looked about 15 or 16, and I seemed to be the oldest. We had no farewell ceremony, but many families and relatives came to see the girls off. I was wearing a black skirt and a white silk blouse, and carried a black cotton bundle which held my underwear, sanitary towels, soap, a toothbrush, a comb, digestive tablets and several sets of winter and summer clothes. All of this, I reckoned, would last me the three years. A man in his fifties met us and handed us over to a Japanese soldier. The soldier put us on board a long train of carriages, and all the other carriages except ours were full of soldiers. In our carriage there were about 50 women, including us. There could have been more women in other parts of the train, but I'm not sure. In ours, the 20 of us who had met at Hamhŭng station soon became friends, but we didn't get to know all the others. The windows were covered with black greaseproof paper which could be pulled down as blinds. Having to leave home made everyone sad, so we sat, rather quiet, lost in our sorrow. Before we pulled away, and as I looked out through a gap in the blinds, I saw the soldier who had led us to the train hand over a roll of papers to a military policeman. He received a second roll of papers in exchange. The two seemed to be exchanging some kind of document. As I watched, my heart suddenly sank. This scene kept recurring in my mind for many years afterwards. I can still vividly remember it. The train was guarded by military police at each entrance; we were trapped.

We couldn't look outside because of the blinds on the windows, nor were any lights put on. So we sat in darkness for the journey. But we sensed that the train was moving northwards. As I had expected to go to Seoul, I felt uneasy when it kept moving towards the north, but there was no one to ask what was happening. Sometimes the train stopped in tunnels, and at nights it didn't speed up; it would creep along slowly. Several times we had to get off and stay in some sort of storeroom. We might have changed trains, but I cannot remember that clearly. We were given a ball of cooked rice with water twice a day. That was our food. We had no way of knowing the hours that were passing, but after about two or perhaps three days, the train stopped. We were herded off the train as a loudspeaker announced something. We asked what was being said and were told that we had arrived in Jilin, China.

In front of the station were trucks, all soiled with dirt and dust, their covers torn. We were divided into groups and pushed on to the trucks. Each of us held on to the bundles containing our belongings. The trucks drove for a few hours, bumping up and down as they traversed a very rough track.

Inhumanity

The trucks put us down at a place where only barrack after barrack could be seen. There was not one ordinary house on the horizon. We were allowed one of the many barracks called a *koya* and stayed there the night. Our *koya* was a roundish hut built of tin. The floor was laid with boards covered with *tatami*. We were each given a blanket and a quilt. But it was so cold that we huddled up to each other to keep warm through the night. At that time I thought to myself that our job must be to cook and wash clothes for the soldiers. There were a few women who had been there when we arrived, and they said to us: 'Poor things, you are dead now.' We asked what our job was, and they replied: 'It is a job, but not a job in the ordinary sense. Just do what you are told. If you don't, you will be beaten to death.'

The next day, soldiers came and took us away one by one. I was taken to an officer. He was sitting near his bed and asked me to come over. He tried to hug me. I resisted, saying that I would do anything, cleaning, washing and so on. But he ignored me and tried to embrace me again. When I continued to resist he slapped me on the face. I begged him to leave me alone, but he told me to do as I was told, to which I replied I would rather die than oblige him. He grabbed my skirt and pulled it so hard that it was torn from the belt. To this point I was still wearing that black skirt and white blouse I had on when I left Hamhŭng and had my long hair braided. Left in my underwear, I knelt before him and pleaded with him to spare me. He grabbed me by my hair, pulled me up and ripped my underwear off with a knife. I was so shocked that I fainted. When I came round, sometime later, he was sitting a few paces away from me wiping sweat from his brow. A soldier came in and took me away. I had to grab my underwear around me and wrap myself in my torn skirt. The women who had been there when we arrived said: 'Do you see what we mean? We won't be able to leave this place alive.'

The officers called for us three or four times a day for the first fortnight or so. The new girls were to serve the officers, as they were virgins. The officers didn't use condoms, so quite a few of us became pregnant quite early on, but we were naïve and weren't aware of it. I was all right, but those who fell pregnant were injected with 'No. 606'. They began to feel chilly, their bodies swelled, and they started to discharge blood. They were then taken to the hospital to have an abortion. After this had happened three or four times, they became barren.

After perhaps a fortnight of this rude awakening, I was moved to a comfort station, leaving my luggage in the *koya*. The station was a makeshift building, and each main room was divided into five or six small cubicles by wooden planks. The entrance to each cubicle was draped with a blanket as a substitute for a door. There were three or four buildings built in a row. I heard that there were more comfort stations in addition to these. There was no sign outside. The cubicle had a wooden floor covered with a blanket and was just big enough for one person to lie down, leaving sufficient room for another person to stand at the side.

Each day when our duties were over, we were supposed to go back to the *koya* to sleep. But often the soldiers came till late at night or all through the night, and sometimes we were too tired to return to our hut. So, more often than not, we slept at the station. It was bitterly cold there with just a single blanket to cover us. We took our meals in an army canteen, and the soldiers cooked for us. The meals were mainly rice, soya bean soup and pickled radish. When we first arrived, we were given baggy trousers, a short jacket, military socks, a cap, black canvas shoes, a padded coat and padded trousers. Later we were given some kind of military training suit. Later still, the supply completely stopped, and we had to wear the clothes that had been discarded by soldiers. When we entered 1945, the supply shortage became so serious that we were not given any clothes anymore. The supply of vegetables also stopped, as did that of soy sauce and soya bean paste. We had to eat balls of rice cooked in salt water. That was it.

There were no fixed hours for the soldiers to visit us, and officers and the rank and file came at the same time. The officers didn't come often, I suppose because they were afraid of catching venereal infection. On weekdays, each of us had to serve 30 to 40 men, but at weekends there were even more soldiers lined up outside the station, some of them with their trousers down and underpants already off. Some got so impatient that they lifted the curtains and entered the rooms while their colleagues were still going at it. If anyone took slightly longer than usual, they would shout at him '*Hayaku! hayaku!*', 'Hurry, hurry'. Those who were facing an imminent battle used all their strength, and some of them wept as they carried on with us. On such occasions I could even feel pity for them. All the soldiers were different. Some came already wearing condoms. Some asked me to put condoms on for them, and some didn't bother to bring protection at all. We were given a box of condoms each, and I initially reckoned that if I didn't have any, many of the soldiers wouldn't come to me. So I threw the condoms away. But the soldiers still came, and I was the one to suffer. While working there, I was never paid. No cash and no tickets were given to me.

During the first year we had to go to the hospital two or three times a month to have medical check-ups. But after that year, a military surgeon came to one of the barracks and set himself up in a room which looked like an office equipped with the necessary bits and pieces. He disinfected us, applied ointment or gave the dreaded 'No. 606' injection. We hardly saw a female nurse. After continuing like this for about a year, not a single one of us remained in good health. Most of us had been pregnant two or three times or had caught various infections. Women with serious problems were put into isolated rooms and were allocated the use of separate bathing facilities and toilets. When they recovered they were brought back. We were treated in this way up to two times, but if anyone came back ill for a third time she was taken away by a soldier and we never saw her again. There was one girl whose lower abdomen began to fester with yellow pus. Her face became yellow and swelled up. She was taken away by a soldier and never returned. Of the 20 of us who had started out together from Hamhŭng station, in the end I alone was left. All the others disappeared. Some became ill and disappeared, and some were moved to other places. Seven new women who arrived to replace them were also taken away one after another, and in the end only seven women were left in the whole *koya*. We were all Koreans, and we were all stricken with illness.

We were given some sort of cotton wool to use during our monthly periods. But the supply of cotton stopped after a year, and from then onwards we either stole someone else's sanitary towel as it was drying on the washing line or collected, washed and used gaiters discarded by the soldiers. If we were caught taking the gaiters, we would be beaten up; the soldiers regarded this sort of thing as unlucky.

The comfort women in the military unit were not treated like human beings. We were beaten almost every day. If we looked at the moon, we were hit as the soldiers asked what we were thinking of. If we talked to ourselves they hit us again, saying we must be swearing at them. We were told to behave as if we didn't see anything or hear anything. So we walked about with our hands covering our eyes. If we tried to take a walk outside the barracks we were kicked back inside. So we had no opportunity to look around at where we were. I don't know what the name of the unit was, nor can I remember the names, the faces or the ranks of the soldiers. I was particularly rebellious, and earned more beatings than the other girls. Even now, my ears sometimes go fuzzy and I can't hear anything for a while. I have strong magnetic strips attached to my knees and hips. If I take these off to have a bath and forget to put them back on, then my knees and hips swell up within five or six hours, and I am unable to sit down.

One day, when I was unable to serve soldiers because my womb had swollen and was bleeding, an officer ordered me to suck his penis. He claimed I was not able to do what he called my 'duty'. I shouted at him: 'I'd rather eat your shit than suck you!' This made him very angry. He beat me and threw me about, shouting 'Konoyaro koroside yarouka', something like 'I am going to kill you, you bitch'. I blacked out, and when I came round I was told that I had been in a coma for three days.

Among the women, there was a girl who had been captured by soldiers on the street when she was in China visiting relatives during the school holidays. She was about 20 by the time I knew her. The women in my koya were all Korean except for one Chinese. Many of the Koreans came from the North, though there was one from Nonsan, in the South. Like myself, most of them had been cheated by being told the lie that they were going to earn money in factories making military supplies. There was no one soldier that I was particularly close to, though I got quite familiar with someone from the medical corps for a short time. He worked in the army hospital and I got to the stage of asking him to look after my friends who were very ill in the koya. I knew him only for a very short time and, besides him, there was no one else I got close to. I didn't have time to feel lonely, since we were kept too busy serving the soldiers.

One day, we were told that some army personnel were moving to a different place, and if we wanted to go with them we could do so. I thought somewhere else might be better than where I was being held and decided to go along with them. About ten of us left together. We were taken on the back of a lorry, but I was so travelsick that I wasn't able to look around. We might have been travelling on a boat for some time. I can't remember clearly. The soldiers dropped us at a comfort station which looked similar to the one where I had been before. I don't know where we were, but at night the bombing was very heavy, and we weren't allowed to put on any lights. There were already a few women there, two Chinese and some Koreans, and these old hands told us that even if we were let out and given our freedom we would only drown. It didn't seem to be an army unit. Most of the men that used the station were sailors, and from time to time we had to deal with military personnel from different units. Here the men were even more cruel; they were savage. Those who knew they were about to go into combat were even worse. It was simply unbearable. After eight or nine months, the unit began a retreat towards Jilin, and I alone followed them, risking my life. In this way I managed to return to the station where I had started from. Sometime after I had got back to Manchuria, Korea was liberated.

Abandoned

One evening, there was no call for supper. There seemed to be nobody around, and it was strangely silent. I crept out of the barracks and could find no trucks, vehicles or horses. There were only mats hanging on the barbed wire, mats being blown by the strong wind. I crept quietly to the dining room and found the place completely deserted. There was not a single human being in sight. Then, as I was drinking some water a soldier appeared. He said he had returned after he had been sent on an errand to some far away, remote mountain, only to find the unit deserted. He said he had been left a memo from his officer telling him to leave this place immediately. He told me 'An atom bomb has fallen in Japan and we have been defeated. It would be best if you returned to your own country. If you stay on here you will be killed by the Chinese.'

I rushed back to the *koya* and told the seven remaining women what I had heard. All seven were Korean. They said they were too ill to go anywhere and told me to leave on my own. I hated to leave them, but I felt I had no choice. I left the *koya* and went back to the dining room, but the soldier had already disappeared. It was quite cold for August, so I put on three training suits abandoned by the soldiers and found an odd pair of *chikadabi* shoes for my feet. I tied my lice-infested hair in a scarf, and began to run.

The unit was much larger than I had expected. I had to pass three gates and then a fourth and final gate of barbed wire. I had to walk about 12 km before I began to see anybody. I walked a little further, and the roads began to be packed with soldiers, labourers and their families. I walked along with them, begging food from people who were cooking on the roadside or from villages. I slept on the road, crouched before fires made by other people as they went along in this mass exodus. As I walked, I changed my clothes into whatever I could find, and got some different shoes. I reached Korea, and around Ch'unch'ŏn I hitched a lift on a cargo train carrying coal. Finally, I arrived at Ch'ŏngnyangni station in Seoul. It was the beginning of December.

I stepped into a restaurant and begged for food. When I told the owner that I had come all the way from Manchuria, she gave me some scraps. As I ate I wept. And I wept. I didn't want to go home in this state, so I told the owner that I had no way of finding my family or relatives. She took pity on me and told me I could stay with her. I had a bath and put on an old cardigan and baggy trousers she gave to me. She cut my hair short, combed out the lice and sprayed my scalp with DDT. I worked in her restaurant for three years and saved a little money. After that I worked in the T'aech'ang Textile Factory until I was 27.

I kept needing treatment for venereal infection with penicillin I could only obtain from an American military unit. It took me a further ten years of treatment to be completely healed. In my third year of working in the factory, the Korean War broke out, and I was evacuated further south, taking only my savings book. On my way I found two orphans and handed them to an orphanage after looking after them for a short while. Later on I came across three more orphans whom I handed over to another orphanage. After the war, I settled down in Ch'ŏngp'yŏng and cultivated a farm for four or five years. I brought the three orphans I had met latterly to the farm and raised them. One of them died, but a boy and a girl have grown up and married. They still come to see me. At times, I thought of ending my life, for it was too difficult to continue living on my own. I came back to Seoul and kept a small stall that sold vegetables. Then I tried selling cooked noodles for a while. At present I run a small café in Shillim-dong, south of the river in Seoul. I manage to make a living, but with some difficulty. I do everything on my own.

Every other morning I rise at 5.00 a.m. and go to the market at either Yŏngdŭngp'o, Karak or Yongsan to buy groceries. I need to have five or six cups of coffee every day to keep me going. My knees often hurt. I had my womb removed some time back. I wonder how I can live the rest of my life without continually being looked down upon and without being ill.

I have lived my life with a resentful heart. I have wanted to tell my government what I have had to suffer, but I haven't been given the opportunity. In November 1991, at 10.00 p.m., I watched Kim Haksun tell her story on national television. The following morning, I rang the number which had been shown, and met up with her. She showed me how to report what had happened to me.

I left home thinking I was doing my duty as a faithful child. But that action ruined my life. From now on, I would like to live the rest of my days without being ignored by others. It is my wish to help poor people and eventually to die without being a burden on others.

CHAPTER 9

I So Much Wanted to Study

Mun P'ilgi

Mun P'ilgi was born in 1925, in South Kyŏngsang province, into a family that was not particularly poor, but was burdened by raising two sons and nine daughters. She wanted to learn so much that her mother sent her to school when she was nine, without telling her father. He was very much against it, and she had to give up. In 1943, when she was 18, a man in the neighbourhood promised her that she would be able to study and earn some money at the same time. She left home and ended up in a comfort station in Manchuria.

I was born in 1925 in Chisu district, Chinyang county, South Kyŏngsang province. My parents kept a small shop selling potatoes, fish, fruits and sweets. It was mainly my mother who ran the shop, while my father either bought the stock or went to sell goods at market. We also owned some paddy fields and vegetable plots. There were eleven of us children, two boys and nine girls. But three of the girls died when they were very young. As my mother didn't have any sons at first, my father had a son by a mistress and brought him home to join us when the boy was six. After that my mother gave birth to her own son. She was 41.

I was called Miyoko when I was little. I wasn't allowed to go to school. When I was nine, mother sold about 10 kg of rice to pay for my tuition and bundled me off to school. My father soon found out. He said that if a girl studied she would become too foxy. He rushed into my classroom, dragged me home and burnt all my books. That was the last of my education.[1] His anger didn't abate with that. He beat me and threw

---

1 In Korea, education was a male prerogative, at least until the late nineteenth century when foreigners set up mission schools such as Ehwa specifically for girls. The attitude that education was wasteful for girls continued to be widely held until after the Second World War, on the grounds that women became mothers and housewives and so had little use for education geared to finding employment. Poverty also had a part to play; given limited financial resources, it was considered better to spend on educating sons who could look after their parents in old age.

me out of the house, and I had to stay at my uncle's for a while. It was only after I promised that I would never go to school again that I was allowed to return home. I resented the fact that I wasn't allowed to get any education and I used to say to myself that I would somehow go on studying without my parents knowing it. I promised myself I would become an intellectual. Then, I used to say, I would be able to live with my head held high. I was quite ambitious. I couldn't see much future in country life, and I thought to myself that I would never allow myself to be married to a rural farmer. I so much wanted to go to school and learn. If I had been a boy I would have been able to study as much as I wanted.

The girls born before me had all died, so I had to do the work of the eldest child. From the age of nine, I did housework at home, helped with the vegetable plot and worked on our cotton field. I did spinning and weaving. I also helped my mother in the shop. The shop sold cooked sweet potatoes, and it was my job to cook them. We employed daily hands for our paddy field and I had to cook meals for them each day. All my work was for the sin of having been born the first daughter.

In our village there was a man in his fifties who worked as an agent for the Japanese. One day he approached me and told me he would give me an introduction to a place where I could both learn and earn money. I had been so resentful that I hadn't been able to study, and his proposition was so attractive, that I told him I would like to take him up on the offer. Somehow I felt that if my parents knew, they would be very angry, so I kept the whole thing a secret from them. It was autumn 1943 and I was 18. The housework was hard, and my father hadn't allowed me to go to school, so I wanted to leave home to study and to earn my living.

After a few days, the man came to see me at dusk and told me to follow him. He said he wanted to take me somewhere for a few minutes. So I crept out of the house without saying anything to my parents. We walked for a little while, to a place not far from home. It was quiet; there were few houses around. There, I saw there was a truck parked, with a Japanese policeman, Tanaka, who worked at the village police station. The two men told me to get on the truck, and the truck drove us off to Pusan. Our departure was so sudden that I had nothing with me except what I was wearing at the time: a dark skirt and a blouse.

The men took me to a hairdresser's shop. They wanted to have my long hair cut short, and though I tried hard to stop them, it was soon done. Then the man from my neighbourhood left me with the policeman and told me I must do whatever he told me if I wanted to study. The policeman handed me a maroon dress and told me to put it on in place of my blouse and skirt. He said the clothes I had were too dirty and I should change into something clean and pretty. There were four more

Korean girls there beside me. One was still wearing a school uniform. We had breakfast in a restaurant, and the five of us got on a train at Pusan station. Some carriages were reserved for civilians and some for soldiers, and we were led to a carriage set aside for soldiers. A Japanese soldier led us inside and made us sit apart from one another so that we couldn't talk. The train passed Seoul, P'yŏngyang and Shinŭiju and then went on to Manchuria. On the way it picked up five or six more Korean girls.

Assaulted

The girls were allocated to different comfort stations in Manchuria. I don't remember the name of the district nor the name of the army unit to which I was assigned. Even when I had actually arrived at the unit, I didn't know what I was supposed to do. The winter up there was very long and bitterly cold. The summer was short and cool, almost like a Korean autumn.

There were about 30 women in my station, and they were all Koreans. Quite a lot came from what is today North Korea, but there were some from Pusan. They were mostly 18 or 19 years old. Among them, some had been students when they had been dragged there. As my name was Miyoko, they called me 'Mich'ang', a sort of Korean equivalent, and Kiyoko became my best friend. She was beautiful and said she had been a *kisaeng,* an entertainment girl, in P'yŏngyang. She said she had come to the comfort station because she had been cheated by a man who told her that she could work in a better place. That man, she said, was one of the Koreans who actually worked at the comfort station. At the request of Japanese soldiers he had gone to Kiyoko's place and coaxed her to come. In the station, there were two men from North Korea, and a Chinese who did the cleaning and various odd jobs. The wife of one of the Koreans came to the station to visit her husband from time to time. When she came, she cooked for us. The soldiers stationed near the comfort station took turns to guard us. The job of the two Koreans was to watch over us and to handle the tickets that we were given by soldiers. The Koreans wore yellow-green uniforms with a badge on the front. One of them didn't harass us, but the other one, the shorter of the two, beat us and molested us cruelly. And if we tried to resist him, or we fought any of the soldiers, he would beat us more severely than ever.

The station was built in the Japanese style, positioned near an army unit. It was L-shaped and had two storeys. Both floors were used for the comfort station. There was a sign at the front gate, but since I was illiterate I still don't know what it said. It was surrounded by a wall. On the ground floor the two Korean men had rooms, and there was a dining room. On the first floor the women had rooms, each one the size of one and a half *tatami* mats. There was a coal-burning fireplace on one wall with which the room was heated. We were given a room each, and in each room was bedding, clothes hangers and some cosmetics.

When we first arrived, we had to undergo a medical examination to see if any of us had venereal disease. They actually wanted to find out if we were virgins. The army surgeon gave me work in the hospital. I learned to dress and bandage soldiers' wounds. I washed clothes and sheets. I did hospital work during the day, and at night I had to sleep with the surgeon. It was he who took my virginity. I had been brought up to value my chastity, and I believed it to be important. So I wept a lot. I thought I was ruined. While I worked in the hospital, I didn't have to serve any soldiers except the surgeon. But after a few months, I was forced to stop working there. I became a comfort woman full-time. Sometimes, when there were many wounded soldiers, I was called back to the hospital to help nurse them.

All of us wore the same dresses. We were given several sets of clothes, so we were not short of things to wear. The fireplace was lit all the time except in summer, so we didn't have to wear warm underwear. We washed our own clothes. Our hair was bobbed. For meals we were given rice mixed with millet, pickled radish and the Korean staple, *kimch'i*, made from white cabbages. For breakfast we had soya bean soup. On Japanese holidays we were occasionally given meat. We had two meals a day, breakfast and supper. We took turns to cook.

My menstruation started when I was already working at the station. I panicked at first, thinking I had caught a disease, but Kiyoko made sanitary towels for me and told me what to do. At weekends, when many soldiers visited us, we had to serve them even if it was the time of the month for our period. Menstruation was the hardest time for me.

On weekdays we usually had to gather in the yard for a morning assembly, and at times the soldiers came to give us air-raid drills. The assembly took place three or four times a week, and all of us had to recite the imperial pledge. We promised to be loyal to Japan and we sang Japanese military songs. The soldiers were out fighting during the day and usually came to us in the evenings. Once in a while a few soldiers were on leave and would come during the day. We had about ten soldiers every evening. On Saturdays and Sundays, the soldiers would come from 8.00 a.m. We were given lunch at the weekends, so we were able to have three meals. But we had to serve soldiers all through the day, except for those few sparse minutes reserved for meals. After 7 o'clock in the evening, the officers would come. They usually arrived early and stayed all night, going back to their units early the following morning.

They were all Japanese. I so wanted to meet a Korean soldier and pour out my sorrow to him, but during my three years at the station I never saw one. I remember that there were some women who said they had met Koreans.

Every time the soldiers came to us, they gave us a brown ticket, half the size of our hand, with the price written on it. The officers' tickets had higher prices than those of the rank and file. Some soldiers tried to leave without handing over their tickets. Those who stayed longer than the allotted time were asked to hand over more than one ticket, and sometimes we sent the odd soldier away without taking any payment when we had taken pity on him. We weren't able to keep the tickets, but gave them straight to the Korean managers. They counted them and recorded them on a big chart that showed the number of soldiers each of us served in any given day. Because I served fewer men than the others I was often told off. I was made to serve about ten men when it was quiet and 40 or 50 on a Saturday or Sunday. We only handed in the tickets; we were never paid. We were never able to save for anything and we never demanded money. And the soldiers didn't give us any money.

On weekdays I washed my clothes. I also washed condoms. I had to wash the condoms thoroughly once they had been used, and disinfect them so they could be used again. At first, I had no idea how to wash them, and it took one month of watching and learning from others to find the best way to prepare them. Each of us kept 40 or 50 prophylactics. When one had been used three times or so, we would throw it away and replace it with a new one. Many of the soldiers had crabs. We often caught lice from them. Kiyoko and I helped each other remove them from our pubic hair with a pin.

The soldiers would queue up outside each door, waiting their turn. There were frequent quarrels as one or another tried to jump the queue. They waited with their gaiters already off. If one of them tried to stay in our room longer than the normal time, the others would make a fuss, knocking at the door and shouting for him to hurry. A low-ranking soldier was allowed 30 minutes, but an officer got an hour. Most of the men finished within five minutes.

The soldiers were meant to use condoms. Most were afraid of venereal infection and readily put one on, and some even brought their own. But there were a few who refused. I would then insist, saying that otherwise they would catch venereal disease from me. Sometimes, I threatened to report them to their superiors. I would plead with them to comply in order that both of us should not be infected. It was bad enough to have been dragged down this far; I didn't want to make my life any worse by catching a disease. So I insisted. After I served a soldier

I would go to the bathroom downstairs and wash myself with water and disinfectant. I was then ready for the next soldier. Among the soldiers were some who, maybe because they hadn't been with a woman for a long time, ejaculated as soon as they entered my room. I fought against any who harassed me or treated me badly, but if I fought, the soldiers waiting outside would shout for us to stop wasting time and hurry up. I was frequently hit.

There were many times when I was almost killed. If I refused to do what one man asked, he would come back drunk and threaten me with his sword. Others simply arrived drunk, and had intercourse with their swords stuck in the *tatami*. This left the *tatami* scarred, but this sort of behaviour was more a threat to make me accede to their desires and give them satisfaction. If that threat didn't work, they would pull the sword from the *tatami* and point it at me. Then, I either had to escape quickly or lie to them in some way, telling them that one of their compatriots was calling from outside.

I had been there for about a year when a soldier threatened me so interminably that I became furious and kicked out at him. He tore all my clothes off, beat me and took out his sword. He rushed out, fetched a red-hot iron bar and pressed it against my armpit. I suffered from the resulting burn for three months. Officers who stayed overnight would also keep harassing me, demanding sex several times, and allowing me no time to get off to sleep. There was one who came totally drunk and would throw up throughout the night, trying to climb on top of me at the same time. I was repulsed by this sort of behaviour and really couldn't tolerate it.

Every time a soldier tormented me, I wished that I had listened to my parents. I would remind myself that I had only myself to blame for this fate. When the sun went down, thoughts about my parents would make me unbearably sad. If only I had listened to them and agreed to get married when they had asked me! What was so good about studying that I had been willing to desert my parents and my home, to come all this way, and to suffer like this? I was in deep despair. I missed home so much that I wept every day, and if I listened to anybody else's sad story I would break into tears. I fell ill, thinking of my mother and my home. I had no wish to live anymore. At times of depression like this the surgeon would give me tranquillizers or herbal tonics.

I went to see a film with the surgeon once. We took a bus to the cinema and watched a Japanese film, *Tsubaki hime*. And once, with his permission, I was able to look around outside the comfort station. Except for these two outings, I never went beyond the confines of the station. The guards were always there, watching us. They were afraid that we might plan an escape together, so they didn't allow us to congregate and talk. As a result we women didn't know each other very well. Once a week we had to go to hospital for medical tests for venereal disease. We had our urine and blood examined. I once caught gonorrhoea and was treated with the injection, 'No. 606', and an ointment which got rid of it. While I was suffering from disease I didn't have to serve soldiers but simply rested, so life became somewhat easier. Apart from this, I was never ill.

Since I was illiterate, Kiyoko from P'yŏngyang wrote a letter for me to my parents. We didn't dare write the sender's address, only the receiver's. I asked a Chinese boy who worked in the station to post it for me. Because I had ended up in such a miserable place, and because this was due to my yearning to study, I asked my parents to do everything in their power to send my brothers and sisters to school. I didn't tell them I was a comfort woman, but simply said I was well.

Back Home

The war ended during my third year at the comfort station. Suddenly, all the soldiers disappeared. Nobody came to visit us. For a while, our nights were peaceful. Then one day, Russian soldiers rushed into the building, pointing their guns straight at us. They tried to get our clothes off. Now that the Japanese had gone, the Russians were trying to rape us! The North Korean proprietor urged us to flee, leaving our belongings behind. He, his wife, Kiyoko and myself put soot on our faces, slipped through the back door of the station, and ran as fast as we could. I don't know what happened to the other women. We all went our own ways running off in different directions. My small group hitched a lift on an open cargo train as far as the Yalu river and then walked to Hŭngnam on the east coast of North Korea. The Korean couple and Kiyoko were from the North, so I said goodbye at that point. Then I walked day and night, without any proper food, through P'yŏngyang and Kaesŏng, until I finally arrived in Seoul. At Seoul station I was able to get a ball of cooked rice and a train ticket home. I felt so relieved when I held that ticket in my hand.

Everyone was shocked to see me. It was as if I had come back from the grave, they said. They thought I had died. I found that my father had passed away a little time before. My mother tried to find me a husband but I had no intention of getting married. I couldn't bear the thought of becoming someone's wife, not with my past as a comfort woman to haunt me. But I couldn't tell my mother what I had been doing. I simply said I had been to school and then had worked in a factory. I couldn't stay at home, and left after a year. I went to my cousin's guest-house in Chinju. I helped her for a while, then left. I wandered about Mokp'o,

Kwangju, Chŏnju and other places, working when I could in drinking houses. But I couldn't stand having men trying to approach me, so I went back home. I moved around in fear that someone might recognize me as a former comfort woman.

I raised some money and moved to Masan, where I rented a house to run as a guest-house and drinking house. People used to tell me that I should get married instead of keeping a place of such low repute like a drinking house. While there, I met a man working in a permanent gang on the railway. I was 36. We moved to Seoul and started to live together. He was eight years older than me, and we didn't ever have much affection for each other. In Seoul he worked on the railway, and I stayed at home doing the housework. Sometimes I had to go out to do manual work, because he didn't earn enough to make ends meet. He drank every day. He caused me much mental pain. He had already been married, and had children, but he initially kept this a secret from me. I tried to leave him many times, but always in vain. We lived together without getting married, and in the end he died of an illness, leaving me just his debts.

At the moment I live alone, but with my sister's grandchild. I was so lonely that I brought the child to live with me when he was four years old. I work on a *Saemaŭl Undong* (New Village)[2] job creation project. I also work in the evenings for my neighbours whenever they need me for 1000 wŏn ($1.25) an hour. I live in a rented, half-basement room, paying 70,000 wŏn ($880) each month and 1,500,000 wŏn ($1900) deposit.

I saw a poster about the Korean Council in a stationery shop in my neighbourhood, and listened to the testimonies of former comfort women on television. To release my pent-up resentment, I reported to the Council in June 1992. I hesitated a lot, but I feel so relieved to pour out the things that have been piled up in my heart for so many years.

---

2 The *Saemaŭl Undong* was initiated in the early 1970s by the South Korean regime of Park Chung Hee as a way of promoting rural development. Based on clubs set up by the American authorities in post-liberation Korea, it aims to increase living standards by supporting the introduction of new crop strains, promoting the building of roads and communal facilities, and actively developing job creation projects.

CHAPTER 10

Return My Youth to Me

Yi Yongsu

Yi Yongsu was born in 1928 in Taegu, the only daughter of a poor family. Due to financial difficulties she had to leave school after attending for less than a year. While she stayed at home, she looked after her younger brothers for her mother. Her mother was a wet-nurse. She then worked in a ginnery for a time. Tempted by a Japanese man, she left home with a friend and was taken to a comfort station in Taiwan.

I was born on 13 December 1928, in Kosŏng ward, North district, Taegu city, the only daughter of a poverty-stricken family. There were nine of us: my grandmother, father, mother, an older brother, myself and four younger brothers. I started to attend Talsŏng Elementary School, but had to give up within a year because my parents couldn't afford the fees. When I was 13 I went to evening classes for a short period, where I used a Japanese name, Yasuhara Riyosyu. I learned Japanese and I learned to sing, accompanied by the organ. I was not very bright at school work, but I did enjoy singing. One of the male Japanese teachers told me that I sang well. Although I attended evening school for about a year, I often missed classes since I had to work in a factory during the day.

My mother was a wet-nurse for a wealthy family who lived in front of Sujŏng Elementary School, and it was my job to look after my younger siblings. The house we lived in, together with the paddy field and vegetable plot we cultivated, belonged to a wealthy family, the same family for whom my mother worked. From the age of nine to 13, I worked in a ginnery in Ch'ilsŏng ward managed by a Japanese man. They fed cotton balls into gins and made cotton wool. The place was full of dust. One day I witnessed a terrible accident. A man was dragged into the machine and his head was smashed. After that I hated working there, but I had to continue as my family needed the money. When I was 15, I was drafted to the training group for the Voluntary Corps in Ch'ilsŏng Elementary School. Boys and girls lined up separately for training, and we did exercises and marched in neat lines. We also had to march home at the end of each day. It was autumn 1944, and I was 16 years old. My father was a casual labourer carrying rice from the warehouse. I had a friend called Kim Punsun who was the same age as me and whose mother sold wine. One day I went to see her for a chat, and her mother said: 'Look at yourself! Poor thing! You haven't even got proper shoes. I'll tell you what, why don't you go somewhere with my daughter? I hear that you can have everything you want there. You'll be able to eat nice food. You can even help your family.' She was talking about Japan. I certainly looked a mess in my rags.

After a few days, Punsun and I were collecting shellfish at the riverside when we noticed an elderly man and a Japanese man looking down at us from the hillside. The more elderly of the two pointed at us with his finger, and the Japanese man started to walk towards us. The older man disappeared, and the Japanese beckoned to us to follow him. I was scared and ran away, not caring about what happened to my friend. A few days later, Punsun knocked on my window early in the morning, and whispered to me to follow her quietly. I tip-toed out of the house after her. I left without telling my mother. I was wearing a dark skirt, a long cotton blouse buttoned up at the front and slippers on my feet. I followed my friend until we met the same man who had tried to approach us on the riverbank. He looked as if he was in his late thirties and he wore a sort of People's Army uniform with a combat cap. He handed me a bundle and told me I would find a dress and a pair of leather shoes in it. I peeped in and saw a red dress. I was so delighted that without any further thought I followed him. Altogether, there were five girls with him, including myself.

We went to the station and took a train to Kyŏngju. It was the first time I had been on a train. In Kyŏngju we were put up in a guest-house. I was washing my hands in the stream in front of the building when I noticed a purple flower on the hillside. I had never seen a flower like it before, and when I asked what it was I was told it was a bellflower. We stayed in the guest-house for two days, during which time two more girls joined us. Now there were seven of us. We boarded a train and passed through Taegu where I could just see my home through the broken window. I suddenly missed it and missed my mother. I began to weep, saying I wanted to go home. I pushed the bundle of clothes away and continued to cry, asking the man to let me get off. He refused. I finally fell asleep in exhaustion as the train just kept on going. We must have travelled for several days.

Beating and Torture
We got off the train at Anju, in P'yŏngan province, and were led to what looked like an ordinary residential house. It was typical, with a thatched

roof and four rooms in the main part, an annexe and a stable. An elderly woman was keeping the house on her own. She wore baggy trousers and a long top, and had her head wrapped in a towel. Food was short, and we were given boiled potatoes and corn. We felt very hungry and sometimes during our stay there we would pinch apples from the tree. The Japanese man who had led us from Taegu punished all of us if any single girl did something wrong. We had to stand on small round clubs, holding large bottles filled with water in our hands. Or he would beat our palms and the soles of our feet with sticks. He would ask one of us to bring him water to drink, and if the girl was slightly slow in doing what was asked, he would beat all of us. Any excuse prompted a beating. We became so scared that we tried not to upset him in any way.

Winter was coming. The ground froze hard and a biting wind began to blow. Every day we had to go out to the fields and collect radishes in straw sacks. We were still wearing light clothes and we froze, feeling ice form all over our bodies. If we complained of the cold, he would beat us. We shivered and tried to keep our frozen hands warm, doing everything behind his back. The two girls who had joined us in Kyŏngju were taken away, leaving the five of us who had set off together at the beginning of our journey. We remained in Anju for about a month and then boarded a train once more to travel to Dalian [Luda]. We stayed overnight in a guest-house in Dalian. The following morning we were given soup and steamed bread. I remember enjoying that meal since I was so hungry and had never had any similar Chinese food before. We boarded a ship and were told that a convoy of eleven boats would be sailing together. They were big ships. We were taken into the last one. It was already crowded with Japanese sailors. We were the only women.

New Year's Day 1945 was spent on board. The ships stopped in Shanghai, and some of the sailors landed for a short break on shore. We weren't allowed to disembark. I was summoned on deck and sang for the men. Afterwards, an officer gave me two rice cakes. I shared them with the other girls. The ships started to sail again but often halted because of bombing. One day our ship received a direct hit. The other ships were destroyed, but only the front of our ship was damaged. Men shouted and screamed outside our cabin. The ship was tossed about, and I suffered with severe seasickness. My head was splitting with pain, and my stomach seemed to turn upside down. I remember crawling towards the bathroom, throwing up as I went along, when I was grabbed by a man and dragged into a cabin. I tried to shake him off, biting his arm. I did my best to get away. But he slapped me and threw me into the cabin with such force that I couldn't fight him off. In this way I was raped. It was my first sexual experience. I was so frightened that what actually happened didn't sink in at the time. I vaguely thought that this man had forced me into the room just to do this.

People kept shouting that we would all die since the ship had been torn to pieces. We were told to put life-jackets on and to stay calm. We thought we were going to drown. Dying seemed better than going on like this. But the ship somehow managed to keep going. Later I found out that I was not the only one who had been raped. Punsun and the others had also suffered that same fate. From then on, we were often raped on the ship. I wept constantly, until my eyes became swollen. I was frightened about everything. I think that I was too young to hold a grudge against my aggressors, though looking back I feel angry and full of the desire for revenge. At that time I was so scared I didn't even dare look any man squarely in the face. One day I opened the window of our cabin and tried to jump into the water. It would have been better to end my life then and there, I thought. But the water, blue-green and white with waves, scared me so much that I lost the courage to throw myself out.

Eventually we arrived in Taiwan. When we disembarked I couldn't walk properly as my abdomen hurt so much. My glands had swollen up in my groin, and blood had coagulated around my vagina. I could walk only with great difficulty, since I was so swollen that I couldn't keep my two legs straight.

The man who had accompanied us from Taegu turned out to be the proprietor of the comfort station we were taken to. We called him Oyaji. I was the youngest amongst us. Punsun was a year older than me and the others were 18, 19 and 20. The proprietor told me to go into a certain room, but I refused. He dragged me by my hair to another room. There I was tortured with electric shocks. He was very cruel. He pulled out the telephone cord and tied my wrists and ankles with it. Then, shouting 'konoyaro!' he twirled the telephone receiver. Lights flashed before my eyes, and my body shook all over. I couldn't stand it and begged him to stop. I said I would do anything he asked. But he turned the receiver once more. I blacked out. When I came round my body was wet; I think that he had probably poured water on me.

The comfort station was a two-storey Japanese-style building with 20 rooms. There were already many women there when we arrived. About ten, all of whom looked much older than us, wore kimonos. There was a Japanese woman, the proprietor's wife. But that same man also had a Korean mistress. He beat both his wife and mistress without any reason. We changed into dresses given to us by the other women. The proprietor told us to call them 'nesang', 'big sister' and to do whatever they told us to. We began to take turns to wash their clothes and cook for them.

The food was again not enough. We ate gruel made with millet or rice. Even now I get frightened easily. I was much worse then and, because I was terrified of being beaten, I was always scared. I was never beaten by soldiers, but I was frequently beaten by the proprietor. I was so frightened that I couldn't harbour any thoughts of running away. After having crossed an ocean and not knowing where I was, how could I think of escape?

The rooms were very small. Each was big enough for two people to lie down in. At the entrance of each hung a blanket in place of a door. The walls and floor were laid with wooden boards, and there was nothing else. We were each given a military blanket and had to sleep on the bare planks. One day, a man came in and asked my name. I was still frightened and just sat in a corner shaking my head without answering. So he said he would give me a name, and began to call me Tosiko. After that day I was always called Tosiko in the station.

We mainly had to serve a commando unit. They were not in the slightest way sympathetic towards us. They wore uniforms, but I had no idea whether they were from the army, navy or air force. I served four or five men a day. They finished their business quickly and left. Hardly any stayed overnight. I had to use old clothes, washed thoroughly, during my period. Even then I had to serve men. I never saw any money. There were frequent air raids, and on some days we had to be evacuated several times. Whenever there was a raid, we were forced to hide ourselves in mountain undergrowth or in a cave. If the bombing ceased, the men would set up make-shift tents anywhere, on dry fields or in paddies, and they would make us serve them. Even if the tents were blown down by the wind, the men didn't pay any attention but finished what they were doing to us. Those men were worse than dogs or pigs. I don't remember ever having a medical examination. I didn't know what condoms were, either.

One day, while we were in an underground shelter, the comfort station collapsed in a bombing attack. Our shelter was buried under the rubble. We dug through the soil, trying to get out. After a while we saw light through a small hole. I was incredibly relieved to be able to look out and shouted 'At last I can see outside!' Then I smelt smoke, and blood gushed out of my nose and mouth. I lost consciousness. The proprietor's wife and mistress, the latter tall and long-faced, died. As the house had collapsed, we were moved into a bomb shelter at the foot of a hill, and there we again had to serve the men. After a while, the proprietor got hold of some material and built a rough and ready house. It didn't take him long. We continued to serve the men. In the end I was infected with venereal disease and the proprietor gave me the injection,

'No. 606'. The fluid had a reddish tint. The disease stayed with me for a long time because I had to continue to serve men before I was clear. So I had to have constant injections. There was no hospital or clinic in the vicinity.

Apart from going to the bomb shelters we weren't allowed out at all. We were warned that if we tried to venture beyond the confines of the station we would be killed, and I was sufficiently scared not to try anything. The men we served in the unit were all young; they seemed to be 19 or 20.

One evening, a soldier same to me and said he would be in a combat later that same evening that would mark the end of his early life. I asked him what his commando unit was. He explained that one or two men would fly an aeroplane to attack an enemy ship or base. They would be suicide pilots. He gave me his photo and the toiletries he had been using. He had come to me twice before and said he had got venereal disease from me. He said he would take the disease to his grave as my present to him. Then he taught me a song:

> I take off with courage, leaving Sinzhu behind,
> Over the golden and silver clouds.
> There is no one to see me off:
> Only Tosiko grieves for me.

Until then I had known we were somewhere in Taiwan, but I had no idea of exactly where. From his song I knew we were in Sinzhu.

When we were evacuated to avoid the bombing we stole sugar cane. We were that hungry. But if we were caught we were beaten. We were not allowed to speak in Korean. Again, if we were caught doing so, we were beaten. One day, one of the older girls who normally hardly spoke a word to us announced that she, too, was Korean. She told me, in Korean, that the war was over. We hugged each other and wept with joy. She held my hand tightly and told me I must return to Korea. We could hear people shouting and running about. This confirmed to us that the war was really over. By the time we had calmed down, the proprietor and the other women who had been at the station before us were nowhere to be found. We walked to a refugee camp by the pier. It looked like a warehouse. We were given balls of boiled rice which had dead insects mixed in. We waited for a ship. I was scared even there in case someone might drag me away, so I sat, shaking with fear, in a corner wrapped in a blanket. I kept crying so much that my small eyes got even smaller.

Return my Youth to Me!

We finally got a ship. When it arrived in Pusan, the barley was green. As we disembarked, someone sprayed us with DDT and gave us each 300 wŏn. There were four of us: Punsun, a plump girl, another girl and myself. We said farewell and went our separate ways. I got a train to Taegu. I kept weeping and tried to hide myself from other passengers in fear that someone might take me away again. I found my house, just as run down and poor as before. My mother asked if I was a ghost or a real person and fainted.

I couldn't dare think about getting married. How could I dream of marriage? Until recently I had suffered from venereal disease. My parents and brothers didn't know what I had been through. My father was upset merely because his only daughter wouldn't get married. Both my parents resented the fact that they weren't able to see me hitched before they died. I worked in a drinking house which also sold fishballs in Hyangch'on ward, Taegu, for a number of years. For three years or so I ran a small shop on the beach in Ulsan. For some time I ran a small stall selling string. Then I worked as a saleswoman for an insurance company. I gave up when I began to get too old.

My parents have died. My brothers long ago became concerned about their older sister living on her own in her old age. People in the neighbourhood were also worried because I lived alone. I got fed up with all of them, and I felt a little sad that I would die without ever having had the opportunity to wear a white veil. So at the age of 60, I married a 75-year-old man. That was in January 1989. I chose an old man because I basically dislike men. But he was jealous of me and he abused me so much that the marriage failed. In February 1992 I divorced, and I now live alone in Taegu. I pay 900,000 wŏn ($1150) every ten months for my housing. I have a small room with a kitchen attached. My brothers help me each month with my living costs.

Now, having reported to the Council and after having poured out my story, I feel so relieved. How many more years can I live? I am grateful that the Council is trying to help us. These days I hum a song, *Katusa*, putting my own words to the tune: 'I am so miserable; return my youth to me; apologize and give me compensation. You dragged us off against our own will. You trod on us. Apologize and give us compensation. This lament, can you hear it, my mother and father? My own people will avenge my sorrows.'

I visited my parents' graves the other day. I said to them: 'Mother, I know you won't come back to life however much I may wish for it. My own people will avenge me. Please close your eyes and go to paradise.'

CHAPTER 11

Taken Away at Twelve

Yi Okpun

Yi Okpun was born in 1926 in Yŏngch'ŏn, North Kyŏngsang province, to well-off parents. She was the only daughter amongst four children. At the age of eleven, she started to attend Nambu Elementary School. A year later, her family moved to Ulsan. About two months later, while skipping with her friends outside the house, a Japanese and a Korean man approached her and told her her father was asking for her. She went with them, was held for three months, and was taken taken by ship to a comfort station in Taiwan.

I was born in 1926, in Yŏngch'ŏn county, North Kyŏngsang province, the only girl in a family of four children. I had one elder and two younger brothers. My father ran a stall in Yŏngch'ŏn market that sold fishing nets and food such as dried whiting, squid, chestnuts, plums and the like. He had two men who helped him. My mother was kept busy at home with housework and weaving. We had a plot of land let out to other people, and we were quite comfortably off. I started at Yŏngch'ŏn Nambu Elementary School when I was eleven. I learned Japanese, and I was quick to read and speak. The grown-ups in the neighbourhood used to pat me on my head and say that if I had been born a boy I would have been successful when I grew up. When I was twelve, we moved to Ulsan. I had just completed the first term in the second grade and was on my summer holidays. My parents were busy as before, looking after the shop. I played with the neighbourhood children every day. We used to skip, jumping over elastic bands singing the songs we had learnt at school. I still remember two of the songs. One ran: 'Mother, what will you do with this baby? Please come with me, you poor thing.' The other: 'Twilight is descending, the sun is going down, temple bells are ringing. Let's go home holding hands. Let's go home with the crows.'

Taken...

It was two months after the move. It was autumn, I think 16 September

1937. I was playing with my friends with the elastic bands as usual. A Japanese man and a Korean, who seemed to be working for him, approached us. The Japanese man wore a pair of work trousers and the Korean our traditional costume. They pointed to me and said that my father was playing *paduk* (*go*) in Cho's guest-house and had asked them to fetch me. The other girls ran away. Although I was only twelve, I looked about 15 since I was tall for my age and dressed neatly. My father had sent me on errands before, so I thought he was doing this again. I trusted the words of these men and went along.

They took me to the guest-house and pushed me into a small room at the rear. Three girls were there who had been similarly deceived. Two were from Yŏngch'ŏn and one from Ulsan. They were older than me, probably about 17. I still remember the Yŏngch'ŏn girls: one was called Tokiko and the other Myŏnggyo. The next day, another girl was brought in from Chinju. Her name was Myŏngnan. I cried and shouted, banging at the door asking for it to be opened, asking to be allowed to go home to my mother. A man unlocked the door and rushed in agitated. He held me by my hair and beat me on my back and bottom. We were locked in that same room for three months, and we dared not cry too loudly. The manageress brought us rice balls and pickled cabbage, *kimch'i*, and we had to use a chamber pot to urinate in. If we had to go to the toilet, the woman would accompany us and keep guard. The manager and manageress watched over us all the time. When I returned home a few years later, I went to Cho's guest-house, ready to demolish the building and beat the couple to death. But the house was gone, and a new building stood in its place.

After three months, the Japanese man came back. He was still wearing work trousers. He took me and four other girls to Pusan. He put us on board a ship. We had to get boarding passes, and because I was smaller than the others he had me stand on a wooden box when the police came to ask questions. He said that if I was asked how old I was, I should say I was 14. It wasn't a passenger ship, but a cargo vessel. There were about 30 people on board, many of them Korean girls. At night I went up on deck, but could see nothing but sky and water. As I cried up there, the Japanese man came looking for me. He was afraid that I might jump overboard into the water. He told us he was taking us to a factory in Japan where we could earn money and go to school.

We left Pusan at about 5.00 p.m., and were told that it was about 8.00 a.m. when we arrived the following morning at Shimonoseki. Without being given any food, we were immediately taken to a big hall, something resembling a warehouse. There were already 33 Korean women there, so with our arrival the number increased to 38. The wooden floor was large enough for all of us to sit down. The man who took us there said that we would soon be going to a nice place. He started to teach us to count in Japanese: one, two, three.... Those who were quick were all right, but anyone who was slow was beaten severely. Then he asked us to raise our hands if we had been to school. I thought that if I raised my hand I might be taken to the nice place he had promised. I was the only one to do so. He asked me to teach some Japanese to the other girls, who appeared to be between 17 and 19. We were watched over by three Japanese men wearing light khaki work trousers. They didn't tell us anything of our fate. We were each given a dress, and for meals we had balls of cooked rice.

We stayed for about a fortnight, during which time I continued to teach bits of Japanese. Then we were all taken back to a ship. This ship was a little larger than the previous one and was loaded with military commodities. There were many Korean women on board, and the men watched them like hawks. We sailed for about three days and landed in Taiwan. We disembarked in the morning and then travelled by train for some time. When we got off we were greeted by more Japanese men. We walked to the place where we were destined to stay. Since I was young, a guard let me ride his rickshaw. It was evening by the time we arrived at what appeared to be a guest-house shaped like a temple. It was a month before we learnt that this was Shyoka.

The house was a two-storey building with a vertical signboard at the gate saying 'Shyoka Comfort Station' in Chinese characters. The station was close to a mountain, and there were many other women there. Some wore kimonos, and some had nice blouses. We found out later that the man who took us there had sold some women from our group to other comfort stations, and the rest of us were sold here. The man who took me from Ulsan and sold me was called Nakamura. There were about 40 in the station when we first arrived, and we were told that it acted as the headquarters of all the stations in the region. Women were constantly brought in and sent on. The day after our arrival, seven moved on. The proprietor was Japanese, in his early forties, and he also wore work trousers. He seemed lost for words when he first saw me, because I was so young. The police issued permits for girls to serve men from the age of 14, and I was clearly too young to get one. So he let me do the washing and run errands.

One day as I was scrubbing the floor and carrying water for the women as usual, I went upstairs and peeked into one of the rooms through a hole. I almost fainted at what greeted my eyes. A Japanese man wearing a *yukata* was clambering over a woman, and right next to him a Taiwanese man with red lips and a Japanese soldier were doing the same thing. I was terrified and wondered how I could survive. I noticed that men paid money to the receptionist at the entrance. There were two more Japanese men working there apart from the proprietor and the receptionist.

I slept in a back room and had to get up at 5.00 a.m. to cook breakfast. If I didn't, one of the women would cook. Over about three months I trained myself not to sleep during the night, looking for an opportunity to run away. One night, at about 3.00 a.m., while the guard was fast asleep, I crept out of the back door, released the bar that locked the gate, and ran away, holding my shoes in my hands.

I kept running, asking those I met on the street the way to the nearest police station. I finally found it, and begged the sergeants through my tears to help me. One policeman looked me in the eyes and shouted 'Aren't you a *Chosenbi?*', a Korean woman. I kept on pleading until a Korean interpreter asked me where I was from. I replied that I was from Yŏngch'ŏn, and they sent a telegram home to check my identity. A month later, no answer had been received. Later, I learned that when a policeman with a sword at his side came by to ask my mother if she had a daughter with the name Okpun, my mother had been so frightened that she denied my very existence. During the month I was in the police station I did odd jobs. When I heard that there was no reply, I again burst into tears.

There was a Chief Superintendent at the station called Hujimoto. He told me that I could look after his young children. So I worked for his wife as a maid. I looked after the children, I cooked and I cleaned. Then the Pacific War broke out, in the winter when I was 16. The Chief Superintendent's wife and family returned to Japan in 1942. I was now 17. I had hoped that they would take me with them. For five years I had not been paid a penny for my work. As my reward, he must have reported to an army unit nearby that there was a Korean girl in his house.

...to a Comfort Station

Hujimoto asked me to mind the house while he was away and suddenly left. I was alone in the house. The next day, two Japanese soldiers on a truck arrived at the door. They were sergeants. They asked me to hurry and board the truck and, although I told them I was meant to wait until my master returned home, they kept on pushing me to get a move on. Eventually I was lifted on to the truck, and we drove off for what I reckoned to be 24 km before we arrived beside a hill. The Kaohsiung Commando Unit was based there. They had dug a tunnel through the hill, and you walked in one side and came out the other. The soldiers occupied an elementary school not far from the escarpment. It was a single-storey building with 17 classrooms. Each classroom was divided into three by wooden boards. There were about 40 women there. In front of the school was a sign saying, 'Commando Unit Comfort Station'. The distance from the barracks to the station seemed to me to be about 2 km.

On Saturdays, the Japanese soldiers formed long queues outside the school building. The ends of the queues were sometimes invisible. They each had a piece of paper with a red chop mark on it. They came from 9.00 a.m. until midnight on both Saturday and Sunday. Sometimes, after the soldiers had returned to barracks, officers came and stayed the night, leaving at about 5.00 a.m. On such nights we got no sleep. Each woman had to serve 20 to 30 soldiers a day. We were already very weak, but going without good food and being forced to serve so many men left some of us half dead. If anyone was too weak to work, the receptionist dragged them out and put a more healthy woman in their cubicle. Three to five weak women were typically kept in a back room without any food. If they thought such a woman could not recover her health with herbal tonics and medicines, she would be loaded on to a truck and taken to a mountain. She never came back. Anyone who died was also carted away to the mountain, the bodies left there, barely covered with grass.

If you wanted to survive, you had to be tactful. If we made faces at the men we were taken to a confinement room by the receptionist, so we smiled regardless of whether we felt like doing so. Each man was given 30 minutes in the cubicle, and I would try to prolong the time in an effort to lessen the number I had to serve, even to lessen the number by one. At first, I got away with this, but later on I was too exhausted to do anything but lie still like the dead with my face turned to the wall, avoiding his stare. During menstruation we had to use cotton wool and continue to serve the soldiers. For my first eight months I only served Yamamoto, the captain of the unit. But once he was transferred to Tayoko, I had to join the other women and serve 20 or 30 men a day. It was better to serve officers, as they would order the proprietor and receptionist not to send anyone else to me until they were spent and satisfied.

During my time there I was called both Haruko and Kohana, whichever name the men chose. We took turns to cook our meals, typically rising at 5.00 a.m. We ate rice with some vegetables or pickled radish as side dishes. Since we were given food only twice a day, we were always hungry. We had breakfast in the kitchen at 9.00 a.m. and supper at 6.00 p.m. We often looked at each other's rice bowl, wishing we could have some of our neighbour's food as well. If one of us was ill or looked extremely hungry, we would each give them a spoonful from our own bowls behind the backs of the Japanese. But if we were caught sharing food, both sharers and recipients got a severe beating. The Japanese had their own rations and didn't have to eat such meagre food as we received.

The tickets, as I saw later, bore the seal of the unit's commander. They were as big as a small pocket diary. The men handed them to a receptionist. There were two receptionists, Eiko and Masako. They passed the tickets on to the proprietor, Itakura. Itakura and Masako shared the same room. Itakura was a sergeant. These three handled the soldiers well, and there were no incidents such as soldiers stabbing us with their swords. We didn't know how they managed money, nor were we ever paid. Other matters were managed by other sergeants. I suppose since there was a war going on, there was no more senior authority watching over us. The cubicles were just large enough for two people to lie down in, and we each had two blankets for bedding. There was a small box for clothes and possessions and a dustbin in each room. Toilet paper was provided.

The soldiers all used condoms. We had a medical examination twice a month for venereal disease in a big room resembling a warehouse more than a hospital. We would wait in a corner surrounded by curtains for a Japanese military surgeon to examine our vaginas by inserting an instrument. There were no nurses. If the surgeon found any of us had caught a disease, he gave us an injection. The shot was so strong that we couldn't eat properly afterwards. It was said that the drug was strong enough to separate the womb from the body. We didn't have any cosmetics, and we were given two pairs of baggy trousers for our clothes in winter, spring and summer. There was a war raging, so we were not allowed to go out. Nonetheless, Yamamoto did take me out occasionally, and we went twice to a Chinese restaurant. Because of the war we had to cut hay during the weekdays, wearing a military uniform topped by a cap. Each of us was told to cut a certain amount of hay. We carried the hay to the roadside and burnt it, filling the air with smoke.

On weekday evenings we were made to sing, dance and play the violin in the bomb shelter. Even there we weren't allowed to sleep properly. The presence of officers in the shelter stopped the rank and file from approaching us. The shelter was huge, 4 km long,[1] big enough to accommodate all the soldiers. We were taught how to play the violin by the soldiers so that we could entertain them. They had eight instruments. If we couldn't play well, we were beaten. The men drank heavily and would quickly become very violent. Because we had to sing to entertain them, I still remember around 50 military songs, one about the commando unit,

1 Yi says '10 ri' in her testimony, indicating a distance which would take about an hour to walk from end to end.

others praising Taiwan, lively Korean folk-songs, songs of blind men, of youth, of comfort stations, of *samurai*, of pilots and so on. The song dedicated to the commando unit went:

> *See the aircraft in the blue sky; my heart flies with it.*
> *The engine has started and I turn the wheel.*
> *Mother, I am going before you: when you hear of my death,*
> *   please record my name in the temple;*
> *When you receive my ashes, please hug them as if you were hugging me.*

The song of the blind men ran 'If I could see I would know what you look like', while the song dedicated to life in the comfort station went something like 'My body is like a rotting pumpkin left out in summer'.

I still have a photograph taken when I was 19. In it I am working, dressed in a military uniform. The woman in a dress standing behind me came from Sariwŏn, Korea. In the original photograph there were many Japanese soldiers surrounding us, but since I hated them I have since cut them out.

The war was coming to an end, and Japan was thrown on the defensive. The soldiers moved about in a frantic muddle. They fought during the day, and at night they hid in caves. As the American bombing raids became more frequent, soldiers could no longer come to the school. Instead, they would abuse us in the caves at night. They demanded that we sing, dance and pour drinks. If a woman was a little slow in meeting their demands, they slapped her face without hesitation. If she cried from the pain, she was slapped again. The comfort station was for the commando unit only, so no civilians were allowed in. Among the soldiers we had to entertain, there were young Korean men who had been drafted as a student corps. We got on very well with the Korean soldiers. We called them brothers behind the Japanese soldiers' backs. We asked them where they were from and talked about our home towns, sitting and smoking together. Together, we wept a lot. If any of them suddenly stopped visiting, we knew he had been killed on the battlefield.

When I recall my life, I feel an unspeakable anger rising in my throat. Whenever any of us were beaten by the soldiers for having shared our rice, I used to grind my teeth together, saying to myself: 'One day I am going to kill you all. I will wipe out your descendants.' At the same time I used to ask myself 'Why is life so tough? Why can't I have my life, instead of living so wretchedly?' I lived each day hating myself that I continued to live. One morning I left the shelter at 3.00 a.m. while the others were fast asleep. I went to the seashore, intending to throw myself into the water, but I didn't have the courage. I tiptoed back and never told anyone.

Return

In 1945, when I was 20, Japan lost the war. When I went into the proprietor's room to clean it – it was my turn to do the cleaning – I heard on the radio that the Emperor had acknowledged defeat. The very next day the proprietor and receptionists packed their bags and hurriedly left. I told the others that our country had been liberated; Japan had been defeated by America. There were about 35 of us, and we all went our own ways. The Japanese left by ship to return to their own land. Although our country had been liberated, we were still in Taiwan and had to cope with the Taiwanese. To make a living I started to work in a bar run by the local people. I entertained customers and sang Chinese songs, wearing a Chinese dress. But I was soon discovered to be a Korean and from then onwards wasn't allowed to work there. Nonetheless, I stayed in Taiwan one more year, working in different bars.

Suddenly, a man began to hand out leaflets. They were written in Korean and asked all Koreans to come to Yasukuni Temple at a certain hour on a certain day. I went and found many of my countrymen already gathered there. One of the draftees came to the front and told us that if we stayed in Taiwan we all stood to be killed. He told us to find our own ways to return to our home towns. And then he taught us a song: 'Asian Coins, we the Koreans, we are smart and gifted...' 'Coins' referred to the Korean people.

I started going around with Kim Nae, the woman from Sariwŏn. We hid in a small cave in Shyoka for a few days, wondering what might be lurking at the far end of the long passageway. Then we started walking deeper and deeper into the cave. We must have travelled several kilometres. Then we saw light, and emerged in an expanse of reeds. We could see water. It was the sea. We couldn't walk any further. Disappointed, we sat on the seashore, looking out to the horizon. There was a ship in the distance. I took off my blouse and waved it about. The ship stopped and a dinghy was let down which was rowed towards us. There were two Korean men in it, dressed in American military uniforms. They asked us our nationality. We shouted that we were Koreans and asked them to help us. They told us to get on the dinghy. We got to the big ship and found many of our countrymen returning to Korea from American refugee camps. There were many women. We were each given a card which we were told to stick on to our chests. It was big enough to cover half my chest, and on it was written: 'This person was dragged away from her home but has survived. Do not accept any money from her.'

To kill time, we held singing competitions. When it was our turn to sing, my friend and I sang the *Song of the Commando Unit*, since we only knew Japanese songs. We were warned not to sing Japanese songs once we got home. After four days we arrived at the southern port of Pusan. I had been taken away when I was twelve and now, at 21, I was finally returning. Kim Nae took a train home. The first thing I did was go and visit Cho's guest-house, but there was nobody left there. I went to Sanakkol, the place in Kyŏngju where my mother's family came from. My father had died, because he believed he had lost his only daughter, but my mother was there with my three brothers. She didn't recognize me. I showed her the birthmark on my neck and cried 'Mother, it really is me. Can't you recognize this?' Only then did she realize who I was and began to hug me. I lied to her. I told her I had been working in a factory. My mother died three years back, unaware to the last that I had ever been a comfort woman.

I stayed with my family for eight years, but when my brother married and began a family, I left and settled in Pusan. I worked as a domestic help and as a cook. I have been running a small café for the past 18 years, ever since I was encouraged to do so by the owner of the petrol station next door.

I have tried to forget my past. What prompted me to give this testimony was an article I read in the paper last year. There, the Japanese government said that comfort stations had been run by civilians and that the government and military had had nothing to do with them. It isn't true. I wanted to prove to those lying Japanese that at least I am still alive and I know what they did. So in July 1991 I contacted the *Pusan Daily News* and told them my story. They did not publish it immediately, but held on until the end of November, when the Japanese Prime Minister visited Korea. I told my story to the National Assembly in December 1991, and I visited Japan in June 1992, to sue them for what they did to me.

CHAPTER 12

Back to My Wretched Life

Mun Okchu

Mun Okchu was born in 1924 in Taegu. When she was eight years old her father, who had been involved in the liberation struggle waged against the Japanese occupation, returned home and died from illness. In spite of her family's resultant poverty, her desire to study was so great that she went to Manchuria with relatives who had promised to educate her. She returned home in secret because they only wanted her to do their housework. In 1940, when she was 16, she was kidnapped by a Japanese military policeman on her way home from a friend's house. She was transported to a comfort station in Manchuria and became a comfort woman.

Childhood

I was born in spring 1924 in Taemyŏng ward, Taegu city. I have lived in Taegu all my life except for the years when I was a comfort woman. My parents came from the countryside not far from Taegu. We still have some relatives there, but I haven't visited them recently. When I was very young my father used to visit us now and again. When I was eight, he came home for good, but soon became very ill and died. My mother explained his absences from home by saying that he had taken part in the liberation struggle against the Japanese occupation in Shanghai and Manchuria.[1] When he became ill, she said he had come home to die. All I remember about him is that he was an educated man.

There were four of us children, with quite big age gaps between us. I had a brother nine years older than me, and when I was three my younger brother was born. I thought there were only three of us until my father died. Then I learned that I had a big sister who had already

1 A Korean government-in-exile was established in Shanghai during the Japanese occupation of Korea. At one point in the early 1920s, Syngman Rhee, later the leader of the Republic of Korea, was elected president. Communist and guerrilla groups also operated in the 1920s in the mountainous areas of what is now North Korea, and across the border in Manchuria and China. Kim Il Sung, later to become president of the Democratic People's Republic of Korea, appears to have been a minor guerrilla leader in the 1930s in one such group.

married and left home before I was born. My father gave my mother her address just before he died.

My mother scraped a living by sewing or working in the homes of others. Sometimes, her own family helped by giving us rice. I was said to be a bright child, and I could remember almost everything I saw, but we were too poor for me to be sent for a proper education. I learned by overhearing the lessons in the village boys' school, and I went to evening classes from time to time to learn Chinese characters, Korean and Japanese. I was very eager to study and can still vividly remember how much I wanted to attend school.

When I was about 13, a relative and his wife who were living in Japan – whether they were directly related to my mother or my father I still don't know for sure – came to the village for a visit. They asked my mother to let them take me to Japan, and in exchange for light house-work they promised to treat me like their own daughter, to send me to school and to find me a good husband. My mother, unhappy at having been unable to educate me, readily gave permission. I left home filled with the hope that I would soon be attending school. They lived in Fukuoka where they ran a second-hand shop and had many men working for them. As soon as we arrived, the wife chopped off my long hair and from then on made me wear a bob. She didn't offer any apologies or any sympathy for cutting my hair, and then started to order me to do the housework. There was no mention of sending me to school, and from then on I had to look after their children, do the washing up, clean the house and do the laundry every day. I must have stayed for about six months. I was angry about the way I was being treated and saved any money I was given for running errands for the second-hand dealers. At the same time I found out from the dealers how to return home. One day, I left without giving any notice. I returned home.

Back in Korea, I went to evening classes and continued learning to read and write. I worked in a factory managed by the Japanese that made slippers. The slippers were made of sedge for hospitals and were very strong. I commuted from home to Taegu and gave every penny of my wages straight to my mother. I felt proud whenever I handed over the money, but the work wasn't regular and I was often laid off and had to stay home. At such times I would go to a hill behind the village. There was a crematorium on the side where the keeper had a daughter, Haruko. She was two years younger than me and, since I often went there, we became good friends. Haruko and her parents were Koreans who had adopted Japanese names. It was her father's job to burn the dead. Just before he put a corpse into the fire, he would always have a ritual with food. I was often able to eat some of the food afterwards.

Food was scarce, but I was able to have enough to fill me whenever I visited Haruko.

In 1940, I was 16. One autumn evening, I left Haruko's, walking home when the sun had almost set and it was getting towards dusk. I had not gone far when a man in a Japanese military uniform, with a red band around his arm and a long sword at his side, approached me. He grabbed me by the arm and muttered something. As we were all afraid of the police in those days, I went with him. He dragged me along without meeting any resistance. He pulled me by the arm for a while and then made me walk before him. I think I was taken to a military police station where I was put with another girl. Without any food, we spent the night on a long bench, first sitting up and then sleeping, the two of us crouched one on each end.

The next morning, the same man took us to the train station where he handed us over to two other men, one a Japanese in civilian clothes and one a Korean. We got on board a train together. The train had a name: *Akachuki*. It kept going north for about two days. From what we overheard as people got on and off we guessed we were passing places such as Andong in Korea, Fengcheng in China, and so on. The men with us were replaced by a single man who spoke Chinese who stayed to the end of the journey. We had no idea who the men were. We wondered if they could be detectives, but there was no way of finding out. They gave us food now and again and one night asked if we fancied something special.

Manchuria

At dusk we got off at a place called Taoansheng in north-east China. The man with us escorted us to a military truck and left us. There were three men in uniform in the front of the truck, and we were bundled into the back. The truck travelled for a while, passing villages and fields, and stopped in front of a house separated and isolated from everywhere else. As we got down, lots of women came out to greet us. They were Koreans. There was a man and a woman who looked about 35 or 36, and we learned later that they were the proprietors. We had to call the man 'uncle' and the woman 'big sister'.

There seemed to be about 20 women, and although I wondered why there were so many in such a place, I quickly fell asleep from exhaustion. The next morning I asked what kind of place this was. Nobody replied. One woman asked if I had been paid to come and, when I replied I had not seen any money but had been captured and brought here, she looked very sad. I asked what was wrong and she told me this was a comfort station where the soldiers came. I asked what soldiers had to do with us. Exasperated, she said that this was a place where the soldiers came to sleep. I was still puzzled. I was naïve, and couldn't see why the soldiers' sleeping place should concern me in any way, nor why the women looked so anguished.

On the third day, the proprietor assigned us each to a room. Each had a mattress, a quilt and two pillows. From then on we had to serve soldiers. This was when I realized why the women had been so anguished. On the day I lost my virginity, everything seemed to black out before my eyes. I wept and wept. Taoansheng was said to be on the border with Russia, and it was extremely cold. The hats and clothes that people wore were all made of fur. My room was one of the many lined up in two rows, and in winter the walls were all covered with ice. There were narrow ditches at the base of each wall so that water from melted ice could flow to the outside.

There were many soldiers. I think we served 20 to 30 every day. It seemed to be the only comfort station in the neighbourhood, and the rank and file and commissioned officers came whenever they had spare time. High-ranking officers came at any time they wished to, but only officers could stay the night. They would sometimes give us money, which was sort of pocket-money. None of them beat us, and none were violent even when drunk. They used condoms, and none of the girls became pregnant while I was there. Not only had we to entertain them, but we also had to make garters for them.

We were to some degree free. The proprietor gave us Korean food prepared with the help of two Chinese cooks. We didn't have any fixed wages, but were given a small amount of money each month. When we received our monthly allowance, we would take a horse-drawn coach to the city and buy clothes and shoes or see films. No one watched over us, but we dared not run away because we simply didn't know where we were or where we could go.

I still remember Kim Kyehwa and Fumiko. There were some women who said they had been comfort women for five or ten years. I already had a Japanese name, Fumihara, but in the station I renamed myself Namiko after a famous actress, Takeoto Namiko. Thinking about her, I remember we used to sing many of the songs that were popular at the time. On the rare occasions when we had something to laugh about in our torturous life, and when we felt lonesome or miserable, we would sing in unison or hum together quietly.

By the time I had become somewhat used to my lot in life I got to know an officer in charge of the provision of military goods. I knew it would be impossible for me to leave the station and return home in a normal way. I thought that if I befriended someone with power among the soldiers I might be able to persuade them to send me home. So I flirted with this officer. I made him special garters and I put them on him. I bought him something special when we went shopping, I bought groceries and I cooked him fine meals in the kitchen. It was around September, and I had been stuck in the station for about a year. The officer asked me to set up home outside the station. Taking advantage of the opportunity this presented I wove a story: 'When I left home my mother was very ill, almost near death. Before I start to live with you, please let me go and see her. I will return as soon as possible and then, surely, I will live with you.' I pleaded with him and, after having made me promise that I would indeed come back, he got me a travel permit.

Home

When I left, I still had some of the money given to me by the soldiers. Before going to my home, I got off at Kŭmch'ŏn to find my eldest sister. Her address is still vivid in my memory: Naedong, Haam village, Sŏbuk district, Kŭmch'ŏn county, South Hamgyŏng province. Her husband's name was Kim Yŏngch'an. I bought a few presents near the railway station and took a taxi to their home.

I got out at Naedong, gave my brother-in-law's name to the villagers who were there and asked to be taken to my sister's home. One rushed off to the field where she was working, and soon she ran towards me, waving her hands wildly. She hugged me and began to cry. At first I hesitated, wondering whether she really was my sister, but I found myself hugging her and weeping anyway. Even though we had never seen each other, we were so glad at last to meet. I couldn't bring myself to tell her about my experiences in China, so I said I had come up from Taegu to see her. I enjoyed my time there. I still think blood ties are the only things you can rely on in life. But that was our first and last time together. I stayed with her for about ten days then returned to Taegu. In Taegu I began to do odd jobs.

I made a new friend in the neighbourhood. Early in July 1942, she asked me if I would like to come with her as she was going to begin working in a restaurant for good wages. Since I didn't think I had much of a future in Taegu, I decided to go along with her. She said she would meet me the following day. I left without telling my family and together we took a train to Pusan. All I wanted was to earn money and help my mother financially. At Pusan station, we were met by a man and a woman. Both were Korean. He was called Matsumoto and, as we found out later, he was to be our proprietor. The woman was actually a comfort woman. They took us to a guest-house. There were already about 15 or 16 women, and one of them was Kim Kyehwa, who had been with me in Manchuria. I was both glad and puzzled to see her. I asked what had happened. She said it was her fate and began to cry. We stayed the night. As we left the next day, I noticed the guest-house was called the Kabŭl Guest-house.

On 10 July 1942, 18 of us boarded a ship at Pusan port. It was part of a navy convoy and six or seven vessels sailed together. The ship we were on steamed at the tail. As I remember it, there seemed to be many women, perhaps 300 or 400, filling the ship. The 18 of us formed one group, and there were numerous similar groups. The ship kept sailing for about two months. Many women suffered from seasickness. I wasn't sick throughout the long journey, maybe because I was so determined to earn money, or perhaps I had very good health. I helped with the cooking for my group, I cleared away the mess they made if they threw up, and I looked after anyone who lost consciousness. When I saw women from other groups, I would ask if they knew where we were going, and everyone replied that we would be working in restaurants. No one seemed to know what our impending fates were to be. We passed Taiwan and Singapore and, after much sickness and trouble, we arrived at Rangoon.

Burma

As soon as we docked, the anchor was dropped. We were told that this was our destination and that we should disembark, keeping in our groups. As we walked off there were trucks lined up across the yard. We all stood in our groups, and the men who had led us so far stood separately. They seemed to be drawing lots. When this was over, the man in charge of us told us that it had been decided we would go to Mandalay.

After a little while, one of the trucks drove towards us from across the yard and as soon as we were all aboard it moved off. It dropped us in front of a two-storey building in Mandalay, again isolated from the residential area. The man told us to go upstairs. We climbed a wooden staircase and found ourselves in a large hall with rows of cubicles on either side. There were about twelve cubicles in total. The whole house was built from wood and looked a little run-down. We were to use the area upstairs. There was an office downstairs, where the proprietor lived. We went down to have meals that had been cooked by a Burmese woman.

The following day, about ten soldiers came with a truck-full of timber and began to work on the house. The first floor was renovated. There had originally been twelve small rooms, but as these would not be enough to accommodate all of us, they put up six more cubicles in the centre of the hall. The soldiers finished their work within a day and left. We were each given one cubicle. On the third day, soldiers rushed in, in large groups. I had been prepared to do any sort of hard work when I had left home, but had little thought I would have to repeat my previous life.

I was dismayed. Ours was the only comfort station in Mandalay. If my memory serves me right, the unit we were attached to was called the 8400th Divisional Headquarters in Burma.

Many, many soldiers came. There was a further unit called the Marusa, and the men from there also visited us now and again. One day, a soldier came into my room sobbing. Tears were streaming from his eyes. I asked him what was the matter, and he said that he was a Korean and had been drafted to the Marusa Unit. There were 50 men in the unit, 30 to 40 of whom were Korean. These Koreans brought tickets and condoms just like the Japanese. We started to serve soldiers from around 9.00 a.m., straight after breakfast. Sometimes the men would queue from early in the morning. The rank and file stopped coming at around 4.00 p.m., and then officers would come until 10.00 at night. After that, some officers stayed through the night.

The tickets were actually brown cards with different prices written on them, according to rank. Tickets for the rank and file cost 1.5 yen while non-commissioned officers paid 2 yen and officers 2.5 yen. Only officers could stay overnight, paying 3 or 4 yen for the privilege. All the tickets were handled by the proprietor. We had one big bathroom which we shared. As it was warm, a mattress and a blanket were enough. We wore Western clothes such as blouses and dresses, or Japanese baggy trousers. Our cook prepared meals with rice. Sometimes we had meat soup, but mostly our soup was made with wild vegetables collected on the hillsides. I continued to use my Japanese family name, Fumihara, but took Yosiko as my first name. I became close to Hondamineo, a man who managed provisions. From my experience in China I knew how useful it could be to befriend such a person, so I made an effort to get close.

I think we stayed about seven or eight months, but the Divisional Headquarters moved to Akyab (Sittwe) and we had to follow. To get there, we used a military truck, then boarded a ship called the *Taihatsu* to cross the dusty, brown sea. The coast was dotted with many islands. As we sailed we had to land on some of the islands to escape shells dropped by American planes. When we landed anywhere, the soldiers stationed there would surround us and welcome us. They would ask us to stay a little while and comfort them, and with permission from higher authorities we would stay one or two weeks. Whenever this happened we stayed right beside the unit, eating and sleeping with the soldiers. When bombing raids took place, we hid in the jungle with them.

At last we arrived at Akyab, where we were to stay about a year in a three-storey building. There were comfort women from Japan and China living there in other houses. We Koreans served low-ranking soldiers and non-commissioned officers while the Japanese served solely officers. Many of the Japanese women had been *geisha* back in Japan, and there was one who looked at least 30 years old. We knew nothing about the Chinese women. Our life was just the same as it had been in Mandalay, except we didn't serve officers anymore. We moved on to other places, but continued a similar lifestyle wherever we went. Not long after we had settled in Akyab, Hondamineo arrived. I was glad to see him. He stayed with the same unit, which meant that he was with us till the war ended.

Then we moved inland to Prome. First, we again boarded a ship at Akyab. We stayed in Prome for four or five months. There were only Korean women there, and our proprietor, who had been with us all the way since we left Korea, disappeared. We guessed that he had run away because the war was intensifying. From then on, the soldiers managed us directly. They cooked our meals and handled the tickets. We were next taken by truck to Rangoon. There, we were put up in a station called the Rangoon Kaikan, which was allocated to us directly by soldiers. It was managed by a Japanese man, and counting those who had been there before us there were about 30 women altogether. Life was a little easier with more women around, but the soldiers seemed more wild. I remember one drunk man who clung to me for more than an hour, hurting me terribly.

One day, a drunk soldier came in and tried to murder me with his sword. I attempted to calm him down, asking how he could do this when I was there to make him happy. He kept threatening me with his sword. So I attacked him, ready to die. He didn't expect this and dropped his sword. Without realizing what I was doing, I grabbed it and stabbed him in the chest. He was taken away, bleeding. I was arrested by the military police and stood trial before a military court. I was so frightened that I was unable to speak Japanese, although I was normally quite good at it. I explained the details of what had happened in Korean, constantly weeping. I was released after a week and started to entertain the soldiers once more. After this, I attempted to return home together with a new friend, Tsubamery, and Kim Kyehwa, my old friend from China. But I failed.

After three months in the Rangoon Kaikan, we were transferred by train to Thailand. We weren't required to serve men there but stayed for about eight weeks. It was temporary. From there we were moved to Ayutthaya on a military truck, where we were to look after wounded soldiers. At first we were trained for a few hours a day to take pulses, give injections, give ice-pack treatments and so on. We had been looking after the wounded for about four months when we heard that Korea had been liberated. We then stayed for a further three or four months, still looking after the wounded. During this time I was the leader of my group. We didn't have to work as comfort women anymore. We weren't paid, but we worked very hard looking after the casualties.

During those three years and four months, except for a year at Akyab, we lived for short periods in many places: Mandalay, Prome, Rangoon, somewhere in Thailand and the old Thai capital, Ayutthaya. Wherever we went we were taunted and despised for being comfort women and for being Korean. We had a weekly medical examination for venereal disease, and the soldiers used condoms. If any didn't want to use a sheath, I would kick them between their legs and demand that they put one on. If a soldier still refused, I would report him to the military police. Some women had babies. I know where some of them live now, but since I don't know why they have not registered themselves with the Korean Council I won't say anything more about them. I will restrain myself from encouraging them to register.

I recall a few incidents that happened in Akyab. Once, I felt life was so miserable that I got drunk and threw myself down from the second floor. I might have covered my head with my arm, for my left arm and shoulder were badly damaged in the fall. The soldiers rushed to me and pulled my left arm in an attempt to put it back into joint. This was so painful that I fainted. I had to have my arm in plaster and stayed in hospital for three months. On one occasion I was missing my family unbearably. I went to the unit headquarters and asked if I could write home since my mother had been very ill when I had left her. They allowed me to write a letter. After some time I received a telegram saying that my mother was indeed very ill and might die soon. This was followed by another telegram that curtly said my mother was dead. I went to an officer in the unit and asked if I could send some money home so that my family could arrange a proper funeral. I was allowed to send some. When we were staying in the temporary place in Thailand, I sent home more money. I still had quite a lot of money saved in my bank-book, but the book was lost somewhere in Burma. When I sent money home the officer recommended I send all that I had, but I wanted to keep some so that I could settle down when I returned to Korea.

Talking about money, I tried very hard to save. When we were in Akyab the officers would compliment me on my good Japanese and singing ability. When they had birthday parties or farewell parties, they would often send for me along with Japanese women. They thought Fumihara Yosiko, me, to be the best Korean. We would pour drinks, dance and sing. There were two or three parties a week, and I was called to every one. They gave me tips, and I saved every penny. I wasn't beautiful but it was said that I was cute. Some officers came to sleep with me on a regular basis. Whenever they were with me, I didn't have to serve the rank and file. I saved money given to me by the officers. I was often able to get free drinks or cigarettes, and I exchanged these for cash, saving everything in my account. I was really upset when I lost the deposit book issued by the Shimonoseki Post Office.

There is also one unforgettable event that happened on the way from Mandalay to Akyab. One of the women was infected with tuberculosis, and she couldn't move any further after we had reached a certain island. All the others left, but I stayed on to look after her. She died within ten days. The soldiers wouldn't come near the body, so I burnt it and scattered her ashes at sea. I saved a few ashes and ground them into powder so that I could later pass them to her family. But, since we were being moved so often, the bag holding her ashes was also lost.

Home Again

After Ayutthaya, we were taken by military truck to a refugee camp. Just before we left, Hondamineo asked me to go to Japan with him. But I just wanted to get home. The camp was crowded. It resembled a large school building, with a playground in the middle. We saw American jeeps arriving now and then. We lived together. After a while, we embarked on a ship bound for Korea. We landed in Inch'ŏn. We were kept busy on board, making flags to use when we arrived. But cholera broke out among the passengers, and the ship had to stay offshore of Inch'ŏn for two weeks. We had to have our whole bodies disinfected when we got off. We all had short hair and wore baggy trousers and *geta*. As we walked down the gangplank, waving the flags we had made, people on shore welcomed us with drums and gongs.[2] We could hear the anthem through a loudspeaker, '…May Korea be protected by Koreans for ever…'. We were moved to tears. Each of us received 1000 wŏn as we disembarked. I went home as soon as I landed, to find my mother was still alive. She said that she had sent the telegram thinking that I would rush home if I thought she was dead.

I had only been back a short while when my aunt by marriage – my uncle's wife – visited and said they couldn't allow someone like me to stay at home and disgrace the family. I was not treated as a human being by my relatives. I was sad and upset, but I quickly grew bold, telling them to mind their own business. I didn't pay much attention to what they thought of me. About a year later, my mother sent me off to train at a *kwŏnbŏn*, a school for entertainment girls, *kisaeng*, in Talsŏng. I was 22.

---

2 Korean percussion bands, known under the umbrella term *nongak*, were a feature of celebrations and festivals until recently.

I learned to be a *kisaeng* over three years, and I paid for my training by working part-time.

After I had finished the course I married a Mr Kim who ran a business in Taegu. He was six years older than me, and his first wife had died. He had a daughter who was already married and two other children, another daughter and a son, still living with him. I lived with them for about six years. But then his business collapsed and he took his own life without having provided for the family. So, I went back to work as a *kisaeng* to support his children and my mother. I must have been 32 by then. In the *kisaeng* house, I met another man. He was running a confectionery factory. He said he was the same age as me, but later I found out that he was three years younger and already married, with a daughter and four sons. He was caring and understanding, and never interfered with what I did. By setting up house with him, I was able to support my mother and the two children of my late husband until they became independent. I also continued to carry out the ancestral worship rituals for my deceased in-laws. When I passed 40, I brought home one of the sons of my companion, and he still behaves as if he is my own son.

There is no single healthy part in my body. I hurt everywhere. There was a time when I suffered severe insomnia. But since I have now poured out my life story to you I feel much more easy. I will be able to sleep and eat much better. Until last year, when I was first encouraged by a friend from my days at the school for entertainment girls to register with the Council, I kept my life in China to myself. I was so ashamed of what had happened that I did not want to let other people know anything about it. So I told people what had happened sparingly. Now that everyone knows the story, however, I feel I have nothing to fear. So, now I have told you everything about myself, I can rest easily.

CHAPTER 13

It Makes Me Sad That I Can't Have Children

Yi Sunok

Yi Sunok was born in 1921 in Yŏngdŏk, North Kyŏngsang province. A relative in the village had been actively involved in the independence movement against the Japanese occupation and, because of him, police surveillance was tight. When she was 17, she heard a rumour that the Japanese government was recruiting girls, and registered herself on paper though not in reality as married. It was difficult for a young girl to pretend to be a newly-wed. So, intending to earn some money, she left home with a man who had promised her work in a Japanese factory. She was taken to a comfort station in Guangdong, China.

Branded and Deceived

I was born in 1921 in Yŏngdŏk, North Kyŏngsang province, the first of four children. I had two sisters and a brother. My father was a farmer who sometimes worked in the gold mines near Kyŏngju and Yŏngch'ŏn. Because I was the first child and was in poor health, my parents took special care of me. They wanted to bring me up gently and then find me a good husband. I didn't help with the farm but helped mother around the house. When I was 15 or 16, I went to evening classes in a thatched house used as the village hall to learn to read and write Korean. The teacher was a young Christian.

About that time, a distant relation lived with his family just behind our house. He had been in prison for taking part in the independence movement against the Japanese occupation while he had been studying in Japan. He and his family had lived in Kyŏngju before moving to Yŏngdŏk. My father treated him well, saying he was intelligent and had great knowledge. The authorities, though, kept a tight watch on us, on the grounds that he was a member of our lineage. If the police visited his house, they would also come to ours and search it. Sometimes my father was taken to the police station for questioning.

When I was about 17, we had to practise drills. These were led by the Korean village head. He frequently made us sing Japanese songs. An alarming rumour was floating around that the authorities were offering Korean girls to their government back in Japan. My father was afraid that I might be taken away, and discussed tactics with my uncle. They decided to register a marriage, in name only, not in actuality, between me and a Mr Pak from Ch'ŏngha district. It was October 1937. My uncle said he had met Pak in Japan while he had been a student and that he had helped run errands for the independence movement. Pak was much older than me and already had a wife and a son, but he had divorced because he had a personality clash with his wife. I never lived with Pak, and I had never even seen his face at this time. It was agreed that when I really married, my registration with Pak would immediately be cancelled. After filling in the documents to register the marriage I went around like a newly-wed, putting up my hair and wearing a scarf. We told our neighbours to say that I had been married off if they were asked about me.

After a short while, my uncle suddenly died. Ever since then we have had no way of finding out what happened to Pak. We moved to Yasa ward in Yŏngch'ŏn, where a married aunt was living. Now there were seven in the family: me, my grandmother, my parents, two sisters and my brother. Another boy had been born just after me, but he died soon after birth.

In Yŏngch'ŏn we lived in the annexe of a big house where some acquaintances of my aunt, the Moritas, lived. They were an elderly Japanese couple who said they had lost their son in the war. Although they were heavy drinkers, they had kind hearts. They spoke good Korean, maybe because they had lived in our country for such a long time. I washed clothes and carried water for this old couple, and they were kind to us. I asked Mrs Morita about Japan. She told me that there were many factories there where girls could earn lots of money by working. She said that everyone worked and earned money, and that no girls of my age were jobless. I had been finding it hard to act as if I was married, with my hair up even though I was still a virgin. I also found it difficult to live in a strange area which was not my home town. So I told the Moritas that I wanted to go to Japan to earn a living. They said my father would be displeased and advised me not to talk about such things.

We kept discussing it until one day a man, a Mr Oh, aged about forty, visited Mr Morita. I was there, listening to them talking about different topics while they drank in the hall. Oh said he had come to recruit girls to work in a factory. Knowing what I wanted, Mr Morita asked Oh if he knew of a good place for me. Oh replied that there was a silk factory which needed many girls, since they had recently opened a new building, and that any young girl could get a job there. He added that the factory would pay travel expenses and that many girls would be going. He also said I could leave at any time if I didn't like the work there. Oh came and asked me if I wanted to go, and I answered that I would like to, given such good terms. My parents were against the idea, but I persuaded them on the grounds that I found it very difficult to act as if married, with my hair up and covered with a scarf, besides which we were very poor. In this way, I left home with Oh. I was wearing blue summer clothes, and it was the season for cucumbers. It must have been early summer 1938.

I got on a train at Yŏngch'ŏn with Oh, and we travelled to Taegu. There, we were joined by Yoshiko from Taegu, Itsimaru from Kyŏngju, Sadako and Masako. These were the names given to the girls later at the comfort station. I was to be called Takiko. Yoshiko was from a *kwŏnbŏn*, a training school for entertainment girls, *kisaeng*, in Taegu. She said she had come along because her foster mother had told her to volunteer for work in a Japanese factory. We had our hair cut at a hairdressers then boarded another train. Oh put us in a cargo carriage, and took himself off to a passenger carriage. We must have been early for the appointed date, for we got off at P'yŏngyang and stayed about a week in a house reached after a long walk from the station. At night, Oh went out to attend to his affairs, and we took baths or washed our clothes. A woman in her fifties cooked for us, making side dishes of fried potatoes and cucumber salad. We slept together in a large room. Namiko, Mitsuko, Yuriko and Eiko from Chŏlla province joined us there.

After a week, we boarded another train at the station. There were many Chinese on it. We got off somewhere, and stayed for a while. A Korean cooked for us there, but the pickled cabbage, *kimch'i*, was terrible. Then we took a khaki-coloured truck covered with canvas. The driver was Japanese and wore a military uniform. Oh sat beside him while we crouched in the back. The vehicle stopped after a short ride. We had heard that Japan was a clean country and we thought it strange, for this place was filthy. Only then did we find out that we had come to Guangdong, in China, not to Japan. From then on, our wretched lives began.

Beaten

When we got off the truck it was cold and there was a biting wind. We were standing in front of a two-storey red brick building. From the outside, the entrance door was very high and big, but inside we found an empty house with no people and no furniture. There were many rooms, each the same size, divided by partitions into cubicles. There was a wooden fence along the little track in front of the house, and a military unit could be seen directly beyond it. There were hardly any Chinese around. We could see no Japanese women, just Japanese soldiers. Once we had all entered, Oh talked to the soldiers then disappeared. The house was cleaned with disinfectant. A woman in her fifties from Chŏlla province came to us. She was obese and had lived in Japan for many years. She always cautioned us to keep ourselves clean. We were to call her *Obasang*, grandmother. She told us not to wait for Oh.

On the day we arrived we were sent to rest in the rooms. The following day, *Obasang* told us to have a bath. The same day, high-ranking soldiers came and stayed the night. I hated what they forced me to go through. It was the first time in my life that I had sex, and I wept a lot. The soldier whom I served first was about 30 years old. He came again after that, once in a while, and was always kind to me, telling me to look after myself, and not to forget to use condoms. He even gave me a ring, which I wore during my time as a comfort woman but which, when I was returning home, I threw into the sea thinking it useless. High-ranking officers hardly ever came; our soldiers were mostly low-grade privates. About 25 came each day, and many more from 9.00 in the morning onwards on Saturdays and Sundays. We waited in the ground floor hall. When soldiers came in, they would choose a girl and go into her cubicle.

We had a box in which to store belongings, and a small cement space for our shoes. My room was on the first floor, and it was about one *p'yŏng*, 3.2 square metres in size. It had straw mats on the wooden floor, laid so badly that the floor creaked whenever I stepped on it. We spread mats and blankets out. We were given four blankets each, two to lie on and two to cover ourselves with. On the door was my name and photograph. Cotton curtains hung at the door which were let down when soldiers came. We were not paid, but soldiers gave us pocket-money once in a while. I owed nobody anything, but those who drank became indebted to *Obasang*. The military police often looked around the comfort station and talked with her. She kept a sword and pistol in her room, and later she would sometimes wear a military cap. If the women didn't listen to her commands, she beat them severely. I was beaten on my abdomen and bottom. If the bedding was dirty or if I refused to serve men, *Obasang* threw my stuff outside.

Among the soldiers, some carried a flask of alcohol at their side. They would get drunk and become violent. Not long after I arrived I was stabbed on the thigh by one. This happened after I tried to refuse him when he went for me several times. I screamed when I was stabbed and the other women and soldiers in the station rushed to my room in surprise. I had to continue to serve the soldiers, even while I was receiving treatment from the military hospital. When this wound had nearly healed, another soldier pushed me backwards for not welcoming him. My hip was hurt, and my thigh began to swell because of the impact. It became so swollen and painful that I had to have an operation. I stayed in hospital for about a week, but was then discharged to rest at the comfort station because of a shortage of beds. The hospital was very small. It only had two military surgeons and three or four beds. After my discharge, I went back to the hospital by rickshaw for treatment. For some time there was a notice on my door that said I could not serve men. While in bed, because I was not serving men, I was given no warm rice, only cold rice with pickled radish.

We took our meals together downstairs. There were long wooden tables and benches in the dining room. Rice and pickled radish were the usual fare. When we served more men than usual, *Obasang* would treat us with a small portion of pork boiled in soy sauce given by the unit. There was no heating at all. When it was very cold, we could have hot water tins, but only those who had been obedient to *Obasang* and had served many soldiers were allowed them. The slightly larger rooms were divided into two by a curtain down the middle. There were about 20 Korean girls in the house, and Chinese women did the cleaning, cooking, washing up, nursing and laundry. We wore yellow underwear and navy long-sleeved dresses. These were issued to us. We also got baggy navy trousers. Later, we were given kimonos and *haoris*. We hung the clothes on the walls. Our hair was always bobbed, and *Obasang* cut it. We went weekly to the military hospital to have check-ups for venereal infection. *Obasang* delivered a box of condoms and cotton wool for sanitary purposes to each of us in the morning. Even during menstruation we had to wash ourselves with an antiseptic solution, insert cotton wool and continue to serve men.

After three years we went to Singapore with our proprietor. We weren't given any notice. Suddenly, one night, *Obasang* distributed cotton sacks and told us to pack our things. Some girls remained, but some volunteered in the hope of seeing Singapore. We heard new girls would be sent to replace us. I kept quiet, saying nothing, but the proprietor told me to go. The soldiers also seemed to be moving on, and we actually went with them. We took a truck, a military train, then a ship. In the truck, there were two soldiers. It was covered, so we could not look out. We were transferred to the big ship by a small boat. There were three or four ships, and all held women in a similar predicament to us. As the ships began to sail in convoy, we waved our handkerchiefs to the girls in the other vessels. We wept, wondering how we would live so far away. We understood that one ship was going to an unknown island and the others to different places. In the main, Japanese soldiers occupied our ship, and Chinese men carried their luggage. We weren't allowed to leave our cabins, and we only managed to look at the sea through a small porthole. We ate in a small dining room and were given cooked rice, pickled apricots and pickled radish. When we were eating, no one else was allowed in the room. The cabin floors were covered with soft *tatami* mats, and the nights weren't cold. I don't remember how long we sailed for. When we disembarked, we used small boats again.

In contrast to the comfort station in China, which had been secluded and had hardly any trucks passing nearby, Singapore was a city hectic with the buzz of heavy traffic. The comfort station was a single-storey long wooden building surrounded by a wooden fence. It seemed to have been purpose-built. Another comfort station could be seen beyond the fence, but I never visited it. Our station had about 30 cubicles. There was an electric fan in the ceiling above every two cubicles. All the women were Korean, and our *Obasang* again managed the place. There was a pregnant woman amongst us, and a girl from Chŏlla province gave birth to a daughter. There was one who had come along believing she was going to an island, and another who had previously worked on another island. We could overhear *Obasang* and the proprietors talking between themselves as they went in and out of the house. They would say 'These girls are obedient', 'girls in such and such a place wouldn't listen to us', and 'it is easy to work the girls from Kyŏngsang provinces'. If a woman drank, *Obasang* reported her to the soldiers, and a soldier would come and give her a mighty beating.

We got up in the morning, cleaned our rooms, washed and had breakfast. Then the soldiers began to come. There were chairs lined up outside the building where we sat, waiting. The soldiers chose whoever they liked and went to the cubicles. There were more women than there had been in China, so we each needed to serve fewer men. We sometimes tried to be clever and serve even fewer. The soldiers would drop into *Obasang*'s room before they came into a girl's cubicle. I don't know if they paid her any money. I don't remember being paid except for occasional pocket-money. Although I had left home specifically to earn money, I had never thought I would end up in this kind of place. In the evenings, high-ranking officers came to stay the night, leaving at dawn. If they came to have a drink, they were given a nice big room. Among the soldiers, there were some who taught us to read *hiragana* and *katakana*, the Japanese writing systems.

It was very hot in Singapore, and there was a downpour every day. Outside the back door of our station, there was a place where we could take baths, and we threw cold water over ourselves once a day because of the heat. Amongst the shower cubicles, one was curtained so that we could wash our genitals. We were given condoms in boxes, as we had been in China, and we had check-ups once a week for venereal disease. Often, *Obasang* did the check-ups herself at the station, but sometimes a soldier came to give us injections in her room. If we became seriously ill, we would be taken to the military hospital for treatment. Our meals consisted of cooked rice and pickled radish. All the time I was a comfort woman, I never ate anything spicy, so I still cannot take hot food. There were many fruit trees and gum trees around the comfort station, and we ate a lot of red fruit which looked like plums, and something similar to pumpkin.

Japan and Home

Fujiwara, actually a Korean from Kwangju in Chŏlla province, was one of my regulars. He was a carpenter and a civilian employee working in Singapore. I earnestly appealed to him, saying I wanted to go home, even if I died in the process. He agreed to help. Some women had already left the station to return, but it was said that ships bound for Korea were often bombed so many died on their way. Even so, I desperately wanted to go home. After a while, he asked me and some of the girls to meet a high-ranking soldier. He seemed to know senior officers quite well, I suppose because of his carpentry work. Six of us slipped quietly out of the comfort station, asking the others to tell *Obasang* we had gone for a walk into the gum tree forest if she came to look for us.

We reached the barracks, and Fujiwara said something to the guard. We were allowed in. We entered and met the officer. He asked us how long we had been there, and we told him six years. We said we wanted to go home to Korea. He told us that a hospital ship was short of nurses and asked if we would look after patients on our way, and enquired whether we would be any good at it. We replied in the affirmative. He told us that it was a Red Cross ship and would leave for Japan in a fortnight, and that we should board it. In this way, the six of us were able to leave Singapore. It was winter 1944. An army official came to the comfort station and told *Obasang* to let us go. She didn't like it, and muttered and moaned. But new Korean women arrived to replace us before we left.

Among my regulars, there had been a Japanese soldier called Haname. He proposed to me before I left Singapore, but I turned him down because I wanted to get back to Korea. One day, he said he would buy me whatever I most wanted and took me by car into the city. I chose a handbag. On the day we were to depart, Haname bade me farewell. He gave me an armful of bananas, but what with seasickness and having to look after patients, I wasn't able to eat them.

I still remember Sadako, Itsimaru, Masako and Fujiko, four of those who left with me. Yosiko, Midori and Eiko had already left, but I had been told that they died in air-raids while at sea. On board the hospital ship, the patients slept on the main deck and the nurses on the lower deck. There were only a few qualified nurses, and numbers were made up with the many helpers like ourselves. The patients smelt and suffered from many different types of wound. Some had lost eyes, some arms, some legs and some their hips. Some grasped photographs of their families in their hands, saying they would remain with them until they died. Our job was to look after these patients. We took a bowl of rice gruel and one pickled apricot to each, and we spoon-fed those who could not eat because their lips had been damaged. For the first few days, I couldn't eat properly because of the strong smell of the patients and their dreadful wounds. The air on the ship was very bad, so the nursing staff were allowed up on deck to get fresh air. I noticed many Red Cross flags, but American planes still flew near our ship, and some torpedoes menacingly approached us. On some days, the air-raid sirens went off several times in an evening. We put on baggy trousers and red socks and held a float in our hands. There were many small boats tied around the ship, and we were told to lower them and jump in if the bombing got too serious.

We arrived at Ōshima, Japan, after 20 days. As soon as we came ashore in a small bay, we had to rush into a shelter because of enemy bombing. The shelter was packed. When the air-raid siren stopped, we told the people who we had joined that we had been looking after patients on a hospital ship and asked where we could spend the night. They led us to the town guest-house. I remember an earthquake that occurred while we were sleeping on the first floor. We thought it was another air raid, but the proprietor came up to tell us what was happening. The next day, we asked how to get to Korea. We were told that Shimonoseki was not far and that from there we could take a ship to Pusan. We were told where to board a train. We had received certificates with the seal of the high-ranking officer when we left Singapore, so were able to travel free if we showed them. In this way, we got back to Kyŏngju. From there I went to Talsan district in Yŏngdŏk county, where my parents were living. I couldn't tell them that I had been a comfort woman.

About six months after my return, Korea was liberated. I worked in a restaurant in P'ohang run by a childhood friend. But the venture was unsuccessful, so I worked with my friend in the canteens of various banks for about six years. We rented a room together. During those years, Sadako and Masako often visited me, but then Masako died following an operation. She had been one year older than myself, and had she still lived, she would have registered at the Korean Council with me. Some of those who were comfort women with me still live in Kyŏngju, but it seems they have not registered. I don't know where Sadako is now, nor how she makes a living.

After leaving the canteens, I sold fabrics back in P'ohang. I carried them on my head to market. Then I decided to return home to live with my mother, who was by then farming. I reported a divorce from Mr Pak in 1960, thereby putting my registration documents in order. When I was 42, through a matchmaker, I became the second wife of an elderly man who already had three sons and two daughters. But I didn't move in with him, and for the next 15 years I stayed with my mother in a village where my sister also lived. I kept a small general store. After my mother died, only then, I moved into my husband's home. But we don't get on well together, so I live mostly at my brother's house.

My brother and sisters encouraged me to register as a former comfort woman, but I felt so ashamed. In this society, people still talk behind our backs. I would feel humiliated, even if I was to receive compensation. But then, I would feel mistreated if I didn't get any compensation. Whenever I think of those years, my heart pounds and my whole body is racked with pain. I live now only with the help of my brother and sisters. My wish is to live the rest of my life on my own in comfort. My greatest regret is that I was not able to have children. This was the result of my life as a comfort woman.

CHAPTER 14

I Came Home, But Lost My Family

Yi Sangok

Yi Sangok was born in 1922 in Talsŏng, North Kyŏngsang province. Her family was comfortably off, but she had to leave school because her elder brother strongly objected to her studying. She was so determined to continue with her education that she left her parents' home and secretly went to live with an aunt in Seoul. She attended school there for four years then, vexed by her aunt, joined what we today might call an escort agency. She left with other women who had been told they would be going to Japanese factories to earn money, but she was taken to the Palau islands, where she became a comfort woman.

I was born in 1922 in Choya village, Talsŏng district, Talsŏng county, North Kyŏngsang province, the first daughter in a family which eventually numbered two sons and three daughters. I was registered under the name of Sangok, but was called Ŭmjŏn at home because I was so quiet and gentle. I was born in the Year of the Dog, and my grandfather used to say that I was an ill-fated child who would have to be a second wife.[1] We were quite well off, since my father was the mayor of the town, and we had servants to work our farm. We even employed a wet-nurse for my brothers and sisters.

Before I went to school, I had attended evening classes, but had stopped going after I became frightened of being attacked by wild animals late at night. I started school when I was nine, and was soon able to read first-grade books. But my brother, who was three years older, stopped me going, saying it was useless to educate a girl. He burnt all my books on the kitchen fire, saying that educated girls ended up leading loose lives. I insisted on going. He took me to the old Confucian

---

1 Yi's grandfather was presumably referring to the almanac and his comment reflects the time of Yi's birth. The calendar is divided into sets of ten heavenly characters and twelve earthly zodiacal animals, which occur in juxtaposition to give a recurring 60-year cycle. The Year of the Dog marks one of the zodiacal animals.

academy,² as he could not beat me in front of our grandfather in the house, and threatened to kill me with a sickle. How I envied the tall girl next door who freely went to school! Since I wasn't able to attend school, I left home without even letting my mother know, in late spring the same year. I decided to go to my aunt in Seoul. I left home and boarded a train. A child, without any money, I was able to travel free. I got off at Seoul station, took a tram south to Ipchŏngjŏng and walked to my aunt's. Her house was in that district.

My aunt was a widow, and though she sold dress fabrics, her living conditions weren't that good. She kept on telling me to return home, and she made me work for my keep. My cousins were older than me, but they took my side, asking if she intended to give me work instead of sending me to school. They pointed out that I had come to Seoul to get an education. So the following year, at the age of ten, I was able to start school again. I cannot remember the name of the place. My aunt paid. I had to continue to clean the house and to sew when I came home, which didn't leave me much time to study. The school was far away, and I had to have an early breakfast and leave. There were some Japanese children at the school, and I still remember my teacher stroking my long hair, and saying I had a good brain. There weren't many girls, but there were lots of boys. Sometimes, on my way home, I used to stop to play jackstones or skipping with other children, arriving home at about supper time. But when I did that I was scolded by my aunt for being late.

I shared a room with my female cousins. One had finished school and was working. I didn't have any pocket-money, and once I bought 5 chŏn worth of sweets with the money my aunt had given me to buy her cigarettes. She didn't scold me, but gave me more money to buy the cigarettes. Since I had begun to live with her, every time she went to Talsŏng to visit my family, my brother made a fuss about me. He would bother her and ask why she had sent me to school. I understand he even stopped my parents coming to get me, saying they shouldn't regard me as their child. To him, I wasn't a dutiful daughter. I didn't write home. I found schoolwork interesting; I read all the textbooks as well as everything else I could lay my hands on.

My aunt paid my school fees up to the fourth grade. Then she told me to return home since she was no longer able to meet the expense. Even before then she had told me many times to finish school. I had cried and said I didn't want to go back to Talsŏng because my family wouldn't

---

2 Confucian academies provided the mainstay of traditional local education until the late nineteenth century, when they were closed by a decree issued by the Prince Regent, the *Taewŏn'gun*.

allow me to attend a school and, unable to change my mind, she had let me stay on. I so wanted to continue, and knew well that my brother wouldn't let me if I went home. I managed to go to school for only four years, even though it was a six-year course.

My aunt bothered me so much that I finally left her. I was 14. I was afraid to go home in case my brother beat me to death. I wandered about until I came to a house where I could hear people talking and singing. The gate was wide open and there was a signboard with the name of an agency, and the name of the owner, Kim Munshik. It was at 123 Ipchŏngjŏng, Seoul. It wasn't far from my aunt's home. I didn't know what the name meant but, hearing the singing, I went through the gate wondering if I could learn to sing. I knew no fear. When I went in, I found women in the hall playing drums and men listening to them. Later, I noticed that the agency called girls and told them to sing: those who sang well were sent away on rickshaws. It was what we today might call an escort agency.

As I entered, a woman asked me where I had come from. I lied a little, saying that my home was in Talsŏng, but that I had been staying with an aunt in Seoul. I said I had done something wrong, and been thrown out. She asked if I would like to stay in her house, and I said that I would. She said she would have to foster me. So I stayed for about a year, cooking and doing the laundry. In return, she fed and clothed me and once in a while gave me 10 or 20 chŏn for pocket-money. I undid the stitches from a corner of my dress and kept the money hidden there. She was the manager, Kim Munshik. She was over 40 and had very little hair, just like a man. While I stayed there I listened to the girls singing and playing the drums and learnt to hum many songs.

After one particular day, girls began constantly to be brought to the house. Every day, one or two came, some of whom had clearly been sold by their fathers. It was said that an elderly Korean man working for Kim and a Japanese civilian employee were travelling the country recruiting girls. The Japanese man wore a brownish khaki uniform with red and green lapels, and a badge depicting something like red seagulls.

I asked the girls where they were going, and they replied that they were on their way to Japanese factories with the Japanese man. I asked if I could go with them, and was told that I could. So I talked with the Japanese man. He said he was glad, and wrote my name on a list. I told Kim Munshik and she said it was fine by her if it was what I wanted. I didn't contact either my parents or my aunt. When there were ten girls including me, we set off with the Japanese man. The girls had come from various districts in North and South Kyŏngsang and Chŏlla provinces. They were 16, 17 and 18 years old, while I was 15 and the youngest. I think it was spring 1936. I wore a lined blouse and a dark skirt. We travelled by train from Seoul to Pusan. We boarded a ferry at once and crossed to Shimonoseki. There, we had our long hair bobbed, after our keepers told us that we would be recognized as Koreans if we had long hair. In the guest-house, whenever the other girls felt hungry, I went out to buy biscuits or eggs since I already spoke some Japanese.

We stayed about a week, and then were told to board a ship once more. We asked where we were going since we were already in Japan. There was no reply. Anyway, it was a very big vessel with a café and bathhouse on board. The ten of us were the only women. Many of my colleagues suffered from seasickness, but after eating the pickled apricots and soya bean soup I brought them they seemed to stop suffering. I don't remember how long we sailed for, but one day as I stood on deck looking at the waves I sang some of the songs I had learnt at the agency. Tears streamed down my face before I realized what was happening. The sailors said that we were going to a place where black people lived naked, except for a few leaves, and that we would all die there. We asked what we would do, and they told us we would work in a factory making pot cleaners, *tawasi*.

As our ship passed by islands, the sailors pointed out Saipan and Yap, then the Palau islands where they said we would disembark. We reached Palau, but the ship wasn't able to get close since there was no proper pier. The ship sounded its horn and a negro came to the ship on a raft. He had no clothes except for a piece of red cloth which roughly covered his private parts. A ladder was let down from the ship and, just as we were about to climb down, the sailors called out jokingly to be careful since the natives used to eat people. We were scared and refused to leave the ship, but they made us hurry down. The raft was very small, just big enough for two people, and it had to make many journeys between ship and shore.

As we landed we noted that the island was undeveloped. It retained its natural innocence. People didn't wear clothes, and women were only covered up to their waists with palm leaves. We walked to a single-storey house built of wooden boards in a long L-shape. It had a big yard with a flower-bed in one corner. The proprietor was a Korean man. He lived with his wife. He was called Hayashi, though we never knew his first name. He was illiterate, but his fat wife spoke good Japanese. He asked us where we had come from and whether our parents knew of our whereabouts. We were hungry and crying by now and didn't have the wits to answer him. The proprietor paid some money to the man who had brought us this far. According to the amount of money paid, the terms of our service were apparently decided: 18 months, two years, three years.

My term was 18 months. I wasn't given any money.

At first we ate a lot of papayas, pineapples and bananas. After about a week, rice arrived, and then we could eat cooked rice and soya bean soup. There was a Korean women in her thirties who cooked for us. She was a relative of the proprietor. To start with we didn't serve soldiers but spent our time talking to each other. When it rained, we collected the rainwater to drink and to wash our clothes in. The weather was like that in May in Korea, and it was cool whenever it rained.

There was a signboard with Chinese script on it but, preoccupied with weeping, I didn't pay much attention to it. A sliding door led into the hall, and the proprietor's room was adjacent to this. Then there was a kitchen and office. Next, there were many small rooms facing each other. When it rained, the water flowed down through the rafters into an underground tank. This water was sterilized for drinking, and was connected to the bathroom through pipes for washing. In front of the proprietor's room was a small tank for their own use. The proprietor said he could only start business when he obtained a licence. This happened about a fortnight later. We didn't know what the business was.

One evening, he asked us to sit in the hall. A little later, soldiers came in carrying their shoes in one hand, and each chose a girl he fancied, walking into her room. It was terrifying to serve a soldier for the first time. I screamed and resisted. He hit me for crying. The soldiers began to come at 3.00 or 4.00 in the afternoon. The proprietor introduced slightly older and more mature girls to the high-ranking officers, but he always introduced ignorant rank-and-file soldiers to me, the youngest. They hit me heartlessly, saying I didn't obey them. Sometimes, if a soldier chose one of the girls and left his shoes in the hall, that girl would take his shoes in her hands and follow him to her room. I served two or three soldiers at the most each day. After only two I was exhausted and had to stay in bed. While sitting in the hall with the others, when the proprietor asked me to take a man in with me, I shook all over and wept. Then he would ask one of the others to serve the soldier. The others had to serve about 20 men. Some of the soldiers had white uniforms and some wore khaki. We didn't see any Korean soldiers. We didn't know where the army unit was, but we heard it was by the sea.

Each soldier was usually allowed an hour. There were some who would remain undressed after intercourse than start all over. I refused men who tried to have sex several times. I wouldn't meet their demands. I screamed and shouted. They would beat me or stab me with a knife. I was struck so many times in those years that I still cannot hear well in my right ear and my body is covered with scars. If I tried to run away, they subjected me to all kinds of abuse, like tying a rope around my neck and dragging me around. The soldiers didn't care whether we were having our periods or not. If I told the proprietor that I wouldn't be able to work because it was the time of my period, he would scold me severely. I didn't have regular menstruation and no one was kind to me. I was cold and resisted them. And they hit me.

The proprietor gave Japanese names to all the girls: mine was Nobuko. I didn't call the others by their names much, so I don't remember them. I remember only one, Hanako, who was from Chŏlla province. She was very pretty and, accordingly, much harassed by the soldiers. The soldiers sometimes paid their money at the office, or they would pay the girls in their rooms. The girls then passed payment to the proprietor. The fee was usually 1 yen, but 3 yen for those who stayed overnight. The currency was Japanese. We each had a room with a small wardrobe and bedding, the cost of which we were told was to be deducted from our income later on. The rooms had *tatami* and were about two *p'yŏng* (one *p'yŏng* is 3.2 square metres) large. My monthly income was said to be 30 yen. But the proprietor provided me with things like clothes, cosmetics and a mirror, and deducted the cost of these from my promised wages. So I never had any money in my hands. He said that we had to keep clean and have nice clothes in which to serve our clients, so he gave us Korean dresses, Japanese kimonos and Western dresses. He also offered us expensive food, but always deducted the expense from our wages.

We even had Korean pickled cabbage, *kimch'i*, with our three meals a day. But we weren't given enough, so we went hungry. We ate pineapples from the trees. The door of the house was always guarded, but some of the more clever girls would bribe the guards with money and go out shopping.

We went to hospital once a week for check-ups. It was a military hospital with one Japanese surgeon and two Japanese nurses. We were examined for syphilis, and the girls who served many soldiers were often contaminated. This was because some soldiers used condoms and some didn't. Anyone found with the disease was hospitalized for treatment. I was never infected. I always washed myself in the bathroom immediately after I had served a soldier. I found the whole sexual act filthy. There were some soldiers who stole my things while I was in the bathroom. Then the proprietor bought what was missing again and told me to take the things to my room. I turned him down and said 'I don't want to buy them. They will only be stolen by the soldiers again. It's like making soup and giving it to dogs.' The proprietor insisted that I should take them and beat me, saying that all the other girls bought them. He asked why I was so persistent. If anyone became ill and was hospitalized, the proprietor would make much fuss. He harassed them, asking how they would pay their debts if they stayed in hospital for two or three months. If we didn't pay him back, our terms would be extended.

The Korean proprietor and his wife handed the comfort station to a Japanese couple after a few months. The new couple were in their forties or fifties. With the change came a new cook and a new manager. But we were treated the same way under the new management. At first there had been just ten of us, but more girls arrived later. Among the new arrivals were some entertainment girls, *kisaeng*, one of whom had been well known in P'yŏngyang. She was older than the rest of us and attracted many men. After her arrival, many men wearing Japanese costume visited. They called for the *kisaeng* and made them sing. Among the men were some who could speak Korean. Some of the *kisaeng* danced well and some could play the zither, *kayagŭm*.[3] One sang popular folk-songs from the Korean south-west well. Even they had to serve the men.

Many people died because of the war, but no girls committed suicide.

I started to menstruate properly when I was 21. One morning, I woke to find blood on my bed, and I thought I was going to bleed to death without even being ill. A girl in the next room came in, and I told her about the blood. She asked how I could be so stupid, rushed out, ordered gauze on the telephone and showed me how to cut and use it. In Palau, just before the Pacific war broke out, I once danced *Arirang* on a stage. I had learnt it from the Japanese soldiers. They would often sing *Arirang*. *Arirang* was a folk-song which became famous as a patriotic song in the 1920s. Sometimes all of us girls, by now 40 or 50, would be drilled, wearing khaki army uniforms and caps, by a Japanese soldier. Even small faults, such as putting on the caps askew or doing up the buttons in the wrong manner, were pointed out. Standing under the sun with an empty stomach I fainted several times. Because of this I was beaten.

When there were no clients, a man in the office gathered us together and taught us to read and write Japanese. I already knew some Japanese, and when I answered him in the language, he told me to go away while he concentrated on the other girls. Not long after we had arrived, Korean pioneers began to move in. They farmed the land, made roads and built houses, developing the island in many ways. Once I went out and saw Korean people working in the fields. The emigrants from Chŏlla province were the largest group. They would visit us, hearing that there were Korean women in the brothel. The proprietor asked us to serve them, but I refused.

3 The *kayagŭm* is a 12-string long zither based on the Chinese *zheng* and similar to the Japanese *kōtō*. For over 100 years it has been common for entertainment girls to sing while accompanying themselves on the *kayagŭm*.

Once, a violent common soldier stabbed me in the chest, arms and feet, and I had to be hospitalized. I still have the scars. There was only one hospital, and it was smaller than the house where we lived. In hospital I cried, calling for my mother, and the Japanese military surgeon asked me where she was. I replied that she was in Korea. Because I was able to speak some Japanese, the surgeon spoke to his boss and got permission for me to work in the hospital. Following his instruction, I helped him examine the women, with an instrument which looked like a duck's beak. We were most busy when women came in for their weekly check-ups. More than 100 women came, of whom about 50 were Korean. While I was working there I learned that there was both a Japanese brothel and a Korean brothel in Palau.

The uterus of infected women was filled with pus and could not be easily cleaned. There were usually ten women undergoing treatment at any one time. A suppository as big as a bird's egg was inserted into the womb, and the vagina was sealed with cotton wool. After 24 hours, the womb was examined once more. Patients with minor symptoms were discharged after two or three days, but severe cases stayed about a month. Through these examinations, I discovered that there were some women who had given birth. My hospital wages were 50 chŏn a month. This didn't leave much after I had bought cigarettes. I smoked furtively. I wore Korean dresses at work, and there too was called Nobuko. Not long after I had started work in the hospital, the doctor, nurses and a few others went with me to Singapore by air. I think it was 1942. In Singapore, I worked in a field hospital.

After a few months in Singapore we returned to the hospital in Palau. But the bombing raids became more frequent, and we often had to run for cover during work. In emergencies we used a motorbike which looked just like a ship's rudder. I helped the doctor and nurse look after wounded soldiers. At the beginning of the Pacific war, the surgeon wrote me a diagnosis and told me to go home. Having lived so long in Palau, he thought I might be susceptible to local diseases. I went to the police with this and began departure proceedings. I packed my bags and was ready to leave the next day, but the ship was bombed. So I couldn't get home until the war was over.

The house I lived in to start with was in an open field and was an easy target for bombs. It now had many holes in it, and many women had died there. I stayed in the countryside, away from it, but even there I was not safe: one day I jumped down from the first floor when I heard the explosion of bombs and hurt my leg. As the bombing became more severe, I left the surgeon and nurses and was evacuated to a place called Iwayama with some other women. We didn't have much food and ate large snails that we found by a stream. The natives didn't eat them for they believed them to be poisonous. Later, we even ate live lizards and rats.

One night, we put our last few handfuls of rice into a *hanggo*, a sort of saucepan which had been given to us by a soldier, and managed to find some water in the dark. We collected wood and lit a fire and then a bomb fell on us. We ran away holding the pan of rice, and found in the morning the rice had turned red. In the dark, we must have used water mingled with the blood of dead soldiers. There were seven of us. We debated whether to eat the rice or not. We had to eat it, as we were almost starving to death, but we did so with our eyes closed. I don't know what happened to the other six who escaped with me. I seem to be the sole survivor. While evacuating, I covered myself with a blanket and walked through the trees trying to avoid bomb shells. The others told me to leave the blanket because the weather was very hot, but I kept it around me. Even in the confusion, some soldiers raped us. Once, one soldier bit my lips so hard that they swelled up. My lower lip still bears a darkish mark.

When the war was about to end, American planes flew overhead and scattered leaflets. They were written in Korean, and said that Koreans should come out from the jungle with their hands up. The Japanese soldiers with us pointed their guns at me and asked what was written on the leaflets, but I misled them, saying I was illiterate and couldn't read. When Japan was defeated, a soldier with us committed suicide by dashing his head against a broken bottle placed upside down on the ground. American soldiers came and made us stand apart from the Japanese. Then the Koreans were asked to move towards a ship, and after some hesitation I obeyed. The Americans gave us cigarettes and asked to swap Japanese watches. So we made the exchange while those who had no watches gave money instead. In this way, we were able to earn a little money.

At night, I slept with the blanket wherever I could find space. In 1946, I boarded a ship bound for Korea with a family who had earlier migrated to the islands. I arrived at Pusan in cold December. I went home to Talsŏng. There was no one there, and neighbours told me that my parents and family had moved to Sangju, my mother's home town. I went there, but no one knew my family. I travelled all over the country looking for them, but in vain.

During the Korean War, I lived in Tangjin, South Ch'ungch'ŏng province, and didn't even attempt to evacuate as battles ranged around me, thinking it couldn't get any worse than what I had experienced in Palau. After the war, I lived in Taech'ŏn and cooked for labourers at the building site in Namhansansŏng, the South Fortress near Seoul. I went back to Tangjin, where an acquaintance from the South Pacific still lived. The friend asked why I was living alone when I was still young, and introduced me to a man. I moved in with him. His wife had died, and he had been living alone with three children. He was very poor, and I was not all that eager to live with anybody, but I took pity on the children and decided to move in. It was 1957, and I was 36. He asked me to marry him, but I thought it unwise to marry someone with three children, so we just lived together.

After I moved in, I got pregnant once. But the foetus was aborted in the seventh month, and I have never been pregnant since. My husband died of a stroke, so I lived with his eldest son's family. But that son flirted with many women, and in the end divorced his wife to live with a mistress. His mistress was violent and treated me badly. So I moved in with a distant relative of my late husband. I have been living in this latter household for the last seven years. Since moving in, the family has become prosperous and are quite well off. But I still receive benefit from the government as a needy person.

Whenever I think of the events of the past or talk about them, I get headaches and am unable to sleep for many nights. Even if I cry aloud, I don't think I can feel relieved. My anger has become a kind of disease. It shoots through me, and even in the depths of winter I can only sleep with my door open. The doctor who sees me often tells me I must not be upset about the past. My right leg gets cramp at night and is very painful. It is because I lost a great deal of blood when I was stabbed trying to resist a man in the South Pacific. These days I feel tired and cannot be bothered to do anything. I started to take Myŏngnang tablets for headaches when I was 20 in Palau. Now I am addicted to them, taking two every day. I also feel very short of breath and need to see the doctor regularly.

CHAPTER 15

Wandering around Manchuria, China and Sumatra

Yi Tŭngnam

Yi Tŭngnam was born in 1918, in Kŏch'ang, South Kyŏngsang province. Her father spent his time gambling and drinking, and he was so violent that Yi looked for an opportunity to leave home. She went to Manchuria to work with an aunt in her café. In 1939, at the age of 22, she left there with other girls who worked in the same place, and was taken to Hankou to become a comfort woman.

I was born on 5 October 1918, the eldest daughter in a farming family in Kŏch'ang, South Kyŏngsang province. I had two younger brothers and two younger sisters. We were poor and never had enough of anything. My father became a heavy gambler and gambled away the crops we produced, even though there were not enough to feed us in the first place. My mother and I would often stay up until late at night, fighting sleep, and wait for him to return home. He would arrive drunk and treat us violently, waking my brothers and sisters. When I was nine, my mother placed me in school without letting my father know. One morning he caught me going out to school. He stared and said 'A girl, studying?' He snatched my school things and threw them on to a fire. He repeated this a number of times, but my mother continued to send me off to school. She said that girls, not just boys, should be able to open their eyes to the affairs of the world. But I found it very difficult to keep up with school work, for I had to try to avoid being caught by my father and needed to help with housework. I gave up school after something like two years.

My father's drinking became heavier by the day, and whenever he saw me he would shout at me for no reason. I hated living under the same roof. One day, I had taken my brothers and sisters fishing and we were on our way home with other village children, when I noticed my father running towards me. He was shouting 'You bitch, you go fishing like a boy? I will kill you!' I was so frightened that I threw the basket holding the fish I had caught down and, without much thought, ran towards my uncle's house across a stream. As I was crossing the bridge, my father threw a stone at me. It caught the back of my head but, without realizing I was bleeding, I ran on. My aunt had been working in her yard and saw me coming. Frightened at the sight, she rushed to me. I hid myself behind her back and wept hysterically. My father followed me in but my uncle, who was also in the yard, scolded him and sent him away. My uncle put some soya bean paste on the back of my head. I stayed with them for a few days until my mother came to fetch me.

The year I turned 17 my parents were talking about marrying me off to a son of the family who kept a fabric store in the neighbouring village. I had the impression that my father wanted to marry me off, as the eldest child, to reduce the number of mouths he had to feed. I felt like I was being sold. So I left home, as quietly as I could, and went off to earn money with friends. We took a train to a fabric factory in Inch'ŏn, the port near Seoul. It wasn't easy to find a job in what was a strange place to us, and we were afraid because we were away from home for the first time. So we returned within a few days. I told my father I had stayed with a friend. After a while, an aunt who lived in Manchuria visited. I asked her to take me back with her, but she refused. At dawn a few days after she had left, I stole money from my mother's pocket when everyone was asleep and boarded a train to follow her.

My aunt kept a café called the New World. She was surprised to see me and asked how I'd got there. I told her I had sneaked away from home. She said I might as well stay a few days since I was there already. I helped her in the kitchen and ran errands for her. She gave me some pocket-money. She tried to send me home, but I refused. So she let me stay on. I stayed about a year before I decided to go home for a visit. My father still drank heavily, and he often stayed away from home whole nights. One day we heard a commotion outside, and looked out to find several men in the yard. They swore and shouted, demanding that we pay back the money my father had borrowed and then gambled away. My mother panicked; my brothers and sisters cried. Looking at her, her spirit seemed to have been crushed, and I made up my mind to earn the money to pay back the debt. After a few days, I returned to Manchuria.

There were two women older than me working in the café, and they were very kind to me. I ran errands for them as I looked here and there for odd jobs. Many Japanese and Korean businessmen came to the café. Among them was one Japanese who frequently came; he was about 31, had a fair complexion and wore thick glasses in a golden frame. One day he told the women he would introduce them to another café, where the pay would be better. He noticed me doing odd jobs in the kitchen and asked who I was. On hearing I was the owner's niece he said I could go along too. The women responded that I shouldn't work in a place like a café, but they knew I had been looking for a job. The girls told me they were moving to a café where they could earn more and that they would make sure I was generously paid if I went along and continued to do odd jobs such as their laundry.

I decided to go with them. It was 1939, and I was 22. We boarded a train for a distant place where we stayed in a guest-house for perhaps a week. The Japanese man bought our clothes and meals. He left us for about three days, then returned with three more Korean women. One said she had come direct from Korea to Manchuria because she had been told she could earn money. I began to feel uneasy. I felt guilty that I had left my aunt without telling her what I was doing. When the man returned, I asked him to send me back. He asked if I realized how much it had already cost to bring me that far. He told me to pay back the expenses for the train and guest-house, then slapped me on the face with his fist. I blacked out.

That night as I was lying on the bed, I overheard the others talking. 'Why on earth did we ask her to come along? We are already ruined, but she is still a virgin...' It was Tokiko, one of the two I had come with. I found out later that they had sneaked out of the New World to sleep with men. But they later told me that they had never dreamt they were becoming comfort women for soldiers. They simply thought they were going to work in a better café. I wept constantly and begged the Japanese man to send me back. Every time I pleaded with him, he hit me with brute force: I still have a scar on my forehead. The day we left the guest-house he brought two Japanese women, so eight of us boarded a train and went to Hankou. There were no seats available, and our feet swelled up because we were forced to stand throughout the journey.

We arrived at Hankou, where the Japanese man handed us over to a Mr Kaneyama. He was a Korean, really a Mr Kim, and he seemed to be in his late thirties. Kaneyama led us to a house which had once been owned by the Chinese, a few metres away from the edge of a Japanese military unit. He seemed to have come from Kyŏngsang province. He had with him a brother-in-law, who looked about 26 and who helped him. Not long after we arrived the brother-in-law left for Korea. Kaneyama was friendly with the soldiers and frequently visited the unit. There were many comfort stations around it. Each room had a bed made from wooden boards. There were 20 Korean women altogether including us newcomers. Ten came from T'ongyŏng. I can still remember Hideko, Asako, Sumiko, Masako, Tokiko, Umeko and Midori, but the rest are blurred in my mind. The youngest was 15 years old, and four were older than me. But most were around my age. The two Japanese women were much older. I pleaded with Kaneyama to send me home, but he said he could do this only when I paid back the expenses he had incurred on my behalf. He told me that since there was nothing else I could do, I should harden myself to the job and earn money.

I sat and cried for several days without eating. Then one day a soldier entered my room. I was frightened and tried to run out, but he seized me and raped me. At first, I tried to fight him off, but finally gave myself up in despair. He tore my vagina, so I wasn't able to serve any other soldiers for about a week. We had to visit the military surgeon for weekly check-ups for venereal disease. Our meals were delivered from the unit. Daily necessities, such as soap, came from the soldiers since we had no other way of getting them. Some soldiers brought their own condoms, and some used the ones I collected. Whenever we served soldiers, we squeezed out 5 cm of cream from a tube to lubricate the condoms. When many soldiers came, we each had to serve about 20 daily. Generally, the rank and file came from 9.00 a.m. to 5.00 p.m. and non-commissioned officers visited from 5.00 p.m. to 8.00 p.m. From 10.00 p.m. until midnight, officers came, some of whom would stay through the night.

The soldiers paid money to Kaneyama down the hall. They took a ticket that showed the number of the room they wanted. High-ranking officers went straight to the rooms of women they liked, and on such occasions we had to receive the money directly from them and then buy tickers from Kaneyama. Every morning we counted the tickets, each of which I think cost about 2 yen. Kaneyama said that he would keep 70 per cent of our income and we would get 30 per cent. He claimed to be keeping a record so that he could give us our money in one lump sum when we left the station. Sometimes, if we asked for money to buy clothes that we needed, he would give us about 20 yen each and say he had deducted it from our respective record. However, he barely gave enough money for new clothes, offering us a little perhaps once every few months. The money I had was given to me by soldiers once in a while. And, even if I wanted to buy something, it was never easy to go out. Kaneyama disapproved of us leaving the station to buy anything from the merchants up the road. He argued that we might miss customers.

In our third year there, Kaneyama said women were needed in Aceh in Sumatra[1] and that he had agreed to transfer our station there.

In 1942, when I was 25, we travelled south. Kaneyama and 22 of us boarded a ship and travelled for some time. We disembarked at Singapore and stayed for two days, then boarded another ship and went

---

1 The Korean text says 'Kutarodja'.

to Sumatra. This last ship was large and belonged to the navy. Many others boarded at Singapore, and we all disembarked at Medan in Sumatra, where many women stayed. The rest of us took a train and went into the countryside of Aceh province. Kaneyama led us to an L-shaped house with red roof tiles which was said to have once been inhabited by Dutch colonists. The two Japanese women, and six women whom Kaneyama had brought who looked like Indonesians, were forced to stay in a house next to ours. Kaneyama thus started business with 28 women, and his system remained just as it had been in China. My room was similar to the one I had had earlier: it was about 1.7 *p'yŏng* in size, with a bed made of rough wooden boards and a basket in which to keep clothes. But it was much hotter here than in Hankou and we had big electric fans and bathrooms. There was plenty of water and we were able to draw it for a bath almost every day. While I was a comfort woman, I saved money the soldiers gave me and now and again posted it to my mother.

There were various units around the comfort station – a security unit, a field hospital, military police and so on. Many soldiers from the hospital came to us. Our meals came from the military unit, but they didn't cook rice well, so we sometimes got uncooked rice from them and prepared it ourselves.

We had a Chinese boy who did odd jobs around the station. He was 17 and local. He was very fond of me, and sometimes cleaned my room and bought me things I needed when asked. With Kaneyama's permission, I visited his family a few times. His parents were farmers and they offered me lovely food whenever I visited. His mother took pity on me and was very kind.

We again had weekly medical check-ups. I paid particular attention to my health, and washed myself thoroughly every time I served a soldier. I was never infected with venereal disease. Even the assistant medical officer complimented me on my health management. But, because my vagina and womb were weak, I was often ill. Once I got very ill, and my vagina swelled up and became very painful. The assistant who treated me told Kaneyama I was unwell and asked him to give me a break. I was able to rest for a week. The assistant was very kind, and I learned how to give injections and from then on would sometimes help him with odd jobs when he examined patients. We were told to be careful with condoms, and we had to wash them and re-use them two or three times. Whenever I washed them, I shuddered as I thought that the more I washed the more men I would have to serve. Some soldiers tried not to use them, but I told them that unless they did I would not serve them. I insisted.

The soldiers were all different. One would blindly demand my services even if I told him I was ill. One would throw a fit if I refused. One would demand I did strange things. One would shout and go into a temper if the man before him was slow. I could go on for ever, relating the stories. Whether here or in China, the violent men were beyond description. Captain Sikai, for instance, was about 30 years old and very eccentric. He was one of my regulars, and he would swing his sword or hit me given the slightest provocation. I had no power to stop him visiting, and I had to please him to survive. On the other hand, there were some who cared for me whom I became fond of. One was a non-commissioned officer called Hara. He was a pilot. We first met in Aceh, and we hated to part. So he would buy more tickets from Kaneyama to prolong his time with me. One day he went to the front line at Sabang to the north, and I never heard from him anymore. There were a few others who were fond of me. One soldier from Osaka asked me to live with him once the war ended. He frequently brought sugar and used to massage me.

We used to go to Medan, the nearest city, to buy clothes and other necessities. It took more than two hours by train to get there. Medan was a busy city that had many more comfort stations than where we were. We went less than four times a year, and Kaneyama still tried to stop us, making a huge fuss. I once had a big quarrel with him and sneaked out without telling him. When we went out, we would always have to rush back. We lived on an island surrounded by water, and the soldiers kept a tight watch on us. Anyone who tried to run away was shot, and anyway we felt the natives were threatening. Our life as comfort women became harder as time went by. Everyone became more and more tense. One day, I went for a bath with some Japanese women in the neighbouring comfort station, and in their conversation I overheard them saying 'Those Koreans, you can't do much about them'. I was angry and shouted at them, asking what it was that they had against us Koreans. They were taken aback by my aggressive response and apologized.

We suffered much from venereal disease and malaria. The woman from P'yŏngyang who had come with me from Manchuria caught a venereal infection from a soldier which lingered and in the end caused her death. Though we had regular check-ups with the military surgeon, they were not much use. Midori, who was two years younger than me, became pregnant. Without knowing, she kept on serving soldiers until she became noticeably larger. It was too late to abort, and she had to give birth. She then had to continue to work and had someone else look after the baby, but it died of sickness after just eight months.

The military units moved more frequently as time went by. We stayed on in the same place, but the bombing was becoming more serious. One of us was almost killed by a bombshell on our way to a shelter. The soldiers became more violent towards us and our life became more miserable with each passing day. I missed home and wept at my miserable fate, especially when we had special simple meals with the army on Japanese holidays. I tried to kill myself once by drinking hairdye, but I kept seeing my mother's face before me, and I wasn't able to see the thing through. A woman from T'ongyŏng took drugs to kill herself, but was immediately taken to the doctor. He managed to save her. The war was getting more fierce, and many were killed. The army used us comfort women as nurses. Five from our station, including Umeko and me, were sent to a field hospital 15 minutes drive away. Since I had learned how to give injections, I was assigned that job. We went every day, did the laundry and helped treat wounded soldiers. In the evening, we returned to the station where we still had to serve soldiers.

Sometime later, a soldier visited and told us that a ship bound for Korea had been bombed with total loss of life. A few months before, Kaneyama had left the station in the charge of one woman, and had taken that very ship. Not long after we had heard of his death, I was told by a Japanese soldier in the hospital that the war had ended. The soldiers left hurriedly, and no one came to our station anymore. After a few days, American soldiers moved us to the hospital where I had been working. A Korean man dressed in an American uniform was put in charge of us. He made us line up and do exercises every morning. He said we would be able to go home in a few months and gave us instructions on what we should do when boarding the ship. We were in a refugee camp where men and women were housed separately, but the number of women only reached about 500. Every day, we quarrelled. Before we left, that same Korean man asked each of us our age and home town. After about three months we boarded a big naval ship. I was still with the women from my comfort station. On the pier, many people milled around, all trying to embark. There seemed to be about a thousand men and women. We got on board but had to wait several days before we started to sail. We stopped in Taiwan for about a week, and now and again the ship would stop here and there.

Whenever we were at anchor, we went to buy salt and to eat fruit from the trees and take vegetables from the fields. Local people would approach us with their goods. They had sweet potatoes and cigarettes, and we bought them with money or swapped whatever we possessed to satisfy our pangs of hunger. After more than a month, we docked at Pusan. We had to stay on board because of an outbreak of cholera. When we finally disembarked we had to go through a formal entry process, and the officer examining our luggage took 500 wŏn from me and returned only 100. Without understanding what had happened, I walked off the pier with my colleagues, and then we all parted.

I was 28 when I returned. I couldn't gather enough courage to go home. I stayed in Pusan for a month, wandering around and living on the money I had brought back. Then I made up my mind to find work, to earn money and then to go home. I looked around Namp'o ward but it wasn't easy to find work. I started a job with a family and in a café. I had worked for a while before I met people from my home town on the street. They told me that my father had died not long before. I immediately went back to Kŏch'ang. My mother started weeping as soon as I entered the house. She was very perceptive, and seemed to have guessed what had happened to me from my letters. She said that she had prayed to the Buddha every day for my safe return. My brothers and sisters asked me where I had been and what I had been doing. The house was in a mess. There wasn't enough food and everyone seemed on the verge of dying from hunger.

I thought I must earn money to support my family, so went back to Pusan. I worked in a restaurant called Sŏngjuk. I also worked in other restaurants, desperately trying to earn whatever I could. Then, on 13 January by the lunar calendar the following year, I heard that my mother had died. I worked for about three more years in Pusan. I was 31 years old. My body, which I had thought would always stay young, became very weak, and I had to give up working. I went to stay with my sister, who had married a man who ran a printing shop in Pusan. I helped with her housework and brought up her children almost single-handed. I liked the city and stayed there for 23 years, after which I moved to Hapch'ŏn. Another sister had opened a guest-house there, which she asked me to manage. She had money. The business prospered for a number of years, but something went wrong and my sister began to issue dishonest cheques. Since the guest-house had been registered in my name, I was the one who went to prison.

Since my release, I have lived on my own in a house my sister bought for 600,000 wŏn for me in Hapch'ŏn. But I have to pay rent, 10,000 wŏn ($12) a month, for the land. I have to fetch water from the well next door. The water is not good, and I have to boil it before drinking it. The local town office gives me rice and barley. Until last year, I was entitled to nothing because I had property registered under my name, but since they found out my real circumstances the authorities have given me some help. I ache all over. I have stomach-aches, and a fever which rises and then drops suddenly. I always feel uneasy. With the after-effects of those years spent in the comfort station, my abdomen used to hurt terribly, as if my womb was being cut away from me. The pain has eased a little now.

People should live in accordance with their fate. If we try to be too ambitious, whatever blessing we may have will run away. I don't have great ambitions anymore. I used to be a spirited woman, but after having wasted my youth as I did, I am afraid to meet people. I just want to live quietly on my own. When I am ill, I feel lonesome, but I spend each day with two dogs who are like children. I only wish I wasn't ill. These days I keep losing weight. I don't know why. I used to weigh 45 kg, but now I weigh just 32 kg.

CHAPTER 16

I Thought I Would Die

Yi Yongnyŏ

Yi Yongnyŏ was born in 1926 in Yŏju, Kyŏnggi province. Her family were very poor, and from the age of eight she worked as a housemaid. Three years later, she went to Seoul to work in factories and as housemaid to other families then, at 14, was sold to a drinking house, where she did odd jobs and waited at tables. In 1942, she was deceived by her employer, and travelled through Pusan, Taiwan and Singapore before arriving in Burma. There she became a comfort woman in the mountains.

I was born 10 January 1926 in Pungnae district, Yŏju county, Kyŏnggi province. I was the second child in a family of five: my brother was five years older but I was the eldest daughter. I am told that my parents originally lived in Yangp'yŏng, where they owned farmland, but my father lost his land gambling. We were very poor, and I never went to school. I began working for other families when I was eight years old. We were so poor that to survive I had to live in someone else's home and work there. The first family I worked for was wealthy and lived in Yŏju township, and I still remember washing floor cloths every day.

In Yŏju we had no land and had to live on rice borrowed from the local authorities. My parents kept on borrowing until the quantity of rice was so great that they could never pay it back. They had no way to make a living, so eventually they packed up their few belongings and moved to Seoul. I joined them, and we stayed with my father's sister in Ahyŏn ward. My aunt let us use one room, but it was too small for all six of us. So I moved out to live in and work with another family, the Ims, while my elder brother was sent away to work. The Ims kept a large draper's shop. I had to work every day, carrying their baby on my back. My back often came out in a rash when the baby wet itself, and in winter my hands bled from washing nappies all the time.

My family moved from one rented room to another until they finally built and settled in a small hut behind what is today Ahyŏn Elementary School. They didn't have much to eat and went without meals as often as not. My mother gave birth to her youngest child. Because she had not eaten properly the baby was very small. My grandmother said I would have to find food for my mother otherwise, having given birth, she would go mad and starve. So for six months I begged for food with which to feed my family. I went from house to house in the city centre with a sack and a basket, and I begged. When I went to prosperous areas such as Sajik ward, people would ask me to live in their homes and work for them instead of begging. I had to turn their offers down, saying my mother had just had a baby and repeating what my grandmother had said. I told them I had to find food, so I couldn't live in someone else's house. Some people would give me cooked rice, and others offered money. A bag of sugar cost 5 chŏn in those days. I would boil the rice I had begged and make it into gruel. I fed this to the baby with a little bit of sugar.

We also bought draff – hog wash – from the brewery and boiled it to eat. Sometimes we would buy Chinese noodles from the factory after they had fallen on the floor and been mixed with dirt. These were very cheap, and we ate them boiled and seasoned. For a short time, my father sold vegetables, some of which we would season and eat. I once got food poisoning from the vegetables. My face turned a sickly brown and I almost died. My father told me that if I lived with a Japanese family, where they would surely eat good food, I would be able to get rid of the effects of the food poisoning. So I found a suitable family, and for a while lived and worked for them. But I soon returned home and began to beg for food again. I would carry water to the top of the hill where we lived. My father always demanded that I should fetch the water, get sugar or feed the baby. Words cannot describe how hard I had to work while I was still a young girl.

When I was 14, I was working in a small confectionery factory located near the Hongje ward crematorium. I had been there for about a year. My father sent my brother to call me, and I arrived home to find a plump and elderly lady dressed in a long coat and wearing gold jewellery. She was waiting for me, and asked me to go home with her. She said that if I did so my parents would be better off and I would be given food and clothing. My mother sat facing the wall and said nothing while my father told me to go with her. I felt I had no choice. Later I learned that the lady had lent my father money which was supposed to be repaid by monthly earnings.

How did this state of affairs come about? Well, the government had given a piece of land to each family who were living in makeshift huts in Ahyŏn ward. At that time, there weren't any houses in Hongŭn ward, only graveyards. The authorities told us to dig up the graves and burn any human remains, then to build our houses. So my father moved our hut to Hongŭn ward. He rebuilt it, so he had to buy timber on credit, and when he was unable to repay the loan, he was told he must either find a way to pay or vacate the house. So he decided to send me away and take my wages in advance.

I followed the old woman to her place – a big bar in front of the prison at Sŏdaemun, Seoul's west gate. My job was to clear tables, set them with wine and run errands for customers. I had worked there for about a year when the woman asked me if I would like to go elsewhere where I could earn lots of money. She told me I would not go alone, but would be with several others, so I shouldn't be afraid. I asked where the place was, and she told me Japan. I didn't ask where in Japan nor how I would travel there. I agreed, given the promise of money, nice clothes and a nice place. My family had always been poor and hungry, and the idea of good food, nice clothes and money appealed. She bought me some herbal medicine and told me to take it and go home. She said I must take it at home if I didn't want to be seasick. She told me to rest until she contacted me and gave me some money. I can't remember how much it was, but I do recall buying a set of clothes for each of my brothers and sisters.

I got home and rested for about a fortnight. During that time I told my friends that I was going somewhere nice, and described the job I had been told about. Two of my friends, Kim Tŏksul and Kim Hakkŭn, had been working in a factory in Seoul and decided to come with me. They were two years and one year older than myself, respectively. We were finally instructed to get ready. It was 1942, and I was 16. I left home wearing a white short-sleeved dress and white high-heeled shoes. I arrived at the appointed place, a Chinese restaurant in Myŏngdong below Namsan, the hill to the south of central Seoul. There were several dozen women already there. My father accompanied me to the restaurant and then went home. Tŏksul and Hakkŭn were with me. We had a lunch of sweet and sour pork with fried rice. I think it was the first time I had eaten anything with sea-cucumber in it. Immediately after eating, we boarded a train for Pusan.

It was night when we arrived at the port, and we couldn't see much. We stayed in a guest-house in the hot spring area of Tongnae for a week or maybe ten days. The day after we arrived, I wanted to go out to see the sea. Our supervisors told me that the coast was at the end of the main road in front of the guest-house, but they wouldn't let me go out. A Korean man and several Korean women were in charge of us. We took baths in the hot spring water every evening and we ate good food, but we weren't allowed out at all. We boarded a large ship at Pusan during daylight. Some of the supervisors stayed behind. I am not certain whether it was a merchant vessel or a navy ship. When the sun was about to set, Japan was pointed out to us across the water. There were hundreds of women on board. At one point we overheard the conversation of Japanese soldiers and learned that we were going to become comfort women. Because I had worked for a Japanese family, I was able to understand them, but none of us had any idea what a comfort woman actually was.

The ship went south, not east towards Japan as we had expected. I suffered badly from seasickness and stayed in bed for most of the time. I didn't eat. We anchored in Taiwan for a short while but weren't allowed on shore. I still remember lowering my hat to buy fruit from vendors. The ship also dropped anchor for a while in the middle of the ocean, while the sun rose from the sea and set in it. We anchored at Singapore, but were again not allowed on shore. We were tired by then and would pass the time of day motionless, as if we were dead. Whenever the ship swayed, we felt sick. It took more than a month for us to arrive at our final destination, Rangoon in Burma. We disembarked and boarded a train to a small village. That was where my life as a comfort woman started. From then on I was called Harata Yōjo. When we were taken, I thought to myself 'Now I am dead!' I couldn't think of anything else. The comfort station was a two-storey building by the road. My room was on the top floor, and had a cement floor. There was a basement where we were corralled whenever the air-raid siren sounded.

The station was some distance from a native village. We didn't know where the military unit was, but soldiers came in the evenings. While we lived there, I became close to Takeutsi, a civilian employee. He delivered rice, groceries, clothes and the other things we needed. He lived in a house that looked like a private residence, not the military barracks, and he normally wore civilian clothes and a white shirt. He asked me to starch and iron his shirts. Among the women, one committed suicide by taking *sake* mixed with opium. The soldiers burnt her body on a pile of wooden sticks, and gathered us in front and forced us to watch. After about a year, we were moved on, this time by truck. As we took a break in the journey, we saw hot water flowing from a spring in a big field. There was nothing around, but the hot water poured out. It was a hot spring. The soldiers collected water in drums and took baths sitting in them, but we women refrained.

We travelled until dusk. We arrived at a small village on a mountainside where there was just a single military hospital. The comfort station was situated across a small stream that flowed right past the hospital, and only soldiers from the hospital seemed to come to us. First we went to the hospital and had our wombs examined with some sort of instrument.

The comfort station was old and unoccupied. We had to clean it out before we could begin to live there. It was a square shaped two-storey building with an enclosed yard and rows of rooms on both floors. It was well built with high ceilings and staircases at both ends. On the first floor there were 20 rooms; mine was one of these. A sign on the gate announced that this was a comfort station, and in front of the gate were many Buddhist figures.

A Korean couple led 50 women to the house, but they disappeared once they had allocated a room to each of us. On the door of each room was a number and the name of the woman, though I can't remember my number because I've been a fool all my life. The room was about six feet by seven. It had a wooden floor, a bed, a bucket and a few other things. There was nowhere to throw away water, so we emptied it straight into the yard from the upstairs windows. There was a dirty and messy dining room downstairs. Three Chinese men cooked our meals. Rice came from the army. We normally wore Western-style clothes that were provided for us. My health deteriorated through not eating properly. About two years after I began my service as a comfort woman, I got malaria. I must have taken too many quinine tablets, because my face swelled and I developed jaundice. None of the women looked after me. I could think of nothing but going home. For about six months I was mentally deranged. I walked about at night looking at the moon and talking in delirium. Once I hurt myself in a fall while wandering, and I still have the scar.

One night, I tried to get into the hospital wearing the uniform of the military surgeon who was sleeping in my room. The guards were about to shoot me when they looked closer and realized who it was. They took me in and gave me sedatives, then took me back to my own room. Some nights, I went to a place where there was some water, sat on a plank and moved my arms back and forth as if I was rowing, telling anyone who came to listen that I was sailing to Korea. No sooner had I been brought back to my room than I would walk out again. I was told about all this when I regained my senses. At that time I was close to a second lieutenant, an army surgeon who treated me. As I began to regain my mind, he gave me glucose drops and swathed me with hot towels. He also forced tablets into my mouth, holding my nose to make me swallow. He would come a few times a week to treat me, and when I was completely recovered he used to sleep with me in my room.

We had check-ups for venereal disease once a week at the hospital. If anyone was infected, a sign went up on her door saying it was off-limits, and no soldiers were allowed to enter. We were given an antiseptic solution which turned water red if you diluted a few drops. If you used too much, the water became almost black, and too little left the water pink.

The solution could kill you if it was swallowed. We washed ourselves with it. As for condoms, some soldiers brought their own, and some used what I had. Everyone used sheaths, and I was expected to put them on for each man. But the surgeon didn't use a condom. He came to me regularly for more than a year until the end of the war. When the soldiers came, they would give me tickets. The tickets were the size of a business card. I received about ten a day, sometimes 15. The largest number I ever received was 20. Those who served more soldiers got up to 30 a day. We collected the tickets and handed them to the office once a week, where they were calculated as money. We understood that the money was being put in a bank, but we neither saw deposit books nor dared to ask for details. The surgeon didn't give me tickets.

The office was downstairs, but I can't remember who ran it. The Koreans who first took us there disappeared without saying anything, and I think Japanese soldiers might have been working in the office. The soldiers who came went into any room where there wasn't a man already. I can't remember whether we had fixed hours during which we had to serve them, but soldiers who were on leave would come during the day. I didn't use make-up. Daily necessities were provided by the hospital. We had a chest to keep our clothes in, and a box and a mirror in each room. I was told that I lined up all my belongings neatly on the floor when I was out of my mind. Three or four women committed suicide. Some left the comfort station to set up home with officers, some died of illness and some ran away, reducing our number to 20. When I recovered from malaria I noticed that the number was much reduced.

We were able to go out only in groups and then only with permission. This was not easy to get. The mountains were rough and the people were of a different race, so we were scared to run away. We were once told to climb a nearby hill to see the body of a white American who had been killed when his reconnaissance plane had crashed. The torso had only thighs and hips but no head or arms. Not long after that, the soldiers suddenly stopped coming. We made inquiries and learned that they had all left.

The war was over. It was about a year after I had regained my mind. The lieutenant I had thought I was close to also disappeared without saying farewell to me. We didn't hear guns anymore. When we were in the first comfort station, we were often evacuated to the basement when the air-raid siren sounded, but we never witnessed any actual bombing. Suddenly, as if from nowhere, some Korean men arrived and led us out. The planes didn't drop bombs, but they flew very low. Whenever we saw one we would hide. We walked through rain, under the scorching sun, and our feet swelled from the constant tedium of the march. When we had to cross a river, we would carry rice, chilli powder and salt on our heads and wade across with the water coming right up to our necks. In some places, we had to cook rice with red, muddy water. We kept on walking day and night, with only an hour's rest once in a while, until we reached Rangoon. We were so excited about the prospect of returning home that we didn't mind the walking. We must have gone on like this for about ten days.

In Rangoon, we stayed in a refugee camp with other Koreans, most of them men who had been in the Japanese forces, and women who had worked as comfort women. There were about 50 women, assembled from all over the place. In Rangoon, we were given cooked rice and side dishes. We even had soup with pork in it. The camp had a big yard which looked like a school playground. We women would be lined up in two rows in the yard, and we were taught how to cross main roads, or we simply ran around. We also sang the Korean national anthem. One evening, a stage was set up, and we acted out plays and sang into a microphone. I sang too. I think I sang a song which began 'No nameplate, no number...'. It was always very hot in the camp. The barracks had a wooden floor, and we slept in rows on a mat. There was a dentist who treated our teeth; he pulled out my back teeth. We were free to go in and out of the camp as long as we returned at a certain hour.

The ship which was to take us back to Korea was huge. We arrived at a pier in Pusan in March 1946 according to the lunar calendar. But cholera broke out among the passengers and we had to stay on board for several days. The ship then set sail again for Inch'ŏn, where once again we weren't allowed to disembark. We were told we could only disembark if we gave in all our rings and money. So we handed in all that we had. In return, as we landed, we were each given 1000 wŏn.

Tŏksul was with me when we finally disembarked. Somehow her mother and brothers had found out about her arrival and had come to meet her. There was nobody there for me. I went home to Hongŭn ward, but my family had moved. I felt helpless. Fortunately, I was able to track down a friend of my father who used to live in the same neighbourhood, and he took me to my brother in Ŭlchiro. I learned my father had died on 2 December 1945, in the same year that Korea was liberated. He had sold vegetables and other things, carrying them around on his back. Then, he had bought a little grocery shop, but he gambled away all the money he had, turning a blind eye to his starving family. He had been so irresponsible that before I left Korea I had once asked why he didn't just die. But when I heard that he had actually passed away, I was sad and felt guilty for saying such a nasty thing to him. I discovered that my younger brother was now disabled, having wounded his leg while working on a building site managed by the Japanese.

I was 21. I started to work in restaurants and in the homes of families in order to make a living. I was distressed, so I drank a lot. I drank two or three bottles of rice wine, *makkŏlli*, daily. When I was drunk, I would cry aloud lamenting my lot in life. My teeth are now rotten and I can't eat anything either too hot or too cold. I also have a bad stomach. I never dreamt of marriage. When we were fleeing south during the January retreat in the Korean War, I met a man 17 years my senior in Ch'ŏngju and started to live with him. We were never close, since I felt I could never like men. Of course I couldn't have children. My companion died five or six years ago when he was 74. I treat his son like my foster son, and we live on despite our many difficulties.

All I want is to have my own room and to live the rest of my life at ease. The Japanese occupied our country and abused us. I don't mind whether I am well off or not, but I want them to compensate us for the sacrifices we were forced to make when we were still virgins. They took us completely under their control, but now they are making feeble excuses about the recruitment of comfort women, and they say that we volunteered. It was their politics that drove us to the place of our deaths. I want to tell the Japanese government that they must not evade the issue any longer.

CHAPTER SEVENTEEN

Death and Life Crises

Kim T'aesŏn

Kim T'aesŏn was born in 1926, in Kangjin, South Chŏlla province. After her parents divorced she was brought up by her uncle. Her father was an opium addict and quickly disappeared from family life, and a few years later Kim's mother died. When she was 18, two men visited her uncle and promised Kim work in a Japanese factory. Trusting their word, she left home, passed through Pusan Refugee Camp, Osaka and Saigon (Ho Chi Minh City) and finally ended up at a comfort station in Burma.

I was born on 20 February 1926, in Hangmyŏng village, Kangjin county, South Chŏlla province. I was the youngest of three daughters. My father helped on a farm owned by his elder brother. Whenever his legs ached from neuralgia, he took opium. My mother tried to stop him, believing drugs were bad for his health, but he beat her severely if she said anything. She found it impossible to live with him and eventually left home for Kwangju, the provincial capital. My father sold our house and promptly disappeared. I followed my mother to Kwangju and attended Pokchŏng Elementary School for four years. My eldest sister was already married, and my second sister lived with an aunt in Haenam, a town further south. When I was twelve, my parents formally divorced. I went to live with an uncle, another of my father's brothers. He ran a business in Kwangju but, unable to make a good enough living, moved back to Kangjin. I went with him and his family. My mother died a few years after the divorce became final, but by that time nobody knew where my father was or even if he was still alive. My uncle consequently took over all responsibility for me. He tried to find me a husband, and I had to meet several young men he arranged for me to see. He couldn't find a suitable young man, so I continued to live with his family.

It was some time early in September 1944. I was 18. My uncle had told me of a rumour about men taking girls away and one day, when I returned home from outside, he told me to hide myself immediately. I went to the attic, and continued going up there every morning after breakfast until 2.00 or 3.00 p.m. for about a week. One day, when I was still hiding during the morning, I became so hungry that I came down and had lunch with my uncle and his family. A Japanese man in his thirties, dressed in civilian clothes, and a Korean man in his forties and wearing a Western suit, kicked our brushwood gate open and entered. Both spoke good Japanese, and at the time we thought they both were native Japanese. The Korean was really called Mr Ch'oe but went by a Japanese name, Iwaoka. Later, I asked him if he was Japanese, and he shook his head.

Ch'oe urged me to quickly finish lunch. It was September, and we had left the door open, so I could see from the room the two men sitting at the end of the hall. As soon as I had finished, he asked 'Wouldn't you like to earn money in Japan? Come with us and work in a factory for a year where you will earn lots of money.' They grabbed me by both arms and marched me out. We walked for about 30 minutes to the bus station. We took a bus for Kwangju, where they led me to a house which looked like a guest-house but had no signboard. There were four girls there already from Naju, Posŏng and Yŏsu. As we were all from the Chŏlla countryside we soon became friends. We stayed the night, and the next day walked to Kwangju railway station. We took a freight compartment with Ch'oe and the Japanese man and travelled north to Seoul. There we took another train in a further freight carriage and went to Inch'ŏn. There were civilians and soldiers on the trains. In Inch'ŏn, the port to the west of Seoul, we were taken to a place which looked like a hostel. There were two or three rooms, and in one about 20 women waited. Some were young and unmarried while others had already had children. Some came from Kyŏnggi province in central Korea and the Kyŏngsang provinces in the south-east, but the largest number came from Chŏlla.

In Inch'ŏn, I took the Japanese name Mizuko. This name reflected Kwangju, the place where I had come from. I had adopted a Japanese surname, Kanetani, in Kangjin. Even here, the two men told us that we were going to factories in Japan. They said there were many factories and that we would work as factory hands. We were given clothes: two pairs of dark baggy trousers, two blouses and two sets of underwear. The blouses were of many different colours, but I asked for white ones because it was my favourite colour. When I had been taken from my uncle's home I had been wearing dark baggy trousers and a long-sleeved blouse. All the others seemed to be wearing *geta*. We stayed a week at this house, during which time we were subjected to medical check-ups. Two doctors, one Japanese and one Korean, examined us with a stethoscope. They looked down our throats and a few of us were diagnosed as having lung problems. We didn't have gynaecological examinations. I was healthy, 160 cm tall and weighed 55 kg.

We boarded small ships, 20 to each, and sailed around the coast to Pusan. We arrived on or about 20 September and were led to a camp that housed many women. It was a large prefabricated building which looked like a warehouse, and it was sited some distance from the pier. There we were each given a ball of cooked rice. We asked once again where we were going, and were told simply that the factories were in Japan. The factories in Pusan, we were informed, couldn't employ many more people. We were watched by a Korean man, not a Japanese. He kept a close eye on us, and even followed us when we went to the toilet. He wore a Japanese military uniform, and talked with Japanese soldiers in their own tongue. I think we stayed about a week. Around the end of September, we boarded trucks and were taken to the pier, where we embarked on a ship. About 40 of us were to be sent to Osaka, and about 20 to Shimonoseki.

I was in the group sent to Osaka. There, we were housed in a relocation camp, alongside a Japanese military base. Besides the 40 of us, there were about 50 more Korean women who had arrived earlier. We stayed in this place for two weeks, and still had not seen any factories. Ch'oe said we would have to go on to another place. We responded that we had come as far as Osaka for the factories, and asked why he was proposing to take us elsewhere. And we asked how much longer we would have to wait before we got our jobs. He said a ship would come within a week, but in actual fact we waited about a fortnight. After the beginning, no, in the middle of October 1944, about 100 of us boarded a large boat with five decks called the *Arabiya Maru*, with its name stencilled in Japanese script. We women occupied the first, second and third decks. I cannot remember whether I was on the second or the third. As we sailed south, about 60 women were taken off at Okinawa. The ship sailed only at night because of the danger of daylight bombing raids. There were soldiers on board.

We travelled as far as Saigon. I think it must have been around the end of October. When we arrived, there were already other women there, so the total number rose to 100 again. It was here we learned for the first time that we were going to comfort stations. We were watched even more tightly. Guards followed us to the toilets, our meals were brought to us. Even when we were asleep, they kept up their surveillance.

We were divided into three groups, and my group of 20 were sent to Burma. I don't know where the others went. The Japanese man and Ch'oe, the two who had brought me all the way from Kangjin, came with us. We arrived at Rangoon either at the beginning or towards the middle of November. It was very hot. When we disembarked, a truck was already waiting, and there were Japanese soldiers on it. We travelled north along a road clinging to the mountainside for two or three hours, and arrived at a house with a signboard saying it was a comfort station. It was dusk. The station was situated on a wild mountainside. We could hear the soldiers moving about in the nearby army unit. We could even hear bombs falling. The unit sent enough cooked rice for 20 of us: it could not have been far from the comfort station. Two Burmese women cooked for us in a kitchen.

The station comprised two long buildings separated by a road. There were ten rooms in each building, giving 20 in total. It was new and had no gates or fences, so people could walk in and out freely. There was one dining room and two bathrooms. Each room was the size of one *tatami* mat, and the walls and floor were built from wooden boards. Each room had two blankets. Of the 20, I was put in room number 3, which was not far from the office, perhaps 7 or 8 m away. Each room had its number, and under my '3' was written my name, Mizuko. The entrance to each room was closed by a curtain. All we had with us was a small bundle of belongings. There were thousands of mosquitoes, which tortured us day and night. We were watched closely, and couldn't run away.

We had to begin working the very next day, and this was the first time I had had sex with a man. The first client was a soldier about 25 years old with an Osaka accent. When he came into my room, he said he was glad to see me and shook my hand. He told me he had to rush because there were so many men waiting, and he just opened his fly and finished what he had come to do in no time. Because this was all so sudden and I had to serve so many men from then on, my abdomen hurt and I began to bleed. I couldn't lift my legs up because my body hurt so much. Ch'oe said 'You won't become pregnant or get an infection so long as you use condoms. Just tolerate the pain for a little while, and soon you will be all right.' The young soldiers were very excited and ejaculated in a very short time. I think that was the reason why we were able to serve so many men and yet survive. Nonetheless, it was sheer agony for a week or so. We had breakfast around 7.00 and started to serve soldiers from 9.00. We had to serve the lower ranks until 3.00 p.m., then non-commissioned officers from 3.00 p.m. to 7.00 p.m., and officers until 10.00 p.m. Some officers stayed overnight, leaving at about 6.30 the following morning. We were given three meals a day, usually a ball of rice cooked in salty water which was so meagre it could almost be blown away, pickled radish and soya bean soup. When it was very hot, we were allowed a bath, using water from a pump which had been installed outdoors.

The soldiers waited outside the huts in orderly lines. When they came in, they would keep their shoes on and just pull their trousers down. They wanted to save time. I, too, just pulled my underwear down. On busy days, I had to serve 20 of the lower ranks, five or six non-commissioned officers and three or four officers. The smallest number I ever had was about ten regulars during a day. The soldiers' Osaka accents were very noisy, and sounded rather like a Korean Kyŏngsang accent. They were unkind to us, probably because they were staring death in the face, and some kicked us as if we were little more than animals. There were, however, some officers who tried to comfort us. Some just sat and talked then left without doing what they had supposedly come for in the first place. After about a month, I became somewhat used to this life. Some soldiers would return and visit me again, and I would then help them take off their shoes or clothes, or put on condoms. This made them come more quickly. Sometimes, the kinder officers and non-commissioned officers brought large strawberries or grapefruit carefully wrapped in paper.

When we were ill, we received some treatment. I suffered for about a week, and was given ointment for my soreness and allowed to rest. Although illness and so forth meant that some rooms were gradually vacated, no new women arrived. The Japanese man who had brought me all the way from Kangjin took tickets off the soldiers at the entrance to the station, and Ch'oe told them which room to go to. When officers and non-commissioned officers came asking for me, Ch'oe would lead them to my room after making sure I was alone. It was Ch'oe who kept a record of the number of soldiers we served. I kept my own record, dividing it into the number of privates, non-commissioned officers and officers served each day, and would show this to Ch'oe. We didn't receive any money from the soldiers. The station was on a mountainside, and if we had got money, we would have had nowhere to spend it because there was nothing to buy.

Condoms were distributed to us and we used them on soldiers who didn't bring their own. But there were never enough to go around. So, we collected used condoms in a jar and washed them with soap in a nearby stream whenever we had time. We would dry them in the sun, then spray them with a white antiseptic powder to use again. This was the worst of the jobs we had to do, and I hated it the most. I saw one soldier wash his penis with a blue antiseptic fluid after his condom burst. Even when we were menstruating, the soldiers didn't pay any attention and just kept going at it, as if they were oblivious because they had condoms on. The Japanese man and Ch'oe, the two men who controlled us, shared a room. They didn't sleep with any of us. I worked for about a month from the middle of November 1944.

After 10 December, Allied bomb attacks became more frequent. The army told us to get ready to leave, since they would be moving in about ten days time. Three days before the predetermined move, we were having our supper when an officer from the unit visited the station. He confirmed that we would be leaving, and when we asked him where we were going he responded that we just had to follow the troops. Ch'oe suggested it might be better if we ran away. He told me in confidence that I and my two best friends, Haruko from Kyŏngsang and Kimiko from Chŏlla, should be the last to board the truck on the day of the move. On the allotted day, the comfort station was completely demolished. A truck drove up and we hurriedly packed our clothes and boarded it. I waited with my two friends until the others had leaped aboard. Countless trucks seemed to be rushing here and there and, while we hesitated, all of the others drove off. We were left alone, Kimiko, Haruko, Ch'oe and I. We sat down and discussed what we should do. All through the night we walked and came to the conclusion that, since the troops had moved to the front line, we would die if we followed them. We began to feel that whether we died from bombing at the front line or from being shot while trying to escape, we would soon perish anyway. So we determined to run away as far as we could get without being caught. We had also realized that if we didn't hurry we would all die where we were crouched.

We began walking south. The bomb attacks were too serious during daylight, so we walked only at night. During the day, we found whatever shelter we could. At one point, we walked into a Burmese village to ask for help. We managed to find some rice and fruit. Ch'oe had money he had received as his wages, and he exchanged this for red-coloured Burmese currency. Being able to use local money certainly helped us as we walked along. After about ten days, we came to a large river. The year of liberation, 1945, began some time then. It was New Year, but we still hadn't reached Rangoon. We attempted to cross the river on a small boat, but it capsized. There were about 20 of us on it and we all fell into the water; people threw ropes to us from the bank. Ch'oe managed to get to the bank and threw us a rope. He called out to reassure us that the river wasn't deep and that we would survive so long as we kept hold of the rope. But Kimiko was weak. She couldn't catch hold and drowned. I held tightly until, in the end, Ch'oe and a Burmese man pulled me to the bank. We had to cross many rivers, both big and small, after we left the comfort station.

There were three of us left: Ch'oe, Haruko and me. Then, cholera reared its ugly head. We knew that the disease could kill us, but we had no medicine. We were determined to survive, but Haruko died. The bomb attacks ceased in May 1945. Ch'oe and I walked into Rangoon. We had wandered around the front line for six months.

British and Indian soldiers were in Rangoon. Ch'oe and I went to the British camp. A Korean-born British soldier interpreted for us. We told them how we had run away from a comfort station. They didn't ask anything about out personal background. So far as I know, I am the only surviving woman from the station. I was already infected with cholera, but the British gave me antibiotics which helped me recover. The camp was clean and had nice rooms. I think we stayed for about a month. Then we took a train to Bangkok. In the autumn, Ch'oe and I boarded a large ship off Bangkok and sailed back to Pusan. On board were Korean and American soldiers and about 20 women who like me had served as comfort women. Two held tiny babies. We had medicals on board, and we were all disinfected. We disembarked after a week and were taken to a refugee camp where we received a further check-up because of the prevalence of cholera. It was breezy and cold when we arrived back in Korea.

Ch'oe originally came from Seoul. Although he was the one who took me to the comfort station in the first place, I don't think he had any choice at the time about it.

I went to Inch'ŏn from Pusan and worked in a restaurant for about three years. My employer introduced me to a man in 1948, when I was 22. I lived with him quite happily. We had two girls, and it was only when I went to register their birth on the family registration that I learnt my husband already had a wife. So my daughters were registered under his first wife's name, and so far as my family registration is concerned, I am still unmarried. Both daughters graduated from high school. My husband died of stomach cancer, and I have worked and lived with a family as their domestic help for the past 20 years. I have been going to church for a decade. I now blame my past on my ancestors. What happened occurred because my country was poor. I sometimes wonder if I would have become a comfort woman had I been married at the time my uncle tried to hide me. I think it was my misfortune to have been born when and where I was. My daughters know nothing of my past. I don't think it is necessary to tell them.

I pray to God every day, but I will never forget those months. I feel relieved, now, as I pour out the story of my past. I am now receiving medical treatment because I have trouble with my colon.

CHAPTER 18

Hostage to My Past

Pak Sunae

Pak Sunae was born in 1919 in Muju, North Chŏlla province, and married an extremely poor man at the age of 16. When she discovered his poverty she left him, and in 1936 became the second wife of a more wealthy man. Two years later she gave birth to a son. In 1941 she was sold to an introduction agency by her husband, who had always been suspicious of her chastity. There, she heard that a comfort group was being recruited, and volunteered since she felt this was a way she could earn sufficient money quickly so that she could live with her son. She was taken to Rabaul in New Britain.

Sold

I was born in 1919 in Muju county, North Chŏlla province. I was the third of six daughters. My mother was extremely capable, and bought five *majigi* (about 2500 square metres) of paddy fields with money she had earned from weaving linen and cotton cloth by hand. My father cultivated the fields with the help of a farmhand and provided just enough food for the family. My elder sisters helped with the paddies, but I was a small child and simply used to run out and play. My parents loved me just as I was and never scolded me, since they thought I was sickly. I went to an elementary school for two years. Even then I used to play truant and climb a hill to play instead of going to class. Whenever my mother saw me coming home with mud on my pants, she simply told me I could give up school if I wanted to. So after two years I gladly stopped going. I had been taught Japanese at school, but I wasn't particularly good at it. After a while, I started to go to evening classes to learn how to read and write Korean.

When I was 16 I was married. My mother consented to an arranged marriage on the understanding that my new husband's family was well-off. But there were nine in his family and they turned out to be very poor. My husband was also illiterate. All we had to eat every day was a gruel made of barley and wild vegetables. Neither my husband nor any-one in his family abused me, but I couldn't endure the poverty. So I ran away to Kŏch'ang where a cousin lived. I stayed for some time, but I knew I couldn't stay indefinitely so I agreed to become the second wife to a Mr Kim. He lived in the same neighbourhood. It was 1936, and I was 17. My husband wanted to remarry because his first wife had had an affair with a man next door. His family was quite nice and they were well off, but Kim himself was always suspicious of my fidelity and would often beat me when he got drunk. If he became violent, I would run to my father-in-law, who was always kind and told me to try to be tolerant of my husband for him, and such things. I stayed in this marriage because of my father-in-law; I thought he would live for ever.

I gave birth to a son in 1938. My husband was over 30 and was happy to have a son. He brought home some kelp for me, food which was very scarce at that time. I think we were the only household in Kŏch'ang whose rice chest was always full. Then he became ill. He heard of a good doctor in Yŏngch'ŏn, and went to him, taking all the money he made by selling our house. I was forced to move in with my in-laws. He was soon cured but, instead of returning home, went to Japan. When our son was three he returned, bought five *majigi* of paddy fields and left again for Japan.

When he returned once more he started to beat me. His suspicions about my fidelity were aroused once more. I had had some of my hair cut because it had become too full, and wore what was left in a bunch. My husband found fault with this and kept criticizing me. Then he took my child away and handed me over to an introduction agency. It was around October 1941 by the lunar calendar, and I was maybe 23 years old. At the agency were many women who had run away from their homes without taking anything. We were fed and clothed, but the agency charged a large sum if our own family came to take us home. So once you were in there you had little chance of returning home. Most of the women were sold on and taken to Manchuria. I was passed to a fur-ther agency in Seoul.

The agency was housed in a large building with a thatched roof and four rooms in Ahyŏn ward, Seoul. The owner was Im Manjun. Dozens of people dropped in, and sometimes the Japanese police would come to visit. There were quite a few of us there. I met a woman named Kŭmsun who had lost quite a lot of weight and most of her hair because of a fever. We became friends and waited for some job for us to do to turn up. Whenever she had any information, Kŭmsun would tell me. She had heard that if we went to a place where the war was going on, we could earn a lot of money in very little time. We became very close, almost like sisters, and I decided to follow her. People came from all over the place to buy us as cheap labour. The agency staff told me I wouldn't be able to pay back the debt I owed them if I stayed on and worked in Korea. I only learned that I actually owed them something when I arrived in Seoul. I knew some money had been given to my husband before I left Kŏch'ang, but I had no idea I was the one meant to pay it back. I was told the sum would be enough to buy five *majigi* of paddy fields. Once I knew about the debt, I wanted to repay it as soon as possible. I just wanted to earn enough so that I could live with my son.

Some time later, we heard about the comfort corps. It was said that the corps' duties were to wash clothes in field hospitals and to look after wounded soldiers for a term of three years. We heard that the term would enable us to pay off our debts and still have a lot left over. We were told they were recruiting 25 women. Kŭmsun and I, alone in the agency, volunteered. The others told us that we would be going to a nice place. It was December by the lunar calendar. We stayed on, waiting for our departure. Pak, who recruited us, bought us each a pair of pink shoes, a blue dress and a small suitcase. When we arrived at Seoul station many women were already gathered. As we left families, who had come to see their daughters and sisters off, were in tears. One girl, Sumiko, was an only child, and her parents wept a lot as she boarded the train. There was no one to see Kŭmsun and me off. The train went to Pusan.

Twenty-five of us left Seoul led by Pak, Kim and Cho, and another 25 were led by a man known as Hayasi. We arrived at night and straight away boarded a ship. We sailed to Shimonoseki and anchored there for a day. As soon as we arrived, vendors gathered around. We lowered money to them on string, and they tied dried squid and whatever they were selling on the string in return. The ship then sailed south until we arrived at our destination. It was a navy ship with a restaurant, cinema, hospital and bathrooms, and it even had horses quartered on board. We took turns to bring meals up from the kitchen. Two of us would get cooked rice and soup in wooden buckets and sufficient bowls for each meal. The ship went here and there to avoid torpedoes, and arrived at Rabaul in New Britain after about a month and a half.

'Sizuko'

It was a bright afternoon at about 4 o'clock when we reached Rabaul. It had been planned that we should stay the night on board, but ceaseless bomb attacks made the ship sway so much that we couldn't stay. At dusk, a cargo truck came, we disembarked and were taken away. We watched the bombing, which looked like a grand firework display, as the truck took us and dropped us in front of a two-storey house. It seemed to have recently been occupied by white people. They must have kept a shop, because we found books and soap on display. You entered the house through a gate that opened straight out on to the road, and there was an office right beside it. The building was then divided into two parallel sections with one storey on the right and two on the left. Rooms on the ground floor opened directly into the courtyard. The staircase was at the end of the building on the left. Twenty-two women had rooms downstairs, and only three, including me, were housed upstairs. Below the staircase were a kitchen and a small store-room. A larger store-room and a toilet were sited behind the buildings across the road.

We had never dreamt we would have to have sex with soldiers. We knew only what we had been told: we would do laundry and look after wounded patients. We were, thus, perplexed when soldiers began to come into our rooms. We all frantically fought them off to start with. We confronted the men who had taken us there and told them we had not come to do this sort of work. I locked my room and didn't venture out except to go to the kitchen for food. The proprietor was furious and told me I would never be able to pay back my debt. Sumiko, who was barely 17, resisted for two weeks. But with constant abuse from the proprietor and soldiers all around us, we couldn't keep up our resistance. Even running away was impossible, because the place was surrounded by water on all sides.

Our lives as comfort women started. We would begin work at 7 o'clock in the morning, serving the rank and file until 4.00 p.m., non-commissioned officers until 7.00 p.m., and then officers through until 10.00 p.m. Some officers stayed overnight. The soldiers were brought to us in vehicles, and we had no idea where their unit was. We only served the military, but once in a while Korean civilian employees same. The latter wore shabby clothes and were not supposed to visit the comfort station. But they would sneak in occasionally.

The soldiers bought tickets before they came to our rooms. The regular soldiers had white tickets, non-commissioned officers blue tickets, and officers red tickets. They were priced, respectively, at 2 yen, 2.5 yen and 3 yen. Those who stayed the night paid 6 yen if they arrived before midnight, but a different rate if they came later. Sometimes officers would stay the night without tickets and give us money directly, but we had to hand this in to the office without fail. Pak, Kim and Cho worked in the office, counting the tickets every morning. I don't know about the others, but I took no interest in the number of tickets I collected. I just handed over what I received. The men in the office calculated the money daily, giving us a token amount but keeping the rest with the excuse that they were saving it for us. I cannot remember how much was meant to have been saved on my behalf. At first we women would sit in the office for soldiers to select. But after some time, the soldiers knew which rooms we occupied and came in directly. There were name-plates on each door, and I was called Sizuko.

When there weren't many soldiers, we served about 20 each per day, but when things were busy we would serve over 30. They were allowed an hour each, but no one stayed that long because there were so many others waiting in the corridor in orderly queues. On Sundays especially, the soldiers crowded into the station like ants. We normally wore dresses, but on busy days we had no time or energy to bother to wear pants. My abdomen swelled and my womb throbbed. Life was so hard that I would plead with any man who seemed like he might be kind-hearted to help send me home on a plane. The reply was invariably that there was no room for women on planes.

The Japanese were terrified of venereal disease, and a medical team would come once a week to give us check-ups. Three or four doctors came, but we never saw a female nurse with them. We lay on a bed, and they examined us with an instrument. They made the soldiers use condoms so that we would neither become pregnant nor catch disease. Some soldiers brought their own sheaths, but the office supplied them to us for those who didn't bring any. We had to put the condoms on, and about one in twenty tried to refuse to use them. I refused to serve men who didn't wear protection, and they would then often become violent, slapping me on the face and shouting at me. The doctors gave us tablets to dilute in water which provided an antiseptic solution with which to wash ourselves and even some of the more dirty soldiers. There was a water-tank on the top floor, and we would use water from this when it had anything in it. I was absolutely determined to look after myself and as a result never caught venereal disease. Once I got malaria, but Lieutenant Abe, one of the surgeons in the field hospital, looked after me well. There were two sisters who had come to the station together. The younger one gradually lost her sight. She had to depend on her sister even to go to the toilet. I wondered whether syphilis had caused her blindness. Anyone infected with venereal disease received treatment for about a week, and had a sign posted on their door saying it was closed. I put this sign up when I had my period. The hospital gave us balls of cotton wool to which threads were attached to deal with menstruation.

We were taught simple Japanese phrases and were told to use the language to address the soldiers. I was not good at it, and I can still remember how I used to repeat to myself '*Iratsyaimase, iratsyaimase*', 'Welcome, welcome', as I went up and down the stairs. The proprietor wore a Western suit and he made much fuss of arriving soldiers, shouting

'*Iratsyaimase!*' Food was provided by the army. An elderly Chinese man cooked rice, but it was difficult to eat without side dishes. Water was also supplied by the army. Soldiers shared their ration boxes with me a few times.

When I had resigned myself to my fate and had begun to adapt myself to this lifestyle, I gained enough composure to look at my surroundings. When I had a moment to spare, I would look out of the window. I could see Hayasine next door. Though we were neighbours with just a wall separating us, we didn't talk to each other. I could see a person going in and out of the rooms shouting that the time was up and asking men to leave. Sometimes I could hear women singing in the courtyard, and some of them sang really beautifully. Though I couldn't sing well, just watching them seemed to release some of the resentment which knotted my heart.

I felt like I was in a prison and wanted to escape to get a breath of fresh air. But a military police check-point was posted right in front of the house, and we weren't allowed out. We needed a permit to venture beyond the compound, and we were intimidated into staying put by being told that in the compound we were protected from the natives who would otherwise rape and kill us. So we didn't go far, though we did occasionally sneak out to a store across the street. They sold goods such as clothes and small umbrellas. Our work started after 9.00 a.m., and we were able to sneak out straight after breakfast. With the small amount of money the proprietor gave me, I could sometimes buy high-heeled shoes or colourful sunshades. The comfort station was located right in the town centre, and we could see two-storey shops and many people from different countries – natives, Chinese, Japanese and whites. Not far from the station was a building with white people which made much noise; it could have been a factory. The sea was not within sight. There were no military units around us, and the only permanent residents appeared to be natives. The men didn't wear shirts and walked around barefoot, while the women wore vests. They were given jobs such as cleaning and running errands for the Japanese.

The officers sometimes took us on outings with the permission of the military police. One morning, at around 8.00 a.m., Lieutenant Abe came for me and took me out in a car driven by a private. It had a canvas roof and was big enough for four people. Abe had a picnic basket with biscuits, wine, bananas and other food. We drove towards a smoking volcano. It looked quite near, but we had to drive for a long time. I wished to go nearer, but Abe said it would be too hot if we went on any further. In the evening, he stayed the night with me although everyone else had left, and a private came to fetch him the following morning. Lieutenant

163

Abe came to see me regularly, and when he came he looked after the ill among us. Consequently, the proprietor treated me well. Seeing how I was treated some of the women accused me of sleeping with the proprietor. My room was upstairs and I didn't talk much with the others. I couldn't understand why some would fight with the soldiers or would be beaten by them. They seemed to quarrel with the proprietor a lot.

On public holidays, we gathered in a big hall with a stage. None of the rank and file were there, only officers we had not seen before. We were there from morning until lunch time, and the officers recited the Oath of Imperial Subjects and lectured us. We sang the Japanese national anthem, and sometimes the Korean folk-song *Arirang*, on the stage. There were some Japanese women, although we never knew where they came from. Most were older than me. Once, this ceremony was interrupted by an air-raid.

In Rabaul, I missed my son so much. One night, the moon was shining brightly and I sat on top of the bomb shelter across the courtyard thinking of him and my home. It was about midnight and I had finished work for the day. A soldier approached the shelter and went inside. As he came out he was struggling to put his jacket on. I heard something fall on the ground, but he didn't notice it and just went his way. I sat for a while, then as I made my way down to go back to my room I picked up what he had dropped. It was his wallet, complete with an ID card and money. The following morning, I handed it in to a military policeman. He made a telephone call and, a few minutes later, a soldier came and thanked me, politely bowing several times. There had been 50 yen in the wallet, and the policeman told the soldier that since I had been honest I deserved to receive the money, and asked him to give me half. I turned his money down.

Later, when I returned to Korea, a citation came to my mother's home one February. It was issued because the money I had turned down had been donated to the state by the soldier in my name. I kept the citation in a chest, but it was burnt with my other things in air raids during the Korean War. I wrote to my parents while I was in Rabaul but they, ignorant of my actual situation, used to write back and say they would love to come to visit me but could not afford to. The letters came via Shimonoseki.

Air raids got more and more serious, and we were anxious to return home. We often confronted the proprietor and demanded he should let us go as our terms were well over. He refused, saying he could not let us go because no replacements had been sent. Sometime later, we were somehow allowed to leave even though nobody had come to replace us. All 50 of us left together. Just before we boarded a ship, the proprietor gave us each a savings book. He told us we would be leaving within a week, and should keep the books secret, not let on about their existence to spies. He advised us to hide the books around our waist. Each book was a reddish colour, and we were told we could draw money from any post office with it. I think something like *Arai Kiyoko* was written on the cover. None of us had ever visited the post office in Rabaul.

The ship was as large as the one we had taken to get to Rabaul in the first place. One morning, when we had been on board about seven days, Akiko, whose real name was Ch'oe Kŭmsun, and I were on breakfast duty. We had just finished eating and were about to return the buckets when, suddenly, water surged into our quarters. The ship must have been hit by a torpedo. We had been told to keep life-jackets on all the time, but we weren't wearing them because of the heat. The water kept pouring in, and a woman from Kwangju was washed away. Her abdomen burst open as she was carried off: she had been pregnant. There was a huge creaking sound and the ship split into two. We clung to a rail as the ship rocked terribly. We tried to stay on board, but in vain. Women were being swept away by the tide. Akiko, too, was lost. I fainted, and when I came to I was holding a piece of wood, floating in the middle of the ocean. I heard someone shouting '*Kochi koi, kochi koi*', 'Come here, come here', in the distance, and saw a soldier swimming towards me. Each soldier had a rope around his waist, and the one who shouted to me threw the end of it to me. By grasping it, I could gradually move towards them. It was a rule that we should have a small white flag to call for rescue, but no one had anything. So I took off my white underwear and we used it as a substitute.

A boat came to our rescue. It could not approach us easily because of the bombing and Allied fire. It was about 4.00 in the afternoon by the time a navy ship managed to get close enough to us. We had been in the water for eight or nine hours and barely managed to climb on board, holding fast to the ropes. We were given a bowl of gruel. Those who had been wounded groaned and screamed, while others were busy trying to tend to them. It was a chaotic scene. I had bruises on my arms and hips, and there was a wound from shrapnel on my forehead.

The vessel returned to Rabaul. Only 15 of us had survived. Sadako had broken her shoulder and Kimuyo's leg was so badly damaged that she had to have it amputated. We took turns to look after the injured. Once Kimuyo recovered to some degree, she worked in an office. Kim, Pak and Cho, the men who had taken us to Rabaul in the first place, had gone, and a Japanese man aged about 60 managed us. We called him 'Father'. There were three Japanese women there – we had no idea where they had come from – who disappeared once we returned.

'Father' told us that since we had come back we could not return to Korea unless we completed a term again. We thought this very unfair, but had no choice. We started to serve again. All our luggage was lost in the shipwreck, and we had no possessions left. There wasn't even much food. We exchanged cigarettes for papayas and bananas. If we had lived just on the food given to us at the station, we would all have starved.

Air raids had now become extremely frequent. Attacks were so severe that sometimes we had to run around to avoid the fire. During raids, we would open our mouths and cover our eyes and ears. Most of the Japanese soldiers we served died as soon as they went into battle. Not long after my return, Lieutenant Abe also died on the front line. New soldiers arrived from Manchuria and they were much more rough with us.

Home

We were finally allowed to leave because Japan continued to suffer defeats. The ship was again wrecked by bombing, but this time we were rescued straight away without suffering any fatalities. We didn't return to Rabaul but went to the Palau islands, where we stayed about a week. It was more peaceful there; there were buildings with pointed roofs and functioning theatres. Several Japanese women joined us. Some women remained behind in Palau to earn money. The one I remember most clearly was Hitomi. She said she would work in a brothel to earn money, because she thought it would be too dangerous to return to Korea by ship. I hated being there and wanted to get home, even if I had to risk my life. I don't remember how long I was on the next ship, but I arrived at Shimonoseki on New Year's Day 1944. The two women who had been severely wounded earlier were with me and remained in Shimonoseki to receive further treatment. I went on to Pusan. I don't remember how I managed to pay my fare, since I had no money. It is possible that we were given free passage because we had been at the front line. My friend Kǔmsun, who had taken the Japanese name Hanako, and I travelled together by train to Yǒngdong and then went our separate ways. I haven't heard from her since.

When I returned home my parents were still alive. If I had had any money, I would have tried to bring up my son. But I had lost my savings book and wasn't able to do anything for him. I wanted to see him so much that I tried to go to Kǒch'ang to visit, but my mother stopped me. She had seen how my husband had beaten me, and said he would hold me a virtual prisoner if I went to him, and that he couldn't be considered a human being the way he behaved. He realized that he had been cheated by his uncle once he had sold me to the agency, and I hear that he beat up his uncle. That should never happen. My parents had many problems because my father kept a mistress in his old age. I couldn't stay at home, so in that same year I became mistress to a man who worked in the town office. He thought I had been working in a hospital in Rabaul. I didn't think I could have children, but as soon as I started to live with him I became pregnant. I am deeply sorry that I never had a normal married life. I regret the fact that I ruined my children's fortune.

After Korea was liberated, the man I was living with resigned from his work, and we spiralled down into abject poverty. I did all kinds of work to support and educate my children, but things didn't work out well. I sold *insam* (ginseng). I helped with housework and I sold vegetables, often leaving my youngest daughter alone at home. Life was very hard. I have three children, but I am listed as single on my family registration. I have recently been living on government aid for the poor.

My cousin's wife, who lives in Sŏngnam to the south of Seoul, reported to the Korean Council on my behalf. I decided to report my past in the hope that my case might be of some help to my country. I think that Korea should never be controlled by another country again. I have lived with resentment buried deep in my heart for what I was made to go through. I am grateful that the Council is now trying to help me release this pent-up resentment.

CHAPTER 19

Silent Suffering

Ch'oe Myŏngsun

Ch'oe Myŏngsun was born in 1926 in Seoul. In early 1945 a Neighbourhood Community Centre official came and suggested it would be good for her to find work rather than stay at home doing nothing; at home, she might be drafted by force into the Women's Voluntary Corps. She considered this for a few days, then left home with him. She arrived in Japan and became an officer's mistress. After pleading to be sent home, she was handed over to a Japanese army unit and became a comfort woman. Later she married and had children but, because of diseases contracted at the comfort station, her eldest son became mentally unstable.

I was born in 1926, so am 67 this year (1992, age according to Korean reckoning). Through the course of my life, I have suffered every possible hardship a woman can possibly endure. Because of this, I look about 80. In this report I will grasp the chance of releasing the resentment which I have buried deep within my heart, living for so long in fear that my children or husband might find out about my past.

I was born in Tongja ward right in front of Seoul station. I had an elder sister and two elder brothers. My father stood as guarantor for someone else's loan, but it was not repaid, so we had to move from one rented room to another. I hardly remember my father being at home, and I don't remember what he was like or what he did for a living. He was away for many months at a time, and when he came back he stayed only a short while before he upped and left yet again. My mother had a hard time feeding us children, and she worked for other families in order to bring us up. When I was about nine, my brothers and sister were already in school. My sister was eight years older than me. She was very pretty, and neighbours often said that I would be lucky if I grew up half as pretty as her. But one day she disappeared. My mother travelled around all over the place looking for her. My sister's school friends also tried their best to find her. Our neighbours were concerned, too. My mother wept daily, and my father returned for a few days, but then left again in anger. We didn't move, but stayed in the same room anxiously waiting for her return.

After two or three years, she came back, looking for all the world like a beggar. Our neighbours crowded into our house to look at her. She was nothing but bones. The neighbours said that a pretty woman's destiny was to endure misfortune. Then, when I was out doing an errand for my mother, I overheard some neighbours say how my sister had been taken away by the Japanese police. Soon after this, we left the neighbourhood. My mother was scared of something, but she never told me what and didn't allow me to go out to play unsupervised. I started school when we had moved to Sogong ward. I was eleven or twelve, a little old to start school. I went to Hwagang Elementary School in Sup'yo ward, but I had to give up in the winter of my fourth year after we moved further away from the school, to Hongje ward. By this time, my mother couldn't afford school fees any longer. I left my school and my friends in tears.

My sister was now very ill. My mother gave her herbal medicines and went to shamans to get them to perform rituals.[1] My sister took to her bed, gradually getting worse, and she died during the winter of the year she returned home. Her body was buried in Kŭmgok, where my maternal grandparents had lived. My oldest brother was by now married but had no permanent job, and my second brother was working in a printing shop. I was particularly close to my second brother. I did whatever he asked me to do and he, in return, would do anything for me. I was more attached to him than to my parents, but he was drafted into the military when he was just over 20. Shortly afterwards, my oldest brother moved with his wife and family to Manchuria in search of work, and I was left alone with my parents. I missed my second brother very much, although he wrote to us from Hiroshima. I was gradually getting more and more fed up with our life of poverty.

It was January 1945, and I was 19, when we moved once again, this time to Tadong. A Neighbourhood Community Centre official visited me and asked if I had thought of finding work. He said that if I stayed at home with no job I ran the risk of being drafted into the Women's Voluntary Corps. I could avoid this if I went to Japan to work, and at the same time I would be able to earn money. I said I would discuss his

---

1 The indigenous ritual specialists in Korea are often referred to as 'sorcerers'. Since early in this century, it has been common among folklorists and anthropologists to label them as shamans. Koreans use the term *mudang* to denote a shaman, and those practising in and around Seoul experience the possession and trance which characterize classic Arctic shamanism.

proposition with my mother when she returned home. I happened to be on my own at the time. He came again a few days later, urging me to make up my mind quickly. I hadn't said anything to my mother, but one evening I told her about his proposal. She told me not to do anything, then added, somewhat curiously, 'Oh, dear! We will have to move again!' I didn't agree with her, because at that time I didn't understand what she was worried about. After all, she was our sole bread-winner, and I thought if I worked it would ease our financial difficulties. Not only that, if I went to Japan as the official had suggested, I would be able to meet my brother. So I began to direct my thoughts towards going abroad.

My mother insisted I shouldn't go, but I thought about it overnight, then packed some clothes and left while she was at work. I went to the Neighbourhood Community Centre. The official and I boarded a train for Pusan the same day. We journeyed through the night, and in Pusan he handed me over to two Japanese men. I was scared. I had learnt some Japanese at school, so I understood a little, even though I pretended not to. I was afraid they might start talking directly to me if they found out that I knew Japanese, so I just followed them without saying a word. They led me to a ship. There were about ten Korean women on board, all of whom looked older than me. They sat silently, and none of us had any idea where we were going. I went to the toilet. I felt sick. I went up on deck to look out. We were in the middle of the ocean. There were no houses or mountains in sight, only an aeroplane circling around in the sky above us. One of the Japanese men came up, said something, slapped my face and grabbed my hand. He broke my hand! As a result of that brutality, my knuckles still jut out. He seemed to think I was about to throw myself overboard. I went back below and lay down as he ordered. I now regretted that I had left my mother. I hadn't listened to her. I began to weep.

Some time during the evening, we disembarked. The journey seemed to have taken about eight hours. As I walked on to the dock I heard we were in Shimonoseki. The name of the place was strange, but I tried to commit it to memory, repeating 'Seki, Seki'. I was worried and wanted to return home. I didn't know where I was. The other Korean women disappeared, and I was left alone with the two Japanese men. We boarded a train on which all the windows were blacked out. I had no idea where we were going. All I could think was that I was finished and would die without seeing my brother. My situation looked dark and bleak. The train stopped, we got off, and went to a certain house. A Japanese man of about forty appeared, apparently very pleased to see me. The men talked together briefly, and the two who had brought me left.

The new man pointed me to a room and asked me to enter. I soon summed up his situation: his wife was ill and bedridden, and he had a son about 20. I went in, ate supper brought in by a maid and stayed still, afraid of doing anything. The maid came back in the evening, spread bedding for me and told me to lie down. I sat still for a while, not knowing what was going on. A little later, the man came in, lay on the mattress and pulled me to his side. I shook my head and tried to resist, but he forced me to the floor and began to take my clothes off. I was too scared. My head was stunned, and my body turned so stiff I couldn't move. Something was entering me, and at first I thought it was his knee. It hurt so much that my head swam. Blood flowed, wetting the mattress. My womb hurt as if it was going to spill out. I realized I had been raped. He continued to sleep with me. But when he stayed away from home, I didn't have to go through the ordeal. He hardly visited his sick wife's room. Even in the midst of that hateful nightly ordeal, I felt guilty and sorry for her and I thought about the agony she must be going through.

His name was Suhara; his son Ziro. He was a soldier, and his uniform had a rank badge with stars on a red lapel. He wore the uniform to work each morning. The house had three rooms, and I still remember photographs, a whip and a long sword hung on the walls in the hall. The family also kept a horse. I lived there, waited on the wife and helped with housework. I was not allowed to help cook and nobody else in the household abused me. I often heard the sound of bombing. I asked him, using sign language, where I was, and he replied Hiroshima. I pretended I didn't know any Japanese. But when I heard this was Hiroshima, I wanted to see my brother. After a while, when I was less scared, I said my brother was in the same city and asked him to help me find him. I showed him a letter from my brother which I had brought with me when I left home. He nodded and spread four fingers, indicating so far as I knew that I could meet my brother in four days' time.

Suhara took me by car to a building which looked like a factory. I met my brother, though I don't know what he was doing there. When he saw me, he asked what I was doing in Japan and told me to get back to Korea quickly. I told him how I had been brought there, bursting into tears. He was upset and told me to leave by whatever means I could, for this was not a suitable place in which to live. We wept and talked for three or four hours before Suhara came to take me home. We hugged each other and bade a tearful farewell. Back at Suhara's house, I did my utmost to please him, constantly asking to be allowed to go home. I asked his wife to let me go, telling her that her husband didn't come to her because I was there. If I went back to Korea, I said, her husband would love her much more. I took Japanese lessons from their son for an hour or two every evening, and I asked him, too, to help me get home. For two months or so, I kept pestering them, and the wife began to get fed up with me. She became nasty, but I kept on pestering her from morning until night. Suhara normally gave me anything I asked for, but if I asked to go home he would quickly become angry. One day, after Suhara had left for work, I begged both the wife and son to let me go. They talked together, then the son told me to pack. I was grateful and excited, so I packed my belongings. We left for a railway station. There, the son met two Japanese men to whom he talked before handing me to them. He shot me a quick glance as he left. The men held me by my arms and tried to take me away, but I resisted them, shouting that I was on my way back to Korea. One kicked me hard in the thigh and told me to follow them. I was dragged away.

I was taken to a small building which looked like a warehouse. There was a row of perhaps ten rooms, and I was taken into one, about one *p'yŏng* in size. It had nothing but a blanket. Soon, a Japanese woman appeared with food and waited on me. I thought Suhara must have felt guilty to his wife for having me in their house, and that he was leaving me here until he could send me back to Korea. I expected to see him in the evening, but the same woman brought me a basin of warm water to wash in. I washed and was ready to leave at any time. Soon afterwards, though, a strange soldier came in. I thought it was at last time to leave. I thought he had come to take me off to Suhara. But instead he smiled and asked me to lie down. I clutched my bundle of possessions on my lap and pushed him away, shouting at him to go away. He pulled me to him and tried to pacify me. He pushed me on to my back and raped me even as I clutched the bundle. I still hoped he would take me home after he had done this, thinking merely that he must have been desperate for a woman. But then my new life began, a life which I had never imagined possible. I shudder and feel repulsed at the mere recollection of what happened. Even now I regret that I pestered the family to let me go, since if I had kept my silence I would not have gone through that awful ordeal. It would have been easier to stay with one than to serve so many men.

We got up at about 9.30 or 10.00 in the morning for breakfast. Soldiers would sometimes come before lunch, but mostly they visited during the afternoon. On Sundays they crowded in from morning onwards. They queued and each man spent about five minutes, or ten at the most, with a woman. They kept coming in one after another, and my living hell ended only at about 10.00 p.m. On days when there were not many, I would serve 20 soldiers.

Because I didn't do as I was told, I was often beaten. I would faint and, when I did so, I was given injections to bring me round. If I lay still, wetting myself and with my womb bleeding on to the ground, some men would just kick me and leave. I was beaten so often because I would lie with my face covered by my skirt, because I would not suck them off when I was ordered to, because I spoke Korean not Japanese, and so on. I was beaten so much that I seemed to lose my spirit. I just lay like a corpse, with my eyes open but not focused on anything. When air-raid sirens sounded, the soldiers all disappeared, locking my door from the outside. I was scared at first and banged the door to be released, but soon enough I just lay there staring at the ceiling.

Some soldiers ejaculated quickly and left, but some took longer and were unable to finish. If one stayed for more than ten minutes harassing me, I would faint. If I did, the Japanese cook would douse me with cold water and feed me rice gruel. I couldn't imagine ever surviving. I just ate whatever food was placed before me and served soldiers whenever they came. Three or four soldiers guarded the entrance, and these seemed to change often. They would beat me if I tried to go out for fresh air. The soldiers who came for sex seemed to pay the guards money. Only recently did I learn that they could have paid either in tickets or in cash. All I was given to wear was an outer garment. I didn't have any underwear.

The woman who cooked and did our washing never changed. She was Japanese, and about 40 years old. She tried to console me. She helped me because I fainted so easily. Whenever I came round, I would ask her where Shimonoseki was and beg to be taken there. Instead of responding, she would try to calm me down and wipe the blood from me. Even though she was Japanese, she was kind. She was the only person I felt I could trust. When I asked where I was, she told me I should not ask such questions. But I think she once said I was in Osaka. I never spoke to any other women there. I bumped into one only once, on my way to the toilet. I wanted to ask where she had come from, but I passed by silently in fear that I might be noticed by a guard. I was beaten so frequently if I ventured out that I stayed in my room except when I had to visit the facilities. My meals were brought to the room.

The soldiers were all different. Some behaved very badly and were simply less than pigs or dogs. There was one man who would just hold me in his arms without demanding my body, and one who just talked to me, saying he would come back for me once the war ended. One officer tried to be good to me. He slept with me only once, and on subsequent visits just talked and left. He even washed my womb when he saw what a mess I was in. But I didn't get to like him, and I refused to talk to him since I was suspicious he might send me to another, even more awful, place. Every soldier seemed to bring his own condom, and some used them while some didn't bother.

Because I was forced to serve so many men, my womb became raw, red and swollen and began to smell badly. A military surgeon came and gave me injections, but nothing improved. Even in this state, I had to keep on serving men. Once, a soldier was about to get down to his business when he saw how red and swollen I was. He swore and pricked me with something sharp, perhaps a nail. The wound became infected, covered in blood and pus, but I still had to serve the men. The soldiers weren't human beings, and tried to enter me as they had come to do even after they had seen the infection. Pills and injections didn't improve my symptoms. I don't know what the injections were, but they made me feel sick and a nasty taste would retrace its way back to my mouth and nose. The surgeon said that drugs and injections wouldn't heal me. Once, the kind officer came along with the surgeon and said something. It seemed he asked him to send me away. I thought he wanted to send me to another place.

One day, the cook told me I would be going back to Korea. She said they were releasing me because I was sick. When I heard this, I began to think that I should have died earlier instead of surviving for so long. I felt resentful towards the cook because she had brought me back to consciousness whenever I had fainted, instead of leaving me to die. Of course, I am grateful she looked after me and I am grateful that I was able to leave, even in the sorry state I was in. Looking back, the officer must have helped me return home.

The surgeon gave me a piece of paper with some writing on it. A soldier took me to a pier where a ship was berthed. I showed the paper and boarded the ship with a guide. Once on board, I could think of nothing except that I was alive and was about to return to my mother. I disembarked at Pusan and the guide helped me get a train then left. I arrived in Seoul alone. I had left for Japan after New Year's Day 1945, stayed at Suhara's house for two months, served soldiers in Osaka from March to July and now was returning after more than six months. When I got to Seoul station, I was penniless. I walked to Tadong where we used to live, with no luggage except for the clothes I was wearing and a pair of flip-flops. My abdomen hurt every time I took a step, and I had to sit down frequently and rest. Fortunately, my mother was still living there. I opened the gate and walked in quietly, and found my mother sitting on the threshold of the room. She saw me, rushed out, grabbed me and wept, saying she must be dreaming. Because I had a diseased abdomen, she took me to hospital, trying to keep my illness secret from the neighbours. She deliberately didn't ask me where I had been. It seemed that she knew everything. She used to weep, saying that her two daughters had been ruined in the same way.

My abdomen hurt very much, and my mother felt me and said she thought I must be pregnant. At the hospital a doctor examined me and announced that the baby was already dead in my womb. It had been a boy, and half of the foetus had already rotted. The doctor said that germs had caused it to die. The foetus was six or seven months old and had been dead for about a month. He must have been Suhara's child. I never had a period while I was in Japan. My mother borrowed money from here and there and took me to several reputable hospitals. Finally I was treated in the Obstetrics and Gynaecology Clinic owned by Yi Kwangsu and my infection was, to a certain degree, cured.

My mother heard that the Women's Voluntary Corps were again recruiting in our neighbourhood. She panicked and married me off to a man who had lodged next door. I didn't know what his job was. Shortly afterwards, Korea was liberated. My infection was never completely cured, because I married before my treatment was finished. I lived with my husband for a few months before he started to beat me and threw me out of the house, saying that he had got syphilis from me. I went home to my mother, pregnant again. I seemed to get pregnant easily, for I had lived with him only a few months yet was so soon with child. I was afraid that this child too would die. My brother returned. He had been injured when the atom bomb fell on Hiroshima and came home with his body burnt. He suffered from radiation sickness, his ribs crumbled into small pieces that looked like chipped teeth, and he died within a year. That same year, I gave birth to a boy in my mother's house. The child seemed to be healthy, and I felt a great sense of relief wash over me. I stayed at my mother's, doing housework and raising my child.

One day, the mother of a friend introduced me to a man, saying that I was good looking and should re-marry even if I already had a child. So, I met and married my present husband. His parents and sisters treated me harshly simply because I already had a child and I was thrown out of the house many times. I cannot describe in words how sad I was. I was mistreated, and the backs of my hands were torn and constantly bled because I was never allowed to use warm water to wash the cotton clothes with, even in mid-winter. My husband must have married me just for my looks. He changed completely after we married and often stayed away from home. He had affairs with other women and he tormented me while he was young, but I was in no position to complain. I kept having children, and I had to do all kinds of odd jobs to feed them and support my in-laws. My first son was badly treated by his stepfather. I wasn't able to educate him properly. He managed to complete primary school, and then did all sorts of odd work. He went around, almost begging, but I wasn't in any position to look after him.

When I turned 30, I began to develop restlessness and to become mentally confused. I would suddenly hate my husband, my blood would run hot and cold and I would throw a fit, shouting at him to get away. He scolded me, asking if I intended him to become a monk. I would be restless whenever I heard people talking or heard the radio or television. I would lock the door and refuse to let anybody in. I fainted when I heard gunshots. I got scared when I met people, and shuddered when I heard any loud sound. I stayed indoors for 30 years, crawling on my knees. It has only been in the last four years that I have started to walk properly. I still take medicine, tranquillizers, without which I would be restless.

I have had four children with my present husband, three daughters and a son. They are now all self-sufficient. I live with my youngest daughter, but I used to live with my first son. Even though he only went to primary school, he learned much by working for different people and used this knowledge to set up and run his own business. This became quite prosperous, but suddenly he developed mental problems when he was over 40. He was confined in Ch'ŏngnyangni Mental Hospital. I was called to see the doctor. He made others leave the room, and asked me if I had had my son while infected with syphilis. I dropped my head, wept and left, unable to say anything. I am to blame. I have ruined my son's life. I little imagined that my past could make my son mentally ill after so long: hadn't he been born normal? Hadn't he grown up normal? He has now been released, but he has a fit about once a month. I am sure the doctor did not tell him anything, but last year he threw plates and dishes around and tried to attack me. He said he had gone mad because he had been born illegitimate and shouted that he would kill me. I was so scared that I left the house and moved in with my youngest daughter. My daughter-in-law had already left home.

I have lived looking forward only to death, and without telling anybody my story. My tribulation has remained buried deep in my heart. Now I have reported to the Council and I take part in various activities of theirs. But I am anxious in case anyone recognizes me. I have a husband and children, so I cannot bewail my life and be so resentful in public. If, by any chance, my children's spouses and families discover I was a comfort woman, what would become of them? I look normal on the outside, but I suffer from a nervous disorder and from diabetes. I am unable to live without medicine. Who would be able to guess what inner agony I suffer with this awful story buried in my heart? My story, as hidden as it is from those around me, will follow me to my grave.

CHAPTER 20

From the Women's Volunteer Labour Corps to a Comfort Station

Kang Tŏkkyŏng

Kang Tokkyong was born in 1929 in Chinju, South Kyŏngsang province, and lived with her grandparents after her father died and her mother remarried. Her grandparents were well off, and she was sent to elementary school. In 1944, when she was 16 (in Korean age) and in the first year of high school, she was sent to Japan with the first group of the Women's Volunteer Corps to an aeroplane plant in Hujiko. Life there was too hard, so one night she ran away. She was captured by a soldier who took her to an army unit where she became a comfort woman.

The Women's Volunteer Labour Corps

I was born in February 1929 in Sujŏng ward, Chinju, South Kyŏngsang province. My father died when I was young, and my mother remarried, so I was brought up mostly by her parents. My grandparents were comfortably off. Pongnae Elementary School was not far from where I lived, but I was sent to Yoshino Elementary School, now known as the Chungang Elementary School. I am one of those who graduated in the thirty-first year of the school's existence. After six years of education, I stayed at home and did nothing. My mother didn't think this was good, and sent me to a new secondary school. The school was founded the same year I began to attend, and it had only a single class of about 60 pupils.

In June 1944, when I was still in the first year of classes, I joined the first Women's Volunteer Labour Corps and was packed off to Japan. My teacher was Japanese, and he came to me and told me to join the Corps, saying I would be able to continue my study and earn money at the same time. My mother was strongly against it, and wept and pleaded with me not to go, but I had made up my mind. Two girls from my class, the head girl and I, went. The head girl was the brightest of all of us, and came from a wealthy family. Fifty girls from Chinju were gathered to join the

Corps. Fifty more boarded our train at Masan, and there were 50 more waiting when we arrived at the port of Pusan, making 150 in total. Before we left, we all trooped to the county office. A farewell ceremony was held in the yard which the county head attended. My friend read the Corps' statement of allegiance. We didn't have any ceremony when we left Chinju. We left by ferry the following morning. As we boarded the ship we began to weep. Two army ships and a number of planes formed our escort. Our ship had three decks, and we were stationed in the very bowels.

We arrived at Shimonoseki, boarded a train and were taken to an aeroplane plant in Fujiko City, Toyama prefecture. We were greeted by a middle-aged couple as we arrived. They showed us round the plant, and demonstrated how to work a lathe. The place was huge: it looked larger than the whole town of Chinju at that time. And there were many, many workers there. It was surrounded by walls, and guards were posted on the gates. We reached the plant by walking from our dormitory. We were given brownish uniforms and caps. The jackets had *Women's Volunteer Corps* sewn on them. We wore clothes we had brought with us in the dormitory, but we had to wear uniforms in the plant. We also had to don caps whenever we worked. One girl who did not wear her cap caught her hair in the machine, and she was dragged in and killed.

Our dormitory was near the main gate. The supervisor was a man, but we had a few female supervisors who helped instruct us. Before we started work, they took us on an outing to the coast near the border of Shinminato and Fusiki where many Koreans lived. We went to a village to get water, and were welcomed by Koreans, who asked if we had come from the homeland. We were delighted to meet them and there were hugs all round. The food in the plant was too bland for us, with no seasoning, so we asked the Koreans for salt. We also noted where the village was in case we ever got the chance to return.

We worked twelve-hour shifts, switching from days to nights every week. Our job was to cut components on the lathes. We had to do this with great care. Sometimes the material was so hard that the bit burned, and we would have to wait around for the machine to be repaired. All of us from Chinju used lathes, while the girls from Chŏlla cut steel. Once, I found some of the steel so attractive that I took it back with me to the dormitory. But a supervisor took it from me, saying I could be arrested as a spy. I remember hearing that our wages would be saved, but we never saw any savings books. The work was hard and we couldn't tolerate the hunger. We were given cooked rice, soya bean soup and pickled radish, but in tiny quantities. We would sometimes count each grain of rice so that we could savour it, or we sometimes gobbled the whole lot in just three spoonfuls. Some girls saved some of the rice to eat later. For lunch we would get three small slices of soya bean cake, *tabu*, which we often ate before lunch because of our ever-present hunger. When we were on night shifts we got breakfast after work then nothing until the evening. We were so hungry we some-times stole food meant for different rooms. We little thought that the girls in other rooms might starve because of us. I was so hungry I sent my grand-parents a postcard asking for food. They sent salt and beans, which tem-porarily appeased the hunger. I regretted the fact that in childhood I had often worried my grandmother by refusing to eat properly.

There were three older Japanese women who worked in the plant. They commuted from their homes and brought packed lunches. Sometimes I sent a postcard asking my grandmother to send washing soap, and exchanged this with the Japanese women for rice or salt. Because of hunger and overwork, one of the girls from Chŏlla went crazy and was sent back home. Later, another girl pretended to be mad, rolling about on the road, but the supervisors realized she was only pre-tending and didn't let her go. We spent the winter in the plant. The snow was piled so thickly on the roof that it hid the structure. They made a canopy along the road from the plant to our dormitory. Whenever we worked on night shifts the Japanese workers had supper at the appropriate time, but we ate only soya bean cake rations meant for our tea. We would cry ourselves to sleep, crouched around the stove.

The dormitory rooms were the size of twelve *tatami* mats, and a dozen or so girls slept in each. We each had three sets of bedding including mats and quilts. The dormitory was so huge we never saw all of it nor knew who slept where. There were no Japanese women, and we Koreans were grouped according to our home towns, Chinju, Masan, Chŏlla province, and so on.

Amongst those of us from Chinju, my friend was named captain and I her deputy. I don't remember who gave us these nicknames. I don't remember that we did anything special, except that we wrote the words to a song, which I can still remember. The words were in Japanese and accompanied a military song we had learned earlier in our school:

Ah, across mountains and seas,
We, the Women's Volunteer Corps, have come thousands of miles.
The Korean peninsula, seen far away on the horizon,
Our mothers' faces shine from there.

As the snow fell, we Chinju girls would walk around singing.

Once, the girls in our room staged a strike. We agreed to stay in bed and to refuse to get up one morning. When the supervisor came to wake us, we remained with our eyes closed, pretending to be sleeping. The set hour when we were meant to start work passed and we didn't go. But we received no food and were heavily reprimanded. About two months after we arrived, we had become so hungry that we tried to run away early one morning. My friend and I ran to a Korean in Shinminato, whom we had met before. However, the supervisors somehow found out where we were and came for us. We were taken back and slapped on the face many times. We were scolded severely, and told we should set a good example not try to run away. Fifty more girls came from Chinju later. Among them, Kang Yŏngsuk was one year younger than me. I scolded her and told her she should never have volunteered, saying how hard life was. We looked for an opportunity to run away, and after a while my friend and I seized our chance again.

A Comfort Woman
It was night. We sneaked under the barbed wire, and ran in the opposite direction from the one we had taken during our previous escape attempt. We wandered around not far from the plant but were seized by a military policeman. We had promised to stay together whatever befell us and held hands tightly, but I found myself alone when I was thrown into a truck. I was left alone with the policeman and a driver.

My captor had three stars on his red lapel. I didn't know his name or rank at first, but later found out his name was Corporal Kobayasi Tadeo. He sat with the driver through the journey, but half-way through stopped the vehicle and told me to get off. It was very dark; nothing was visible. He raped me. I had no experience of sex, so I was too scared even to try resisting. If such a thing happened now, I would kill myself by biting my tongue off. But at that time I was scared and helpless.

We got back on the truck and rode further until we arrived at an army unit. Two guards stood outside, and behind the buildings was a tent. My captor took me there and told me to stay put. There were already five or so women there, who looked at me in a daze and said nothing. Soon, day dawned. The tent was partitioned into five or six cubicles. Mine was the size of one and a half *tatami*, but had no actual mat. I slept on a simple military bed. Most of the women were older than me, and at first I was scared and not sufficiently composed to talk with them, so I didn't realize what we were there for.

Some three days later, Kobayasi came and had sex with me again. Then, other soldiers began to come. I served about ten a day. No one came during the day, although they would visit on Saturday afternoons. No one stayed overnight except for Kobayasi. He came often. We women generally slept in one place. Our number was less than the number of soldiers, so we couldn't have any days off. I remained scared, and my abdomen hurt a lot, so I didn't get a chance to think about anything else. The soldiers from other units would sometimes take us out. I was called Harue, and if a soldier called one of our names, that particular woman had to follow him, carrying a blanket. We had to serve countless soldiers on the wild mountainside. My abdomen, my womb, throbbed with pain. I had to serve so many men. Afterwards, I would be unable to walk back to the tent, and the soldier would have to drag me off the mountainside. I can't describe in words the misery I endured.

Kobayasi brought me clothes, and I also had the clothes I had been wearing when I ran away from the plant. Our food came from the army, and I remember balls of cooked rice. We ate on a low table on the ground. Kobayasi sometimes secretly brought me extra balls of rice and dried biscuits. I was scared at first, but later I stopped being afraid of him. I didn't get any medical examination. After some time, the army unit moved. The soldiers boarded a long, khaki vehicle which looked like a posh taxi and three trucks. We women got on one of the trucks with other soldiers. We moved in the dark.

It probably took less than a day to arrive at the next site. As we drove along, I could see a river on one side and mountains on the other. The new site was near water, perhaps a lake or a broad river, and was surrounded by fields and trees. A lot of snow had fallen. The army compound was huge with flat-roofed low buildings built haphazardly. Unlike where we had been before, there were quite a number of private residences. We were taken to a house which also had a flat roof. The entrance led to a corridor off which there were many rooms. Each had a window facing the back yard. Each had *tatami* mats. There were about 20 of us housed there, in quite crowded conditions. Those who had been there when we arrived often went out, on some days leaving just five or six of us. The unit was large, but not many soldiers came. We served maybe five or six a day. Some stayed overnight. There was no exchange of money or tickets.

To the left of the entrance was a large room, and to the right was a row of small rooms. We would usually sit in the large room while the soldiers queued up outside the door then walked in. Each soldier would call out for the woman he wanted, and go with her into one of the small rooms. Each room was big enough for two people to lie in, leaving just a small space. Each had a mattress, blanket and hot water tin. We were told to place the tin under our feet or to cuddle it when it was cold, but I don't remember a very cold winter when I was there. I had regained my bearings somewhat since the move, and now began to ask questions of one of the women, Poksun, or of Kobayasi. Poksun and I lived in the same building. She said she had been there the longest of all of us, and she certainly looked over 30. I asked her how far we were from Toyama and where exactly we were. She replied that she didn't know Toyama and told me the name of the place where we were, although I can't remember it now. She also said that the civilian bastards who controlled the station kept all the money involved although they were meant to give it to us. She said 'Poor you, you were seized by a soldier, yet you don't get paid'.

I tried to befriend Kobayasi, believing that I might be able to run away if I coaxed him sufficiently. I smiled at him for the first time, and asked if it was far to Toyama. At first, he refused to tell me anything, saying our location was a military secret. But later he told me this was a place prepared for the Emperor to escape to. He said the Emperor would be coming. On some occasions he refused to say anything, claiming the answer to my question was a military secret, but at the same time he promised to let me go home soon. Once he asked if I had worked at the plant. I think he knew my past. I didn't speak to any soldiers except Kobayasi. I fell ill and, in my misery, wrote a song with a borrowed pencil.

> *Ah, crossing from one mountain to another,*
> *I came to the Women's Volunteer Corps a thousand miles away from*
> *   home;*
> *But I was captured by a sergeant*
> *And my body torn asunder.*

I set these words to a military tune I had learnt at the plant. One day, I sang it to Kobayasi, but he quickly stopped me. From then on, he didn't visit me as frequently as before. I don't think I spoke to anybody except for Kobayasi and Poksun. Whenever I bumped into any of the other women, we would exchange glances and nod. I remember hearing their names, Meiko, Akiko, and so on, when soldiers called for them. I lived in my own world.

I remember several men who wore khaki but no rank badges and who visited the comfort station often. They brought our meals, but we women didn't eat together. The rice was always short, although we also had soya bean soup and pickled radish. Once in a while they would give us fried plants culled from the mountains. Once, Kobayasi, in a somewhat drunken stupor, brought me *sushi*. Poksun sometimes went out in the evening, to where I don't know, and came back having had a good supper. When asked by the others where she had been, she would simply say 'the house over there'. Sometimes she brought some garden vegetables back. Kobayasi continued to bring me clothes. I didn't wear a Japanese kimono, but rather blouses and skirts. I was always ill and wanted to stay in bed, so I hardly ventured outside. I found it difficult to walk straight because of the pains in my abdomen. Poksun sometimes told me that many soldiers would soon come from the south, and I became scared of Saturdays, when most of the men came, more than death. I stopped thinking about anything except running away.

Return

One day, it fell strangely quiet. I walked with one of the women to the unit. There were no guards in sight and inside all the soldiers were weeping, crouched on the ground. We couldn't understand what had happened, so walked to the street, where we heard people shouting in jubilation. There was a Korean on a truck, holding a flag, and the street was crowded with people from many places. They seemed to be men drafted by the Japanese. I grabbed another Korean and asked what was going on, where he was going, and pleading with him to take me with him. He reeled back in surprise and asked what I was doing there. I didn't tell him I had been a comfort woman. I just asked him to take me to Toyama, since I thought Koreans lived only in the area around Shinminato. He said he would take me to Osaka, and I rushed back to the station, quickly packed and jumped on his truck. Two or three of the women took the truck together, while the others went their own way. In Osaka, the driver gave me some balls of cooked rice and asked someone to take me to Shinminato by truck or train.

I went to Pang, the man who had given me food when I first ran away. He asked me where I'd been and what I'd done, and I told him. He let me stay until I could leave for Korea. I helped cook and launder for four or five months until, in the depths of winter, Pang, his family and I travelled to Osaka. We boarded an unlicensed ship. His wife had died, and he was living with his children. He was dating a Japanese woman in the neighbourhood, and she also came with us. It was this woman who noticed I was pregnant, even before I knew it. When I had first been seized by the military police, I had never had a period. I had begun to bleed a little when I was in the second comfort station, and I must have become pregnant almost immediately afterwards. I tried to throw myself off the ship as we crossed the sea to Korea, but this woman sensed what was going on and followed me everywhere, making it impossible for me to take my own life. Pang came from Chŏlla province, and we went to the town of Namwŏn when we got to Korea. Returnees were put up in the Kuksu guest-house, which had been run by the Japanese during the occupation. The repatriates stayed in one section while the National Defence Corps were billeted in another. I gave birth in January 1946, and Pang's woman helped with the birth. I stayed on for a few more months. Although the woman loved Pang and had willingly come to a foreign country to live with him, she found it difficult to settle down and decided to return to Japan. On her way to Pusan to find a ship bound for Japan, she took me to Chinju.

When I got home, my mother told me I couldn't live at home with my son. She was sorry for me, so asked a distant uncle to take me to Pusan. He went with me to a large orphanage managed by the Catholics, and I left my child there. He found me work in P'yŏnghwa restaurant in Ch'oryang. From there I could visit the orphanage to see my son every Sunday. But when I got there one day I noticed another child wearing my son's clothes, and discovered that he had died of pneumonia. He was only four years old. I never saw my dead child with my own eyes, so I found his death difficult to accept. I have never married.

From then on I did all kinds of work, waiting in restaurants, selling things, helping with housework, keeping a boarding house, and so on. Maybe I am ill-fated, because something would go wrong or I would be taken ill every time I was about to be able to save some money. I don't even have a proper house that I can rent now. I become ill very easily. When I was young, I used to roll around my room with period pains. I had to have injections to relieve the throbbing. And I bled copiously. I went to herbal doctors and to a gynaecological surgery. I would even have danced naked if I could have been relieved from so much suffering. The doctors told me that the lining of my womb and my fallopian tubes were infected. My periods, which had started properly only when I was 18, stopped before I reached 40. Since then, I have had no monthly pain, but I have been hospitalized several times with bladder infections.

The reason I came forward to report to the Council was to pour out my resentment. I have tried to write down my experiences several times, but because I have had to move so often, I kept losing the notes. I am telling my life story so that nobody else will ever have to go through the same things as me. I think we must try to get what we justly deserve from Japan: a proper apology and proper compensation. There are still some who say that what we did is shameful, but they are indeed ignorant people.

CHAPTER 21

Shut Away Close to Home

Yun Turi

Yun Turi was born in 1928 in Pusan. Her father was a fairly prosperous builder, but her brother became mentally deranged after marrying and left home. After her father died, the family fortunes sank and they were soon living in poverty. In 1942, Yun went to work in the Samhwa Factory and then in a complex that made military uniforms. In the latter place a Japanese manager harassed her, and she looked around for an alternative job. As she passed the railway station an officer called to her from the police station, and when she followed him inside she was forcibly taken to the First Pusan Comfort Station.

I Was Born Into a Prosperous Family, But...

I was born in 1928, the fourth child in a family of three boys and four girls. My eldest brother finished secondary school, but the rest of us only managed to finish or only started elementary school. I was sent to Ch'ŏnyŏn Elementary School in Seoul, whereas my brothers and sister all went to schools in Pusan. I was born in Pusan and lived there until I was eight, but then I moved to my aunt's in Seoul from where I went to school. The reason for the move was because a fortune-teller told my family I would not live long because I had a short upper lip, and so to avoid misfortune I should live apart from my parents.

My father was in the building business. He didn't drink and treated his children very well. We owned a number of paddy fields and vegetable fields, which, rather than farm ourselves, we let out to tenants. Our house stood in front of the Chosŏn Fabric Company and was huge; it was about 200 *p'yŏng*, 720 square metres, in size. But after my eldest brother married, trouble set in at home. Only a month after the marriage, he became mentally disturbed and would frequently leave home. Then my father died, and the family fortunes began to sink rapidly.

In 1941, when I was 14 years old, I went home to find all our fields gone and the house sold. My family, my sick father, mother, two sisters and a brother, were living together in a single small room. The day after I returned, my father collapsed at the breakfast table and died. My mother suffered from kidney trouble, and my sister married in March the same year, leaving me as the eldest child with the responsibility of keeping things going. I found work in a factory to support my family. In February 1942 by the lunar calendar I started work in the Samhwa Rubber Factory. My job was to stick soles on shoes, but the glue had a strong pungent smell which made me feel dizzy and sick all the time. So I learnt to sew in my breaks and was moved to the sewing department. I worked there for about five months then moved on, to Nishimura Garments, a company which made military uniforms, where I could earn more money. The workload was heavy, and we had to work until 9.00 at night since we couldn't finish our allotted work by the proper knock-off time, 6.00 in the evening. It would be almost 10.00 p.m. before I got home. By the time I had tidied up for the night, the buses had stopped running, so I had to walk home, a young girl alone at night. One Japanese manager, with evil intent, seized me three times on my solitary walks home. When I turned the corner he would grab me and drag me to a hillside. However, each time Korean technicians and team leaders, who worked at the same factory and happened to be in the vicinity, came to my rescue. I worked there until August 1943.

The manager kept up his harassment until I felt I couldn't continue working there. I decided to leave and went to a glove-making factory in Ch'oryang to see if they had a vacancy. I was on my way home at about 5.00 or 6.00 p.m., and was passing the Nambu police station in front of Pusan railway station, when a policeman on guard duty called me over. He asked me to go inside, and I dutifully followed him in, thinking nothing could happen because I hadn't done anything wrong. It was some time in early September 1943. There were three or four girls of my age already inside, and the policeman asked me to sit down. When I asked why, he said he would find me work in a nice place and told me to wait quietly. The Japanese occupied Korea, so we obeyed them. At about 11.00 p.m., a military truck arrived, and two soldiers loaded us on board. I asked where they were taking us, and the only reply was that they were going to give us good jobs. It was night and we didn't know where we were.

We travelled for a little while then got off at some unknown place. There were five women waiting. With the five of us, ten in total slept in a room which resembled a warehouse. The following night we boarded a motor vessel which looked as if it belonged to the police. There were now about 50 girls, all of whom looked to be under 20, and three soldiers. The boat went to Japan, but I don't know what part. We kept crying as we held each other on the boat. We got off, were marched for a while and then led into a room which again looked like a warehouse. There were many young women already there. We stayed overnight. The following morning, we sang a song, recited the Oath of Imperial Subjects and were divided into groups. The 50 girls from Pusan were divided into two groups of ten and two of 15, and I was in one of the smaller groups with Sunja, who had left with me from Pusan. Sunja was 17, a year older than me, and already had the Japanese name Kanemura Zunko. Her home was in Kugwan in Pusan, and she said she had also worked in a factory and been seized on her way home. My group was the second to reboard the very same boat that had taken us to Japan. We were still accompanied by the three soldiers. The boat travelled for some hours and returned to Yŏngdo, an island just off Pusan. We were told to wait quietly as they were going to find us good jobs. We told them we already had jobs and pleaded with them to let us go home. Eventually, we all ended up in the First Comfort Station in Yŏngdo, Pusan. It was September 1943.

The Comfort Station
On the day of our arrival, we stayed overnight downstairs. The following day, a Korean told me to follow him. He was an agent for the Japanese, who cooked for the women and watched over them. He said a Japanese soldier had asked for me and told me to go upstairs. I found a soldier who looked like an officer sitting, waiting. I was afraid to go into the room and asked why he had asked for me. He shouted, saying I shouldn't ask for reasons. I tried hard to resist him, but in the end he managed to rape me. My vagina hurt so much that I refused to serve soldiers for a few days and earned myself a number of beatings. As things progressed, some officers stayed overnight, and we had to serve soldiers all day long except during our meal breaks. There were 45 comfort women in the station, and all were Korean. Those from Kyŏngsang province around Pusan made up the majority, although some came from Ch'ungch'ŏng, Chŏlla and Kangwŏn provinces in the centre, south-west and east of Korea. The girls mostly came from farming families.

For our meals, we were generally given rice mixed with barley or the dregs of sesame seeds, with Korean *kimch'i*, pickled cabbage, and Japanese-style pickled radish for side dishes. We occasionally got bean sprouts, but typically it was just rice and two side dishes. On Japanese public holidays, we received scraps of pork. I wore the black skirt which I had worn when I was caught and things given to me at the station. I was given baggy trousers and a cotton jacket with an open front, much like a modern tracksuit top. We were never short of clothes since they were supplied each season. For underwear we were given pants with elastic at the waist and the legs. Our daily necessities – soap for washing clothes, face soap, gauze, cotton wool and tooth powder – were supplied by the station. We women pooled these things in one place and shared them. We washed our own clothes during the quiet periods when no soldiers were visiting.

While I was a comfort woman, I received no money, nor any tickets. Sometimes, Yosimura, who liked me, gave me money to buy food. I hid it. If we had money, we were allowed out to the shops on the street beside the comfort station, but I felt too ashamed to go out. The others were too exhausted, and nobody hardly dared go to the street to buy anything to eat. The comfort station building had been requisitioned from a Korean who had formerly run it as a guest-house. There was a red-light district nearby called Hibarimatsi, about 500 metres to the left of Yŏngdo Bridge, the bridge which connected the island to Pusan proper. If you passed that area and walked on, you would eventually reach the comfort station. The building was separate from the military barracks. It was a two-storey building with eleven rooms downstairs and twelve upstairs. Each was 2.5 *tatami* mats in size. There was one room with underfloor heating on each floor, in which medicine was kept. A person who did odd jobs for us lived in each. My room was upstairs and had nothing but bedding in it. There was another single-storey building, with about 20 rooms, next door. This had been the residence of a Korean family, and the rooms were larger, but partitioned to give many smaller cubicles. There you could hear exactly what was going on in adjacent rooms.

The proprietor was Takayama, a Japanese man, but the army managed the station's affairs. A Japanese civilian employee, Yasimada, sat in the hall and allocated soldiers to rooms when they entered. A Korean man cooked and watched over us. There were three or four other soldiers who took turns to guard us.

I served, on average, 30 to 40 men daily. They were mostly sailors and soldiers posted to Pusan. When a ship came into harbour, many sailors visited us. At weekends, many more would come than on weekdays. When I had to serve many men, I would go out of my mind. The men would enter my room one after another, and it was impossible to count them. After I had served a soldier, I went downstairs to wash myself with water mixed with creosol. Then I returned to serve the next man. To lessen the number I served even by one, I insisted on washing each time and tried to prolong the time I took cleaning up after each. The soldiers were supposed to use condoms, but many tried to avoid them. Many of them were nasty. It was quite common to be asked to suck their penis. Some wanted to have sex while standing up. There were all sorts, and words fail me if I try to describe much of what they did. Some brought an erotic book with them, the *48 Rules*, published in Japan, and demanded I should follow its instructions and pose for them. I would swear at them in Korean. Even today I still can't drink milk because it reminds me of sperm.

Some soldiers were kind. Yosimura came to see me often, and he took pity on my plight and did not try to sleep with me. He was a soldier. He took my photograph and said he wanted to marry me once the war ended. He said that he would take me to Japan after his country won the war. I tearfully pleaded with him to help me leave the place, but he replied that he lacked any real power. He couldn't do anything because I was there on the orders of his superiors. He sometimes gave me sweets or money. After Japan lost the war, he went back to Japan alone. There was another man who often visited me. He said he had Korean parents, but that he had been born in Japan and was now a sailor in the Imperial Forces. His ship came to Pusan once a month, and he visited me each time. Once I went to the harbour with him to see his ship. He, together with several other officers, got permission to take us out and bring us back. That was the only time I left the station. Others went out occasionally with soldiers for short liaisons but, in principle, we were not allowed out.

I never got pregnant at the station, but two others did. One died while having an abortion. The other grew quite large with the baby, and tried to commit suicide by hanging herself from a banister. But she was discovered by a soldier and taken away. I don't know where she ended up. Nobody had any children at the station. When we had our monthly periods we were given gauze in lieu of sanitary towels, which we used whenever we weren't serving the soldiers. But we were made to serve soldiers even while menstruating, so we had no time to keep the towels in place. I can't describe in words how dirty and miserable the whole thing was. When we had to continue having sex while menstruating, we rolled the gauze up and inserted it deep into our wombs. Once I couldn't get it out again, and became very worried. In the end I had to go to hospital to have it removed.

The hospital was right next to the comfort station. It had a male doctor and a nurse who gave us check-ups for venereal disease once a month. The doctor looked into our insides, inserting his fingers. Anyone infected with gonorrhoea was given the 'No. 606' injection. This hurt your arm so much that you felt it would drop off your body. I was infected once. I went to the hospital for injections and took a lot of medicine. Even after I left the station, the infection would flare up whenever I became weak.

Many officers stayed the night. When they stayed over, in what was euphemistically described as 'sleeping the long night', I would leave the bedroom and stand out in the hall even in the cold winter to reduce the hours I had to spend with them a little. Once a week, when there were no officers staying overnight, I was able to sleep comfortably. Those who stayed left at five the next morning. Then we could sleep better, but we had to be up at 7.30 a.m. We had to gather in the yard, sing the Japanese anthem, and recite the Oath of Imperial Subjects. Only then did we get breakfast between 8.00 and 9.00 o'clock. We had a break for an hour and then the soldiers began to arrive. The largest number would arrive at between 3.00 and 4.00 p.m. We were allowed 30 minutes for meals, during which time we weren't forced to serve soldiers. Of the women in the station, I still remember Yun Yŏngja, who had the Japanese name Yamamoto Eiko, Umeko and Sunja.

A fortnight after my arrival, I tried to escape. Sunja said she knew the area around Yŏngdo, so we tried to run away together. I was the one who suggested it. To get past the two guards, we pretended to be nice to them and offered them cigarettes. We asked if we could go out to get some fresh air, but they wouldn't allow it, so we offered them drinks, after which they sat down in the hall and began to doze. We sneaked out, pretending we were off to the toilet, and then ran. But the road outside the station was longer than we had thought, and we were caught before we had got more than a few steps. After that I was hit hard three times on my hip with a gun, and I fell on my belly with blood pouring from my mouth. The wound on my hip left a big bruise and became infected, giving me an accompanying high fever. I was unable to lie on my back, but even in that state I had to keep on serving soldiers. The wound festered and became rotten. Only then did the soldiers take me to the hospital to have the rotten part cut out. I was allowed to take a break for three days. Then, even though it was still impossible for me to lie on my back, the soldiers started to visit me again. This was the hardest time of my confinement. It was too painful to serve soldiers when I couldn't even lie on my back. All the women harboured thoughts of running away, but after they saw me beaten and suffering, they gave up. Nobody attempted to flee anymore.

There was no single happy moment during my life as a comfort woman. When the soldiers didn't visit us and we were left on our own, we talked of our homes and wept. When the Japanese soldiers did visit, they often lined us up and took photographs. I would sing my two favourite songs, *Arirang* and *To My Mother*. When I missed my mother, I sang the latter song and cried. We had to sing anything in Korean in secret, since if we were caught we would be severely reprimanded. I never wrote to my family nor received a letter from them. No correspondence and no visits were allowed. But I once heard news. I was looking out of the window when I saw a pedlar from my neighbourhood. I asked him about my mother, and he told me she was selling herbs. I wept a lot when I heard this.

I now know that, when I didn't return home that fateful day, my mother and sister had gone round trying to find me. My sister even came to the comfort station in case I had been taken there. Since the building had once been a guest-house it was on the street and we could see passers-by from the windows. They came by again on a day when no soldiers were visiting, and I saw them while I was looking out of the window. I rushed down to greet them. My mother saw me and tried to take me back, but the soldiers pushed them both away, and we were parted without being able to say a single word to each other. After that my mother was so upset she became ill. There was a signboard and guards, so they must have realized I had become a comfort woman. There was also a second comfort station in Pusan, in Taesin ward. I hear that there were about 40 to 50 women in that place.

Back Home, But...

We hadn't heard that Korea had been liberated, but it was very noisy outside. We were finally able to get out to see what was happening and learned the news. The proprietor, Takayama, and the Japanese soldiers who had been posted in Pusan left for their country by boat. We all went our own way. I intended to go home but found myself penniless. Before I was taken, I had been the main bread-winner in my family, and I felt I couldn't go back without any money. Since I had heard that my mother was selling herbs to make a pitiful living, I thought I should get some money before I returned to her. So I started to work as a waitress in a restaurant right in front of the comfort station for a month, then moved to another restaurant for a year. Only then did I return home.

My mother was out selling vegetables at a market, and my younger sister greeted me with tears in her eyes. At 6.00 in the evening my mother, haggard and with a faded dark complexion, came home. To see her like that broke my heart. She wept. I wept. She wept, saying that she had thought she would never see me again. The following morning, she was ready to go out to sell her vegetables, but I stopped her. With the money I had, we first bought rice.

Later, I worked and earned sufficient money to bring up my brothers and sister. My mother was ill, she suffered because of what I had been through, and she died when I was 27. On her death bed she told me that, because I was born at the wrong time, I had to live like this, without getting married. She said she was sorry to leave all the responsibilities to me. And finally she murmured that she could not close her eyes and die without seeing me married. I have never thought of marriage, though, and have always lived on my own. Since I was physically ruined, all I thought of was earning money. At one time I got quite a good living from selling American dollars and goods on the black market, by dealing in opium, by buying and selling through somewhat illegal channels, or by running a guest-house and the like. But I have always been swindled and I am now penniless again.

I lived in Seoul, then in 1980 came down to Ulsan, my father's home town. Though Pusan is where I was born, I don't go there because it reminds me of my life as a comfort woman. At present I live on my own in a rented room, paying 30,000 wŏn ($36) a month and 3,000,000 wŏn ($3600) deposit as key money. I am registered as a First Grade Poor Resident and receive 10 kg of rice, one *toe* measuring cup of barley and 30,000 wŏn every month from the local office. I also have medical insurance granted under the provisions of First Class Home Care, so medical treatment is free. My health is very bad. I suffer from high blood pressure, liver trouble, a duodenal ulcer, arthritis, a water tumour on my right side, hypochondria, a nervous heart and so on.

I want to be born as a woman once again. I want to be able to study more while living with my parents in a good and just society. I want to marry well and I want to have children. When I was young, people told me I would be the first daughter-in-law in a wealthy family because of my healthy, hardy complexion. But what am I now? I am still unmarried. When I wake up at night, I start to ask why I am sleeping alone. Why am I living alone? Who made me feel this way? Why was Korea controlled by another country? I can't sleep. Because I live alone without any children, when I see families passing with their children, I feel miserable. I ask why, if others can have children, my lot is so hard?

Japan ruined my life. How can Japan now dare to evade the issue? They ruined my life. They took away my chance to get married. Could a verbal apology from them ever be good enough? I will never forget what I have had to go through so long as I live. No, I will not be able to forget what happened even after I die.

Military Sexual Slavery by Japan and Issues in Law

Etsuro Totsuka

Litigation in Japan

In December 1991, three South Korean comfort women, victims of sexual slavery by the Japanese Imperial Forces, went to the Tokyo District Court to sue the Japanese government for 20 million yen as reparation. In April 1993, Filipino victims did the same. This provided a forum to reveal the truth about their ordeal, which had been concealed by Japan since the Second World War. The mass media have now reported their campaign, which has resulted in extensive publicity.

Despite this pressure, the prospect of these women winning their case is remote, at least in the Japanese government's view, because of the many loop-holes in Japanese law. Before the post-war Constitution there was no explicit provision in law for the victims to be able to claim damages caused by any wrongdoing of the State. In addition, the Civil Code has a 20-year statutory limitation for victims to sue the perpetrators of torture.

The position of the Japanese government has been that the right to claim of individual victims was not infringed, despite the provision in various treaties in which the governments of the victims' country of origin relinquished all rights of the individual. However, the government is arguing that no individual has a legitimate position to stand under international law before the courts. Furthermore, few observers are confident that Japanese judges would be fair in their interpretation of the law as it affects victims from foreign countries.

It is interesting, however, to note that Article 98(2) of the Constitution allows a court to apply international law directly, regardless of any domestic legislation. Although there was no explicit provision in the pre-war Meiji Imperial Constitution, the authoritative interpretation was the same even before the war. The victims argued in court that the conduct of the Imperial Forces against them constituted crimes against humanity.

In December 1992, an international public hearing of the victims of sexual slavery from various countries and an international seminar attended by five international law experts were organized in Tokyo by the Japan Federation of Bar Associations and the Organizing Committee of the International Public Hearing. Since then, various issues of international law have been seriously debated in the courts.

Disputes at the United Nations

Fierce debates between many non-governmental organizations (NGOs) and Japan have been continuing at the United Nations since February 1992, when I first raised this issue at the UN Commission on Human Rights.[1] By August 1994, about 100 interventions had been made against Japan by about 15 NGOs and several governments in support of the victims.

These NGOs include the International Fellowship of Reconciliation (IFOR), the World Council of Churches (WCC), the International Commission of Jurists (ICJ), Liberation (LIB), the International Association of Democratic Lawyers (IADL), the Third World Movement Against Exploitation of Women (TWMAEW), the Women's International League for Peace and Freedom (WILPF) and International Educational Development (IED).

Originally, the major demand made of the Japanese government by the NGOs was monetary reparation for the surviving victims. As Japan had been rejecting this demand, in February 1994 the Korean victims filed an official complaint for the punishment of the perpetrators of war crimes committed against them. This was instantly rejected by the Tokyo District Prosecutor's Office. Japan has neither investigated nor punished any perpetrator of war crimes committed against the largely Korean victims of sexual slavery. This compares with the punishments, including the death penalty, which the 1948 Dutch military tribunal served on nine Japanese army personnel who were responsible for the sexual slavery of 35 Dutch women during the war period.

This information was received by the UN Commission on Human Rights in February 1994,[2] the UN Working Group on Contemporary Forms of Slavery in May 1994[3] and the UN Sub-Commission on Prevention of Discrimination and Protection of Minorities in August 1994.

On 19 August 1994 the UN Sub-Commission adopted a resolution (1994/5)[4] which decided to recommend that the Special Rapporteurs on the questions of the impunity of perpetrators of violations of human rights take into consideration information on the sexual exploitation of women and other forms of forced labour during wartime.

The Sub-Commission also entrusted an expert, Ms Linda Chavez, who was a member of the Sub-Commission, to conduct preliminary research on wartime slavery, including sexual slavery and systematic rape.[5] As a result, for the first time official investigations by a UN body have started into war crimes committed by Japan during the Second World War. These investigations were previously considered to have been concluded in 1948 by the International Military Tribunal for the Far East (IMTFE).

Legal Issues on Impunity

1. The report on the question of impunity[6] was submitted by the Special Rapporteurs, Mr Guisse and Mr Joinet, to the Sub-Commission in August 1993. In it, the issue of comfort women was not mentioned at all.
2. In August 1993, at the Sub-Commission, Japan formally acknowledged the enslavement of the comfort women by the Japanese Imperial Forces.
3. Legal analysis
  (a) Customary international law
  (i) Crimes against humanity
  These Japanese admissions mentioned above fall within the meaning of 'enslavement', 'deportation', 'inhumane acts' and 'persecution on political or racial grounds' which are the elements of crimes against humanity. I have no hesitation in joining a number of the NGOs in condemning Japan at the UN for the Japanese Imperial Forces' treatment of the comfort women as crimes against humanity.
  (ii) Slavery and the slave trade
  I also believe that the conduct mentioned above violates the prohibition of slavery and the slave trade, which have long been crimes under international customary law.
  (iii) Duties of Japan
  Under the two categories of crimes against humanity and slavery and the slave trade, the conduct of the Japanese Imperial Forces was, and still is, punishable under international law because international law has no time limitation. As a matter of natural justice, Japan is required to take the necessary measures to punish those who were responsible for the crimes.
  (b) Multilateral treaties
  (i) The ILO Convention (No. 29) Concerning Forced Labour
  The Convention was adopted by the International Labour Organization in 1930, and was ratified by Japan in 1932. The first

sentence of Article 2 totally prohibits any forced labour of women. The Japanese government acknowledged that coercion was, in general, employed in recruitment and/or treatment of the comfort women.

Article 24 stipulates that 'the illegal exaction of forced or compulsory labour shall be punishable as a penal offence, and it shall be an obligation on any Member ratifying this Convention to ensure that the penalties imposed by law are really adequate and are strictly enforced'.

(ii) The International Convention on the Prohibition of the White Slave Trade

The Convention was adopted in 1910 by an International Conference held in Paris, and was acceded to by Japan in 1925. This convention is not applicable to colonies and territories, unless notice to apply it is registered by a Member State (Article 2). However, it is applicable to the cases of the comfort women from Korea for the following reasons: Japanese historians have recently discovered that the planning of the comfort women system was conceived and supervised by the Supreme Headquarters of the Japanese Imperial Forces and the centre of the Japanese Government, which were based inside Japan, in Tokyo. Orders, authorizations and permissions relating to the comfort women were directed by these organizations from mainland Japan. In many cases, the comfort women were deported by Japanese ships, which are considered to be Japanese territory. In many or all cases, the recruitment, enslavement, deportation, treatment and supervision of the comfort women was carried out by personnel of the Japanese Imperial Forces. These personnel were acting under the jurisdiction of the Japanese Empire.

Article 1 of the Convention is explicit that those who solicited, enticed or abducted juvenile women with the purpose of prostitution should be punished, even if consent from the woman was obtained. And Article 2 is explicit that those who solicited, enticed or abducted an adult woman using deception or any means of violence, coercion, abuse of authority or any other coercive measures should be punished.

Article 3 obliges the state parties to take necessary measures in order to ensure punishment of the perpetrators of the crimes defined by Articles 1 and 2, as well as relevant legislation.

Many comfort women were juveniles when they were taken. Japan has acknowledged that almost all the comfort women were taken by deception or by other coercive means. Therefore, one must conclude that these obligations for punishment are still binding, even on the current Japanese government.

(c) Legal issues

(i) Time limitation

The offences against the comfort women would have been punishable under domestic law at the time of the Japanese Empire. The problem is that Japan may argue that it is not possible for the Japanese authorities to prosecute any perpetrator by applying the penal law of the time because of the maximum 15-year time limitation under the Criminal Procedure Act. However, there is no time limitation as regards Japan's obligations under international law.

(ii) The possibility of retrospective legislation

Article 15(2) of the International Covenant on Civil and Political Rights, to which Japan is a Party, allows 'the trial and punishment of any person for any act or omission which, at the time when it was committed, was criminal according to the general principles of law recognised by the community of nations'.

(d) *De facto* impunity

(i) Impunity

Despite its obligations under international law, Japan has failed to punish a single perpetrator of the crimes committed against the comfort women. This failure should be condemned as one of the worst examples of *de facto* impunity in history.

(ii) Discrimination against Asian women

The punishment by the IMTFE and other war crime tribunals of the Allied Forces was accepted by Japan in Article 11 of the San Francisco Peace Treaty of 1951. Punishment for crimes against Dutch citizens was carried out by the Dutch Military Tribunal, as mentioned above.

By contrast, Japan has never acknowledged that the very same acts committed against the very same kind of victims constituted crimes, when they concerned Asian, mainly Korean, victims. This can only be described as shameless contempt for and discrimination against Asian women.

Following a long and fierce debate between Japan and many other governments, the June 1994 Second Asia–Pacific Ministerial Conference on Women adopted the Jakarta Declaration for the Advancement of Women in Asia and the Pacific, and a Plan of Action. It included this sentence: 'Governments are asked to strongly condemn the systematic rape of women in situations of armed conflict and war and to support calls for the perpetrators of such crimes to be punished.'[7]

(e) Compensation on the grounds of non-punishment

(i) The proposed UN principles on the right to reparations

The final report[8] submitted in August 1993 by Professor Theo van Boven, the UN Special Rapporteur on the right to reparation for the victims of gross violations of human rights, is based on traditional international law as regards state responsibility. In it, Article 2 of the Proposed General Principles implies that a state is bound by the obligation for compensation if the state breaches the obligation for punishment.

(ii) Expert opinion

Professor Ian Brounlie also supports this view by citing the Janes case from the 1920s.[9]

(iii) Counter-arguments against the Japanese government's defence

Japan refused to admit any legal obligation for compensation of the comfort women in South Korea, saying 'the claims issues between Japan and the Republic of Korea have been resolved by an agreement, signed on 27 June 1965, on the settlement of the problems concerning property and claims, and on the economic co-operation between Japan and the Republic of Korea'. The obligations, however, for fact-finding and punishment were not resolved by Article 2 of this Agreement, as the terms of the Agreement limit the scope to 'the issues as regards properties, rights and profit of both countries and their nationals (including legal persons) as well as the rights of claims between both countries and their nationals'. Japan cannot argue that the obligation for compensation on the ground of non-punishment was resolved by this Agreement as the obligation for punishment, which has no time limitation, was never blocked by the Agreement, and has been breached since 1965.

The Need for an Expeditious Dispute Settlement

Many experienced lawyers in Japan predict that it will take the victims between ten and 20 years to exhaust the civil law procedure and to reach a judgement of the Supreme Court. Considering that the youngest surviving comfort woman is 63, the Japanese government is to be invited to accept the demand for an expeditious arbitration. The Permanent Court of Arbitration (PCA), which can offer services for cases where one party is not a state,[10] could be used in this case.

In May 1994, the UN Working Group on Contemporary Forms of Slavery drew the attention of both parties to the possibility of making an agreement to settle the case before the PCA.[11] Although ten South Korean victims and the Korean Council for the Women Drafted for Military Sexual Slavery by Japan accepted the UN recommendation in July 1994, Japan has not yet responded.

The Power of the UN

The Japanese government argued that the UN did not have the capacity to deal with issues which occurred before its creation. I believe, however, that this issue has already been settled through various practices of UN bodies themselves.[12] These practices, which were instituted by UN bodies and concern slavery and slavery-like practices, such as the sexual exploitation of women and other forms of forced labour during wartime, offer a positive interpretation.[13] The June 1993 Vienna World Conference on Human Rights debated whether only 'current violations' of human rights of women, such as sexual slavery in situations of armed conflict, required a particularly effective response. Following the debate between Japan and several other countries, the World Conference amended the text by concensus to read 'all violations'.[14]

The UN has some precedents for its actions, which include the resolutions of the Commission on the Status of Women and the ECOSOC regarding claims made in the early 1950s for reparations by surviving individual victims of the Nazi concentration camps injured by human experiments.[15]

The Japanese Government's Announcement in August 1994

An announcement was made by the Prime Minister, Mr Murayama, on 31 August 1994. In it, Japan refused to admit its legal responsibility towards the victims and refused to pay monetary reparation to the victims despite the misleading impression given by some elements of the media. Instead, it proposed that Japanese civilians, who were not responsible, set up a foundation by donating money for the victims. Japan classified this money as 'gifts of atonement' to the victims. Besides this, a ten-year, $1 billion programme was announced by Mr Murayama. This, however, is a kind of aid programme, which will never be paid in monetary terms to individual victims.

In a press release issued on 2 September 1994, the International Commission of Jurists, one of the most internationally influential of the NGOs, criticized these proposals.[16] The ICJ said: 'it is imperative that Japan take immediate steps to provide full rehabilitation and restitution. It is clear that Japan has a moral and legal obligation towards the victims.'

Notes

1. I represented International Educational Development up to February 1993. However, at the UN, since May 1993, I have been representing the International Fellowship of Reconciliation in relation to the issues of comfort women and Korean forced labourers.

2. UN Doc. E/CN.4/1994/NGO/19.

3. UN Doc. E/CN.4/Sub.2/1994/33, paras 89–97.

4. UN Doc. E/CN.4/Sub.2/1994/52, page 37.

5. UN Doc. E/CN.4/Sub.2/1994/56, page 124.

6. UN Doc. E/CN.4/Sub.2/1993/6.

7. Jakarta Declaration for the Advancement of Women in Asia and the Pacific and the Plan of Action, VI. GOALS, STRATEGIC OBJECTIVES AND ACTION TO BE TAKEN, E. Protecting and promoting women's rights, 3. Women under war and other conflict situations, Action to be taken, (vi).

8. UN Doc. E/CN.4/Sub.2/1993/8.

9. Ian Brounlie, *Principles of Public International Law*, 4th edition, 464–5. Oxford: Clarendon Press, 1990.

10. A booklet, *Permanent Court of Arbitration Optional Rules for Arbitration Disputes Between Two Parties of which only one is a State*, is available from the International Bureau of the Permanent Court of Arbitration, The Peace Palace, The Hague. An *ad hoc* agreement is possible for any kind of existing disputes, despite Article 1 (1) of the Rules, which is for 'the parties to a contract' (see Article 1 (3) and model arbitration clauses for existing disputes, page 24 of the booklet).

11. UN Doc. E/CN.4/Sub.2/1994/33, paras 101–13.

12. UN Doc. E/CN.4/Sub.2/1994/NGO/30.

13. Recommendations of the 17th session of the Working Group on Contemporary Forms of Slavery (WGCFS) in its report (E/CN.4/Sub.2/1992/34, page 19); Resolution of the 44th session of the Sub-Commission (Resolution 1992/2 of 14 August 1993 on contemporary forms of slavery, para. 18); Recommendations of the 18th session of the WGCFS in its report (E/CN.4/Sub.2/1993/30, page 40); Resolution of the 45th session of the Sub-Commission (Resolution 1993/24 of 25 August on slavery and slavery-like practices during wartime), and Recommendations of the 19th session of the WGCFS in its report (E/CN.4/Sub.2/1994/33).

14. The Vienna Declaration and Programme of Action, II.B. para 40. See the last sentence.

15. Plight of Survivors of Concentration Camps, UN Doc. E/1956, 16 March 1951.

16. Many newspaper articles, including the *Mainichi Shimbun* on the morning of 6 September 1994 (front page) and the *Japan Times* of the same day. The final report of the ICJ, which was published in November 1994, was sent to the governments concerned prior to its press release of 2 September 1994 for comments.